D1495567

A Manager's Guide to Creative Cost Cutting

181 Ways to Build the Bottom Line

David W. Young

McGraw-Hill

New York   Chicago   San Francisco   Lisbon
London   Madrid   Mexico City   Milan   New Delhi
San Juan   Seoul   Singapore   Sydney   Toronto

658.1552
Y69m

The McGraw-Hill Companies

Cku

Copyright ©2003 by McGraw-Hill. All rights reserved. Printed in the United States of America. Except as permitted under the United States Copyright Act of 1976, no part of this publication may be reproduced or distributed in any form or by any means, or stored in a data base or retrieval system, without the prior written permission of the publisher.

1 2 3 4 5 6 7 8 9 0 DOC/DOC 0 8 7 6 5 4 3 2

0-07-139697-7

This publication is designed to provide accurate and authoritative information in regard to the subject matter covered. It is sold with the understanding that neither the author nor the publisher is engaged in rendering legal, accounting, or other professional service. If legal advice or other expert assistance is required, the services of a competent professional person should be sought.

—From a Declaration of Principles jointly adopted
by a Committee of the American Bar
Association and a Committee of Publishers

All trademarked products mentioned in this book are used in an editorial fashion only, and to the benefit of the trademark owner, with no intention of infringement of the trademark. Where such designations appear in this book, they have been printed with initial caps.

McGraw-Hill books are available at special quantity discounts to use as premiums and sales promotions, or for use in corporate training programs. For more information, please write to the Director of Special Sales, Professional Publishing, McGraw-Hill, Two Penn Plaza, New York, NY 10121-2298. Or contact your local bookstore.

Library of Congress Cataloging-in-Publication Data

Young, David W.
  A manager's guide to creative cost cutting : 181 ways to build the bottom line / by David W. Young.
      p. cm.
  Includes bibliographical references.
  ISBN 0-07-139697-7 (hardcover : alk. paper)
  1. Cost control.   I. Title.   II. Title: 181 ways to build the bottom line.
  HD47.3.Y68 2003
  658.15'52—dc21

2002012226

In memory of Guy Lundberg

Contents

Acknowledgments

I'd love to claim that this book was my idea. But it was not. The idea was presented to me by Ela Aktay, formerly of McGraw-Hill. Ela was an inspiration throughout the project. She even suggested some cost-cutting techniques of her own.

The project was completed pretty quickly, mainly because of the assistance I received from Max Bessonov. A former student and teaching assistant, soon to be a doctoral student in management, and a true computer geek if there ever was one, Max scoured the Internet for interesting examples of cost-cutting techniques. How he found such arcane journals as *Air Conditioning, Heating, & Refrigeration News* I'll never know, but he managed to come up with over 100 techniques in just a few weeks.

I relied so much on *Business Week* as a source of good ideas that I think the magazine should be formally acknowledged here. I don't think even *Business Week*'s editors can imagine what a rich source of interesting cost-cutting ideas the magazine is. Some of the ideas were buried in stories about a quite different subject, but they were there nevertheless—most without too much of a stretch.

The last two chapters in the book are substantially more conceptual than the first seven. My coauthor on another book, Robert Anthony, an emeritus professor at Harvard Business School, greatly influenced my thinking for Chapter 8. And Anita McGahan, my faculty colleague at Boston University and my teaching colleague in the second-year MBA course "Competition, Innovation, and Strategy," was extremely patient with me during the past couple of years as I learned about the concepts presented in Chapter 9. I hope I've not done those concepts a disservice.

Clearly, however, despite all this assistance and encouragement, I accept full responsibility for any errors or shortcomings in the book.

David W. Young
Arlington, Massachusetts
September 2002

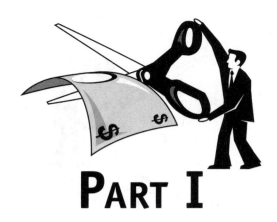

PART I

THE BASICS

This part is called "The Basics" because it focuses on the areas that most people think of when they need to cut costs: payroll, other operating expenses, overhead, and facilities and equipment. In fact, if media stories on cost reductions are any indication, most companies turn first to payroll for quick and easy cost reductions.

However, many companies have found that a reduction in personnel is not the solution that they thought it would be, or that it has some negative longer-run consequences that come back to bite them. The first chapter discusses payroll, shows how some companies have managed to reduce payroll costs in nondraconian ways, and offers a few cautionary notes.

Even if layoffs are made, they needn't be the only technique used. In fact, they may not be the way to go at all. Chapters 2 to 4 discuss some ways to reduce other operating expenses, including overhead, that may be far more beneficial to a company's long-run financial viability than a decreased head count.

1

PINK SLIPS AND RED QUEENS
HAPPY-SIZING VERSUS RIF(ING)
YOUR PAYROLL

"Off with their heads!" proclaimed the Red Queen. The "salaries and wages" line is frequently the largest single item on a company's income statement. For many companies, therefore, it is a logical place to begin a cost-cutting effort. Before you send out the pink slips, however, consider two important caveats. First, unless people have been just standing around, something will not get done when an employee is laid off. If layoffs are to take place, these "somethings" need to drive them. That is, rather than engaging in an across-the-board set of layoffs, managers need to ask themselves, "What is it we're not doing so much anymore, or what is it we do not need to do anymore, and who has been doing it?"

Second, keep in mind that layoffs are not free. Immediately, there may be severance pay or unemployment payments. Further down the road, there may be costs associated with rehiring and retraining that exceed the earlier savings, or there may be new issues raised in union negotiations that will increase costs in the future. All these matters need to be considered prior to instituting layoffs.

Because of this latter concern, some companies have a strict no-layoff policy that they stick to in good times and bad, not so much because they're noble or charitable as because, to them, it makes good economic sense. For example, as other airlines were announcing job cuts of 20 percent and more, Southwest Airlines took a unique approach. In a statement that would make many CEOs shudder, James Parker, Southwest's CEO, stated, "We are willing to suffer some damage, even to our stock price, to protect the jobs of our people." The company was cutting costs, to be sure, but not by laying off employees. In fact, in its 30 years of existence, including periods of jet fuel spikes, recessions, and the Gulf War, Southwest has never cut costs through layoffs.

Southwest is not alone in this philosophy. Other companies, such as FedEx and Lincoln Electric, and even smaller organizations such as Brobeck, Phleger & Harrison, a San Francisco law firm, also seek ways other than layoffs to cut costs. Many of these companies have financial policies that result in there being considerable cash and little debt on their balance sheets, allowing them to weather a storm more easily than their counterparts with weaker balance sheets.[1]

This approach is not exactly altruistic. Many companies claim that layoffs have hidden costs that their policy avoids. Among these are severance and rehiring costs, potential lawsuits from aggrieved workers, loss of institutional memory and trust in management, lack of staffers when the economy rebounds, and survivors who are risk-averse, paranoid, and political. By contrast, they say, the no-layoff policy results in a more loyal and productive workforce, higher customer satisfaction, a readiness to snap back when the economy improves, a recruiting edge, and a cadre of workers who aren't afraid to innovate, as they know their jobs are safe.[2] More generally, a recent study reported in a short (two-page) article in the *Harvard Business Review*, entitled "Look before You Lay Off," made a strong case that layoffs may not be the best way to go.[3] The article contained some data suggesting that companies that didn't downsize consistently outperformed those that did. Moreover, those that downsized did better in terms of stock price appreciation if they engaged in personnel reductions as part of a move toward strategic repositioning rather than simply to cut costs.

The anecdotal evidence confirms this. Palm Pilot, seeing declining sales, cut 15 percent of its workers. Wall Street responded in kind, taking the share price down by a half. Providian Financial cut payroll by 550 jobs in November 2001, and its share price went down by 90 percent within 4 months.

Why does this happen? The conventional wisdom seems to be that job reductions need to be part of a strategic plan, not just a response to a short-term drop in demand. At Sears, in contrast to Palm and Providian, when 2400 jobs were cut as part of a restructuring plan that included closing 89 stores, share prices rose by 30 percent over a 6-month period. Praxair cut 900 jobs in September 2001 in response to the economic decline, but it also invested in new plants. Its share price rose by 30 percent over 3 months. The conclusion: There are good layoffs, and there are bad layoffs. "If the business is struggling, Wall Street wants to see a coherent strategy for fixing the problem— not just a wad of pink slips."[4]

Okay, so you've decided that, despite all these cautions, layoffs must take place. Well, there are layoffs, and then there are layoffs. Some are easier to implement—and easier for employees to deal with—than others. And if revenues are way down, a recovery seems a long way off, and you just don't need the people, some layoffs may be inevitable. But there are many ways to approach layoffs. Let's look at some of the wide variety of techniques that companies have used in reducing personnel costs—or in not reducing them. There are some surprising—and refreshing—approaches here.

✂ Technique No. 1. Link Layoffs to Strategic Changes

Sometimes there is a shift in a company's strategy (or even its tactics). When this happens, it is likely that some positions or some number of positions may no longer be appropriate. When this is the case, layoffs make a great deal of sense. In effect, this is the notion of linking personnel reductions to a move toward strategic repositioning. This approach was illustrated in early 2002 at General Motors. Shortly after taking over as vice chairman for product development at GM, Robert Lutz sent several brand managers to new assignments or had them take early retirement. The number of brand managers fell from a peak of 39 in 1996 to only 26 in early 2002, with more reductions on the way. The reason was not a general cutback but a strategic move on Lutz's part to eliminate GM's so-called "brand-management system," an effort initiated in the 1990s to identify target groups and tailor advertising (and sometimes the cars themselves) to meet the groups' desires.

Technique No. 2. Link Layoffs to Activities

Bad news is never easy to deliver, and whoever delivers the layoff news no doubt will not sleep especially well for a few nights, or longer. One way to make the job easier, and also to make the layoffs as strategic as possible, is to link them to a decline in activities that are associated with certain employee groups. General Electric's aircraft engine division provides an interesting example. The division had been anticipating a production slowdown for 2002, but following the September 11 terrorist attacks, divisional managers realized that there would be more than just a *slowdown* in orders. According to a company spokesperson, there were numerous order cancellations, beginning immediately after the attacks, which were not "anything we saw coming so fast." Layoffs totaling around 4000 were announced in GE's aircraft engine plants in Cincinnati, Ohio, and Lynn, Massachusetts.[5] No one was happy about the layoffs, but everyone, the union included, realized that they were directly associated with the decline in orders.

The concept of activity-based costing (or ABC) can be helpful here. ABC is usually used for manufacturing overhead; it attempts to link overhead costs to the activities that drive their use. While ABC is fundamentally a method for attaching manufacturing overhead to products, it also can help managers to think more strategically about exactly where to target layoffs. For example, if production in a plant is down and if manufacturing overhead is attached to products by means of, say, machine hours, the accounting system provides senior management with little guidance as to where overhead personnel might be reduced. On the other hand, and perhaps counterintuitively, if, say, one driver of overhead costs is material requisitions, it may be that fewer personnel are needed for material requisitions, handling, and processing orders, receiving shipments, and completing the associated paperwork. It might even be the case that the personnel reductions can take place in the administrative offices, as fewer people may be needed to process and pay for orders.

✂ Technique No. 3. Make Layoffs as Painless as Possible

In GE's aircraft engine division, the union was pushing for most of the layoffs to be accomplished by attrition. In fact, the company was offering what will surely become the layoff euphemism of the decade: "early retirement opportunities."

This is not a bad idea, actually. Euphemism or not, the pain of a series of layoffs can be lessened by having some of the affected parties be people who are close to retirement, or who are planning to leave the company soon for another opportunity. A union sometimes can be helpful in identifying those people and working with them, thereby removing some of the pressure from management.

Another way to ease the pain of layoffs is to have a visible sign that senior management is also making sacrifices. Sometimes these "sacrifices" are minimal, but they can have an important symbolic value. Indeed, according to one compensation consultant, in times of drastic cutbacks in a company's labor force, shareholders also will want to see top management "sharing the pain."

As an example of how this can work, consider the case of American Airlines. According to *Business Week,* a few days after laying off 20,000 employees, American Airlines' CEO, Donald Carty, announced that he would give up his pay for the remainder of the year."[6] Now, considering that Carty had earned $4.5 million in 2000, and assuming (conservatively) that he was earning the same salary in 2001, his pay cut, coming just before the fourth quarter of the year, amounted to about $1 million, leaving him with a total salary for the year of about $3.5 million. In short, it is likely that, even though Carty's salary is low by CEO standards, most American Airlines employees would see this more as a symbolic cut than as something requiring the sort of sacrifices being made by the 20,000 laid-off workers. Nevertheless, Carty was, in some sense, "sharing the pain."

 But Beware! In some instances, employee unhappiness can lead to a decline in morale, making it all the more important to consider the consequences of layoffs even when they are linked to activities. For example, in the 1980s, when the revolution in desktop computing and the entrance of new companies into the industry led to a steep decline in IBM's revenue and market share, the company faced a situation similar to that of General Electric. IBM was forced to renege on its no-layoff policy, which led to deep resentment among the remaining employees.[7] Recovering from the resentment and its repercussions took some time.

 And Consider This . . . Downturns in the economy have always been followed by upswings. What then? Will you be able to rehire the talent you need as growth resumes? Will good people be reluctant to sign on with a company that will lay them off when the first economic blip hits the radar screen? Will you incur training costs that will impede your ability to fill orders, causing you to lose some potential business? This is the dilemma that a recent study suggests Boeing Co. could be facing. According to the study, Boeing could be "woefully short of skilled workers if orders rebound substantially over the next few years." Not only do the hoped-for efficiency gains depend on avoiding training-based production difficulties when the company ramps up production the next time, but its unions have been antagonized by what they call "sacrificing people for profit."[8]

✂ Technique No. 4. Restructure Jobs during Downturns

Companies that are in need of new product lines, new business niches, or new markets can use downturns productively. Of course, the balance sheet needs to be strong to support such an effort, but, instead of laying people off, some companies restructure jobs to focus on new activities. When the downturn reverses, those companies are positioned for rapid growth. In fact, some companies even use the "opportunity" of a downturn to recruit talented professionals who can provide a basis for solid growth in the years ahead.[9]

✂ Technique No. 5. Manage Layoffs Creatively

Boeing's unhappy situation described above might have been avoided if the company had separated the layoff from the cost of rehiring and retraining once the economy picks up. At Charles Schwab Corp., for example, the company's severance package included a $7500 "hire-back" bonus that any employee would get if he or she were rehired within 18 months. Schwab considered this a small amount compared to the cost of recruiting and training new employees.[10] From the employees' perspective, the incentive to take a temporary job and return to the old job with Schwab was increased by the carrot of the $7500 bonus upon their return.

With these sorts of concerns in mind, let's look at some options for reducing personnel costs without layoffs. In all instances there are "losers"—people who will not receive the same take-home pay as before—but in almost every instance, their loss is mitigated in some way.

✂ Technique No. 6. Offer Voluntary Time Off without Pay

Rather than being *forced* to work less, some employees would prefer to be given the option. Surprisingly, perhaps, some will take it. Even more surprisingly, it may turn out that they don't *need* to work during that time. At Charles Schwab Corp., for example, management designated three Fridays each month as voluntary days off without pay for employees who didn't need to deal with clients. The company also encouraged employees to take unused vacation days or unpaid leaves of up to 20 days. The technique allowed Schwab to avoid layoffs during that period of time.[11]

✂ Technique No. 7. Create a Paid-Time-Off Bank

By creating a paid-time-off (PTO) bank, a company can cap the number of days off available to employees during the year. The PTO bank can be used for sick days, vacation days, or personal days. The employees know what is available, game playing is eliminated, and the employer can put a clear cap on time-off costs.[12]

✂ Technique No. 8. Offer Key Employees a Partially Paid Sabbatical

Rehiring and retraining costs can be especially high in organizations that provide professional services, such as law firms, consulting firms, and research think tanks. One solution is to negotiate a partially paid sabbatical, thereby reducing but not entirely eliminating some salaries. Accenture used this approach, offering sabbaticals to its consultants during the economic slowdown, which had reduced demand for the firm's services. About 1000 employees accepted. They were allowed 6 to 12 months to do whatever they wanted. One employee, working for only 20 percent of her salary, decided to spend a year with AmeriCorps, a national volunteer group. Accenture continued to pay her benefits and let her keep her work phone number, laptop, and email. Perhaps most important, the arrangement gave her and the other employees the security of knowing they would have jobs after their sabbaticals ended.[13]

✂ Technique No. 9. Take Summers Off

Remember how great it used to be to have the whole summer off when you were in school? Maybe you should return to those thrilling days of yesteryear, either for summers or for some other time periods when employees could use time off and might be willing to give up some pay in return. At Adobe Systems in San Jose, California, for instance, most members of the 3000-person workforce "went fishin'" when the company closed up for the first week of July. At an Intel plant in New Mexico, employees in some departments could elect to take 2 weeks of unpaid leave over the summer months. At Brady Corp. in Milwaukee, a maker of bar code and other labeling systems, 980 employees had an unexpected, and unpaid, 9 days off during the summer. The leave, for some, was not voluntary; in April, the company announced a "summer-hours program" that required these employees to take 9 days of unpaid time off by the end of August.[14]

This seems pretty logical. In many companies, business slows down during the summer, and summer frequently is a time when employees want to spend time at home with the kids. The same might be true over the winter holiday season and during school vacation weeks.

✂ Technique No. 10. Shorten the Workweek

In some companies where reductions in salaries are taking place, morale has been maintained by simply shortening the workweek. For example, faced with declining revenues in the wake of the September 11 tragedy, Nucor maintained its long-standing no-layoff policy by cutting back to a 4-day work schedule. Of course, although Nucor was maintaining its no-layoff policy, it also was asking its employees to sacrifice about 20 percent of their salaries.[15] Better than a layoff, though.

Technique No. 11. Change Your Hours of Service

A 4-day schedule works in manufacturing, but what about companies in other sectors? An approach used by some retailers that avoids laying people off is to change the hours of service. Do you really need to be open on Sundays? Could you close at 8 P.M. rather than 9 P.M.? Could you open an hour later? If your business is seasonal, maybe you can change your opening date. For example, following the September 11 attacks, Colorado's Crested Butte ski resort, which depends on airlines for most of its bookings, postponed its opening day for several weeks to save on payroll costs.[16]

In a similar move, DiamondCluster International, a business strategy and technology consulting firm, asked its 150 newly hired MBAs and college grads to delay their start dates by 3 to 4 months. In exchange, the firm gave them their signing bonuses in advance, a $2000 a month stipend, and relocation expenses. The technique allowed the company to avoid rescinding any offers. Boston Consulting Group used a similar technique, offering its recruits three potential start dates in order to stagger the times when they went on salary. It also offered new hires the option of taking a 3-month intensive language training course prior to their start date.[17]

⊘ **But Beware!** In the midst of negotiations between Boston's hotel industry management and its unions, management was attempting to gain greater flexibility by instituting shifts of fewer than 8 hours. In an editorial, the *Boston Globe* took the hotel managers to task, arguing that not knowing *when* they would work was hard enough for the hotel workers, but not knowing *for how long* they would work was too great a burden for them to bear. Although compromise at the bargaining table was likely, the union was prepared to strike over the issue.[18]

✂ Technique No. 12. Reduce Senior Management's Compensation

In many companies where reductions in salaries are taking place, morale can be improved if employees know that senior management is sharing the pain. Sometimes senior management can absorb all the pain. In Nucor Corporation, for example, the cutback to a 4-day work schedule was accompanied by the elimination of senior management's bonuses. The bonuses constituted some 66 percent of senior management's salaries. Thus, although employees were making a sacrifice of about 20 percent of their salaries, senior management's compensation was falling by two-thirds. In effect, the senior people were making a sacrifice that clearly was more than symbolic.[19]

National Semiconductor Corporation did much the same thing. The company eliminated 2001 bonuses for its high-ranking executives and announced that it would delay salary increases companywide in 2002. The comment of a board member on the compensation committee was telling: "We were expecting a tough time, and September 11 made it tougher." In effect, everyone at NSC—regular employees and senior management—was going to have to share in the hard times.[20]

These are more than just isolated examples. According to *Business Week*'s 2002 survey of executive compensation, the average CEO's pay declined by 16 percent in 2001, to $11 million. Eliminate one outlier (Lawrence Ellison of Oracle, who cashed in over $700 million in stock options), and the average pay declined by 31 percent to $9.1 million.[21] Similarly, Wyatt Worldwide, using a larger sample than *Business Week*, predicted that total pay in 2001—including options exercises—for CEOs of the nation's 1000 largest companies was likely to fall by a third, with the average going down below the $1 million level for the first time since the early 1990s.[22]

But maybe you don't need to reduce work hours, shorten weeks, or institute seasonal unpaid holidays. How about making salaries a variable instead of a fixed cost? This can be pretty easy at the senior management level, since bonuses, in particular, are tied to performance, but it also may be possible to push the shift from fixed to variable costs deeper down into the organization. Consider these sorts of techniques.

Technique No. 13. Trade Salaries for Stock Options and Bonuses

Business Week's 2002 survey of executive compensation contained some interesting data on what, in effect, is pay for performance. Oracle's Ellison, for instance, was one of several CEOs who received no salary or bonus in 2001; all Ellison's compensation was in the form of stock options. Similarly, at Cisco Systems, 3 days after cutting CEO John Chambers's pay to $1 a year, the board of directors gave him $2 million in additional stock options.[23] The message was clear: Get the share price back up, and you'll make a lot of money!

Clearly, this idea could be extended deep into the organization. In a large, multidivisional company where stock options are a major form of compensation, enhanced grants can be substituted for pay raises. Even annual bonuses can be eliminated in favor of stock options.

Technique No. 14. Trade Salaries for Commissions

This is another tried-and-true way to pay for performance, but this one goes deep, deep down into the organization. Sales personnel in many organizations have been compensated in this way for decades, perhaps centuries. In effect, commissions are the ultimate in pay for performance, with the two about as directly linked as is possible. When times get tough, the shift from salaries to commissions becomes increasingly attractive. For example, Executive Clothiers, a men's store in Illinois, was considering lowering base salaries and offering higher commissions. The owner was quoted as saying, "We have to shift more of the risk to employees."[24] Indeed, this is what it's all about: risk and reward.

 But Beware!   One of the problems with commissions and other forms of variable pay is that the money needs to be paid out to employees if they meet the goals or conditions of pay. This is true regardless of how well the company does overall.[25] Make sure you've got the cash to pay the commissions and bonuses!

 And Also Beware!   If commissions become too significant, they may lead to dysfunctional behavior. Sears discovered this, much to its dismay, when state consumer authorities found that the company's commission system at its automobile repair operations in California was leading employees to recommend unnecessary repairs. Sears abandoned the system shortly thereafter.

Eli Lilly has dealt with this problem somewhat differently. Its bonuses are calculated annually, but a portion of the bonus is put in a "bonus bank." Managers can remove funds from their bonus banks only if performance improves each year. If a manager makes a decision in one year that improves performance that year but reduces it in a subsequent year, the balance in the manager's bonus bank is reduced.[26]

Some companies just can't convert salaries to commissions, bonuses, or stock options. For them, if business is down and they want to avoid layoffs, they have to think a bit more creatively. Here are some of the techniques they've found to be successful.

Technique No. 15. Reduce Salaries

Rather than laying off people, some companies have given their employees the option of working for less pay. No one likes a pay cut, of course, but, like the problem of getting older, it's not so bad when you consider the alternative. And, unlike getting older, sometimes it's just temporary. For example, following the decline in travel after the September 11 attacks, the Montrose Travel Agency in California cut the salaries of most of its 160 employees by 10 percent. The owners themselves went without pay. Most of the employees were quite happy to still have their jobs.[27] Similarly, when it became clear that putting projects on hold and cutting back on travel and entertainment expenses to avoid layoffs would not suffice, Charles Schwab Corp. began to institute pay cuts. The two co-CEOs each took a 50 percent cut, executive VPs 20 percent, senior VPs 10 percent, and VPs 5 percent.[28]

United Airlines took a similar approach, but with a couple of interesting variations. First, it needed to negotiate new contracts with the International Association of Machinists (IAM). One result was that United's mechanics received a 37 percent pay increase (which restored their wages to 1994 levels!). Once it had completed negotiations with the IAM's 24,000 nonmechanic members, United planned to ask all 80,000 of its employees to consider a wage cut of up to 10 percent.[29]

Technique No. 16. Reduce Salary Increases

Rather than laying people off or reducing their salaries, some companies have decided that the best approach is to simply reduce the amount of planned salary increases. Again, the post-September 11 period is instructive. A study by Mercer Consulting, reported in *Business Week,* indicated that 19 percent of 340 companies surveyed were planning to cut raises in 2002 from an average of 4.5 percent to an average of 3 percent. Another 11 percent were planning to postpone raises by 6 months, and 2 percent said that they would give no raises at all, including no cost of living increases. Most of the impact was being felt by white-collar workers.[30]

✄ Technique No. 17. Make Strategic Cuts (and Increases) in Salaries

Where is it written that there has to be a cost of living increase, especially in times of low or zero inflation? Who says that there needs to be an across-the-board pay increase? Why not focus your increases or your cuts more strategically? At Electronic Data Systems Corp., for example, less than 40 percent of employees get an annual bonus, and only 75 percent get raises. At Gateway, some employees may get 15 percent raises while others get nothing. Wal-Mart pays bonuses to store managers based solely on store performance. In a recent survey of 721 North American companies by Towers Perrin, the most successful firms were nearly three times as likely to give their best employees massive raises. People who did not get raises in these companies were likely to leave, which in general was viewed as a good thing.[31]

Nordstrom has a similar approach that combines the idea of substituting commissions for salaries with the idea of strategic cuts. The retailer pays its sales staff on commission, but complements this approach by measuring revenue per salesclerk (rather than per square foot, as is common in the industry). Nordstrom prints this number on each employee's check stub and ranks the salesclerk's performance on the employee bulletin board. One result is that the turnover of productive clerks tends to be low, whereas that of unproductive clerks is high.[32]

✄ Technique No. 18. Make Strategic Cuts (and Increases) in Personnel

How about thinking strategically to determine exactly where you need people and where you don't? Trigon Healthcare is a case in point. A health maintenance organization, Trigon faces the same incentive structure as all other HMOs: Its revenues are predetermined, and it must keep its costs below them even if its insured population is less healthy than anticipated. But rather than cut costs everywhere, Trigon has done so strategically. Indeed, the HMO actually incurs some personnel costs that many other HMOs do not. For example, it hires caseworkers to help chronically ill patients (such as diabetics) better manage their conditions. This is not a charitable decision. In the words of Trigon's CEO, "Long term, it costs far less to help chronically ill patients monitor their diseases than to pay emergency room bills."[33] That's actually pretty short term, if you think about it.

Technique No. 19. Grow Personnel More Slowly Than Revenue

This technique is not exactly cutting costs. Rather, it's not letting them grow in the first place. If you're a commodity producer, you need to watch cost growth compared to volume growth very carefully. Apache Corp., a Houston-based oil and gas exploration and production company, has done this quite successfully. The company increased its annual production 20-fold over the 1981–2000 period, yet its employees grew only from 1200 to 1600, a 33 percent increase. Roger Plank, the company's CFO, was quoted as saying, "We are basically taking our fixed costs and spreading them over a greater number of barrels of oil and million cubic-feet of gas produced. Some larger companies focus a lot more attention on cutting costs; our approach to cutting costs is to increase production so that our cost per unit [of production] goes down."[34]

Technique No. 20. Align Skills (and Hence Salaries) with Tasks

While we all need to be good citizens, it makes little sense to have a brain surgeon sterilize the operating room or a drill press operator sweep up the sawdust. This idea lies behind the concept of value-adding work. At Sally Industries, a manufacturer of robots for theme parks, labor cost is a significant percentage of total cost. Moreover, robot manufacture encompasses a wide variety of tasks of varying complexity and sophistication, and Sally has instituted pay rates that match these job demands. Perhaps most important, however, the company has developed a cost system that makes its workers conscious of how they spend their time and that places special emphasis on work that does not add value sufficiently above an employee's pay rate.[35]

✂ Technique No. 21. Distinguish between Labor Wage and Labor Cost

The difference between the two, of course, is productivity, a fact that economists have known for years but that sometimes escapes managers. Perhaps using offshore *adult* labor for manufacturing is not all that it's cracked up to be. Sure, the hourly wage rate is lower, but what's the total cost? To determine this, you need to think about output per hour, error rates, supervisory time, training time, turnover, and a host of other factors that, in the end, may make it more cost effective to stay at home and use local labor.

GE is a case in point. Independent of the home versus foreign labor issue, Jack Welch thought it was possible to pay the highest wage rates while having the lowest wage cost. As a result, during his so-called neutron years, only 37,000 employees left the GE payroll because businesses were sold. During the same time period, 81,000 people—one of every five in GE's industrial businesses—lost their jobs for productivity reasons. Looked at in another way, as those people left, overall productivity increased. Even with wage increases, it is likely that total labor cost fell as a percent of output.[36]

✂ Technique No. 22. Shorten Testing Time

Sometimes enough is enough. How long and how extensively do you need to test a product before it's ready to ship? At Microsoft, the tension between the marketing people and the software engineers is almost visible. The mantra "Can we ship it yet?" is heard pretty regularly around the place as a new product launch nears. But other companies have found that creating similar tension—or just cutting testing time—can work for them, too. At EMC (the data storage company), devices were once tested for 28 days before they were considered ready for market. When a new CEO (Joe Tucci) came in, he felt that that was too long. After 6 months of study, he concluded that quality would not suffer if the testing time were cut in half. The result was some significant cost savings.[37] One would imagine that most of these were in the personnel area, where fewer people were needed.

Technique No. 23. Shift from Full-Time to Part-Time Labor

Maybe you don't need to lay anyone off. Maybe you don't need to reduce any salaries. Suppose your company has seasonality in its operations, and you hire extra people for the high season. What if the high season is not as active as you had thought it would be? Do you lay off some of these extra people? Not necessarily. Belmont Country Club in Massachusetts, which had hired several high school and college students during its busy summer season, found a better way. When business fell off, the club was faced with the need to reduce its labor cost. Instead of eliminating any employees, which might have had repercussions in terms of negative parental reactions or lost goodwill among its members, the club simply reduced the hours of all its employees. Not only were most of the students happy to have the additional free time, but the club did not incur any increase in its unemployment costs.

Technique No. 24. Rent Employees

We're not talking Kelly Services or Account Temps here, but rather "renting" middle management talent with the "option" to hire. PeopleSupport, Inc., a company that provides customer-care services to such businesses as hotels, led the way by cutting back on its hiring of middle managers. Instead, it began using a "rent-to-hire" model. About a dozen or so people at the middle management level and higher in the 500-employee company were "rented" as contractors. The ones who did well would be the first to be hired when the economy improved.[38]

✂ Technique No. 25. Cross-Train

Depending on your company and its needs, it may be possible to eliminate the need for part-time help entirely by cross-training some employees. If the intensity and variety of the job varies by season, for example, cross-training can be extremely helpful. Sometimes this can be as simple as having the school secretary able to do the work for summer camp, and sometimes it can be as complex as training a laboratory technician to process more than one kind of test or a radiology technician to perform multiple imaging procedures. Indeed, in many hospitals, when union regulations have permitted it, some quite significant savings have been achieved by cross-training some of the overhead staff. For example, housekeeping personnel can also work in the laundry department or in the kitchen preparing food to be cooked.

✂ Technique No. 26. Initiate Employee Wellness Programs

This one has a double whammy. Not only can it reduce your healthcare premiums, but it can reduce employee absenteeism and turnover, and possibly increase productivity. At ARAG Group, a Des Moines insurer, for example, the company's 80 employees receive free annual health screenings at a local hospital, for a total annual cost of $8000. Since ARAG established the program, its health-care costs have risen by 7 percent, compared to about 10 percent for all small businesses. ARAG's CEO reasons that much of the credit goes to wellness: If he prevents just one heart attack, he has improved his company's claims history and has avoided a premium increase. Moreover, ARAG believes that the wellness programs have led to a drop in absenteeism and turnover. Last year, its turnover was just 9 percent, about half the industry average.[39]

A focus on wellness can also have some unintended—and admittedly hard to measure—benefits. Take, for example, a smoking cessation program. Most companies and insurers have found these to be uneconomical because of the time horizon for a payoff. For the average smoker, health problems such as lung cancer or emphysema are decades away, and it's hard for a company to justify the expense of such a program. On the other hand, in settings where employees have regularly scheduled breaks, a smoker's jitters for the half hour preceding the break may lead to job-related mistakes or reduced productivity. Under these circumstances, a smoking cessation program may have a relatively easily measured short-term payoff.

General Electric Corp. had a similar experience with employees who were diabetic. These employees had difficulty managing their blood sugar in conjunction with the plant's regularly scheduled breaks. When diabetic employees were allowed to take breaks when they needed them, rather than at regularly scheduled times, they were able to manage their blood sugar levels more effectively, and their productivity improved.

Technique No. 27. Don't Hire Smokers

Here's the wellness idea taken to an extreme. North Miami bans smokers from applying for city jobs. Coral Gables won't allow smokers to join the police force. St. Cloud, Florida, requires applicants for city jobs to swear that they've been tobacco-free for a year, and it tests them periodically to make sure they're not cheating. Why? Fewer lost work days, higher productivity, and lower health insurance costs, says the town. In fact, St. Cloud's HR director was quoted as saying that 6 to 12 percent of the $1.3 million the city spent on health insurance was tobacco-related.[40]

✂ Technique No. 28. Manage Your Email Time

And speaking of productivity, what has email done to yours? Sure, email has some clear advantages in terms of speeding communication, but it also can be extremely disruptive to a person's work schedule. Since productivity is the other side of the layoff coin, it may be worth examining how you manage your email time. Sabrina Horn, founder, president, and CEO of Horn Group, a $10 million public relations firm, is a good example. Ms. Horn found herself spending too much time on email-related activities. She would interrupt her work each time the bell signaled an incoming message.

To solve the problem, she took two steps. First, she separated her work-related email from her personal email by opening a new account. The result was that her time at work was spent on work-related email only. Second, she resolved to check her work-related email only three times a day: first thing in the morning, once during lunch, and once before going home. Her email rules, she claims, have helped her to "find moments of balance throughout the day."[41]

✂ Technique No. 29. Speed Up Your Connectivity

And speaking of email, how long do you spend waiting for a Web page to assemble itself in all its graphic splendor? Many companies have switched from regular phone lines to broadband to speed up connectivity. But the technology continues to advance. Artera Group International in Connecticut has developed a system that it claims can speed Internet access over regular copper phone lines by five times—to 250 kilobits per second (versus 56 kbps on a regular dial-up modem). Fees are expected to be about $175 a month for a three-user office and only \$10 to \$20 a month for homes and travelers. Broadband begone!

Technique No. 30. Follow the 10 Commandments of Email

It's not just the Zen of email that's at issue. The email problem runs deeper than that. We all waste a great deal of time when someone breaks one or more of the following commandments:

1. Thou shalt not send an email without a subject. "Message from the Internet" is useless.

2. Thou shalt not interrupt an email string. When sending a return email, be sure to include all emails on the subject that preceded it. That way, the recipient does not need to dig through old files to find out what's already been said on the subject.

3. Thou shalt not start a new email string with an old email string. When you've got a new subject, start a new string. Don't make it seem as though a whole lot has been said on the matter.

4. Thou shalt not send an unnecessary file. When "File Received" contains exactly the same message as the regular email, it's a useless appurtenance.

5. Thou shalt not have a sender name that bears no resemblance to thy real name. If you do, your message is likely to be deleted on the server.

6. Thou shalt not copy the rest of the planet unless the end is near. Be sure you send copies only to those people who really are interested or need to know.

7. Thou shalt not send arcane software as files. For better or worse, and despite the fact that Word is tantamount to killing a fly with an elephant gun, Microsoft Office is the standard.

8. Thou shalt not send jokes in files in excess of 10 megabytes. If it's not pithy, it's not funny.
9. Thou shalt be wary of email groupings. Be sure that the group contains only those people who are appropriate.
10. Thou shalt curb thy tongue. If you would not say it to the person's face or write it on expensive stationery, you probably should not put it in an email.

Make Sure You Avoid These YGBKs

YGBK No. 1. Cutting Personnel without Understanding the Fundamentals of the Business

Commercial airplanes need a copilot. An operating room needs a scrub nurse. Moving a piano requires two people. And don't suggest that the symphony orchestra eliminate half the violinists while telling the rest to play twice as loudly!

Silly as all this sounds, the reality is painful. For example, in 1990, Tom Werner and his partners bought the San Diego Padres. Three years later, according to Steve Bailey of the *Boston Globe,* "he traded Gary Sheffield, the league's batting champ, and Fred McGriff, the home run champion. He dumped popular shortstop Tony Fernandez, catcher Benito Santiago, and pitchers Bruce Hurst, Greg Harris, Randy Myers, Mike Maddox, and on and on. By the time he was done, Werner had cut the payroll to less than $10 million, the Major League low." It was "one of the biggest salary dumps in the history of professional sports." The result: "Fans showed up with bags over their heads; others filed a class-action lawsuit. The *Dallas Morning News* called Werner "the most hated man in Southern California."[42]

(continued)

YGBK No. 2. Confusing Labor Wage with Labor Cost
You have a complicated patent infringement case, and your patent lawyer charges $500 an hour. But wait: There's a young lawyer who just passed the bar exam who is willing to charge you only $200 an hour. Whom do you hire?

As obvious as the decision sounds, many managers regularly confuse labor wage with labor cost. Assuming comparable outcomes (which is by no means certain in the patent case above), there is still the intervening variable of productivity. If it takes the newly minted lawyer three times longer to complete his or her work on the case, you are better off with the $500-per-hour lawyer. This idea extends into many other matters as well, including such mundane matters as piecework in the factory and maintenance and repair work on the building.

The probably apocryphal story is told of the elderly man who could not start his car and telephoned a local garage. The mechanic arrived shortly thereafter, looked under the hood, pulled out a screwdriver, and made a quarter turn to a screw. The engine then started immediately. "How much?" queried the elderly gentleman. "$25," replied the mechanic. "What, $25 just to turn a screw?" the man asked incredulously. "No, no," said the mechanic. "$1.50 to turn the screw. $23.50 for knowing which screw to turn."

2

CUTTING COSTS WITHOUT CUTTING HEADS
SOME EMPLOYEE-FRIENDLY APPROACHES
TO COST REDUCTION

Obviously, personnel cuts, salary reductions, unpaid time off, and other such techniques are not the only way to reduce costs. There are lots of nonpayroll costs that can be cut. Let's look at them in two categories: direct expenses and indirect, or overhead, expenses. We'll look at direct expenses in this chapter and overhead expenses in Chapter 3.

Something that is a direct expense for one company can be an overhead expense for another. In general, however, the category of direct nonpersonnel expenses includes raw materials, purchased services, perhaps some supplies, and a variety of similar items. The beauty of cost reductions in this category is that they do not affect the labor force, and thus are relatively painless. (Of course, if they're large, they may affect another company's labor force.) The downside is that the savings frequently are relatively minor or may have an impact on the quality of your product. So your goal is to identify the "low-hanging fruit"—those expenses that are either very large, so that there is almost certainly some fat that can be cut, or relatively small but easily cut without having a negative impact on quality.

Be careful with those small items, however. There can be lots of YGBKs. If the amount of the cost reduction is small but the change has a large negative impact on morale, you may be better off biting the bullet and continuing to incur the expense. As an example, a university that was in some financial difficulty told its program heads that they could no longer use their budgets for food. One program director had a regular monthly meeting at lunchtime with students and faculty. To create a relaxed and informal atmosphere, he usually spent about $30 from the program's budget for pizza and soft drinks. When he informed students and faculty that the next meeting would be food-less because of the university's cost-cutting policy, both groups were outraged.

So let's begin with some areas where there is likely to be little outrage or where the outrage is appropriate and well focused. We'll start with customers, then move on to suppliers, and finally look at places where employees can help to cut costs without sacrificing their jobs.

Technique No. 31. Reduce Your Bad Debts

Every company that sells on credit has some bad debt. The question is whether you can manage your customers more carefully so as to reduce the incidence of bad debt. Even if you evaluate your customers' creditworthiness before making the first sale, you need to bear in mind that during a recession a customer who was creditworthy a few months ago may not be so today. So some periodic updating of records is important, especially if the economy is in decline. The one thing worse than not making a sale is making the sale and not getting paid for it.

✂ Technique No. 32. Make 'Em Pay

Okay, so you made the sale to a deadbeat. Delinquencies are an especially serious problem during periods of economic slowdown. Sending out frequent reminders usually doesn't do the trick. Sometimes promises get broken. Sometimes repossession is infeasible or unwise. Adding interest is useless if the debt isn't going to be paid anyway. What can you do? John Meeker, CEO of a Minneapolis executive search firm, has developed the following multistep process:[1]

1. At the beginning of a new relationship, ask the customer to sign a contract that spells out payment terms and obligations.
2. Make sure the contract offers incentives for prompt payment.
3. If deadlines are not met, renegotiate and allow customers to pay in installments.
4. If that doesn't work, go up the chain of command.
5. If that doesn't work, have your lawyer send a letter.
6. Put all collection efforts in writing and keep copies of everything in case you need to go to court.
7. As a last resort, if the debt is not large enough to justify taking the customer to court, turn the account over to a collection agency.

Meeker doesn't count on keeping customers whom he's sued or whose accounts he's turned over to a collection agency. On the other hand, if your customers are flakes, you probably don't want them anyway.

Glenn H. Matteson, in an article in *Air Conditioning, Heating, & Refrigeration News*, has taken this idea to the extreme. He suggests that for whatever amount is not collected, the company should issue a 1099 to the customer, reminding him or her that taxes are owed on the unpaid amount.[2]

But let's assume that you plan to try to keep at least some of your customers. Can you enlist their cooperation in your cost-cutting efforts? It turns out that there are some pretty nifty ways to do this.

Technique No. 33. Give Your Customers Incentives to Save You Money

Who knows better than your customers where you're wasting money? Not only can your customers be a valuable source of information, but sometimes they can be brought into the "family." Here's a neat example from Wal-Mart.

Shopping cart theft costs retailers worldwide about $800 million a year. Each cart costs about $100. Companies have been known to take any number of steps to curtail their losses, from hiring private companies to round up the carts to installing invisible fences at the parking lot perimeter that freeze the cart's front wheels. Wal-Mart came up with perhaps the best approach, however. For every cart that a customer brings back to the store, he or she gets a ticket for a drawing to win a TV. The result was a reduction from 300 carts left outside each day at each store to 100. Even better, one Wal-Mart store reported that it was able to schedule 100 fewer hours per week (at $8 per hour) for cart roundup. Each TV cost the store less than $200.

Technique No. 34. Reduce Shrinkage

Ah, that wonderful euphemism. We're all familiar with the steel cables that hold the leather coats, the changing-room monitors, the electronic transmitters on certain products, the locked cabinets, and lots of other deterrents to shrinkage. Indeed, the use of bar codes has allowed most retailers to know exactly what has left inventory and what has been paid for—and since the two are not necessarily the same, this information lets the retailers target their shrinkage-reduction efforts more precisely. All these deterrents to shrinkage, of course, are ways of working with customers to help reduce costs—although perhaps not the most customer-friendly.

Some companies are more subtle in their shrinkage-reduction policies, though. Did you ever wonder why you're met by a "greeter" when you enter a Wal-Mart store? In part, it is because, in Wal-Mart's view, it's hard to steal from someone who has looked you in the eye and shaken your hand.

But how about the other end—when the thief tries to fence the stuff? XML Global, in Vancouver, B.C., developed a system called Xtract that allows secondhand stores to enter a description of each item they buy into a police database. The police department's software scans the entries for details that match descriptions of stolen property. What used to take weeks with paper records now takes minutes, and stolen property is being recovered much faster than before.[3]

✂ Technique No. 35. Work with Your Customers on Delivery Modalities

Is air shipment essential? Is truck shipment the most cost-effective? What about rail? It's pretty simple to just ask your customer about his or her timing needs, and then think about the best delivery method to use. In fact, it's likely that some customers will appreciate being asked, even if they don't pay the freight. Airborne Express, of course, made a business model out of using a combination of air and truck, keeping costs down as a result, and promising second-day delivery rather than overnight delivery for a reduced price.

This technique can be especially significant for companies that ship heavy loads. Bethlehem Steel Corp. is a case in point. Bethlehem has, on occasion, asked its customers if they would accept delivery by rail instead of truck, or by a combination of rail and truck, when the economics of shipping this way were more favorable than those of shipping by truck alone. With recent improvements in rail service, this modality has become more cost-efficient.[4]

✂ Technique No. 36. Find Out What Your Customers Really Need

You've heard it before: "Listen to your customers." This doesn't always work, of course, since sometimes your customers aren't aware of all their options or don't know what they really need or want. But sometimes listening can lead to some large cost savings. At General Motors, under the leadership of Bob Lutz, the company began an effort to try to determine customer needs in a wide variety of areas. One issue was the number of electrical outlets needed in a vehicle. Did customers really need three outlets, as had been planned for some future models? Using just two would save $4 per vehicle. Big deal, you say? Well, it was. At just $4 a pop, the total savings would amount to $2.5 million a year.[5]

✂ Technique No. 37. Consider Your Features

No, this doesn't mean looking carefully in the mirror. Instead, ask yourself whether your products' features are what customers really need or want. If they aren't, why bother with them? It is reported that when Toyota and the company that manufactures its air conditioners negotiate the price for an air conditioner for the upcoming budget year, one of the items on the table is features. Over the years, the air conditioner manufacturer has engaged in extensive reengineering to reduce costs as much as possible. At some point during the negotiations, the air conditioner manufacturer's representative might say something like, "It currently takes 7 minutes from the time the driver turns on the air conditioner until the car reaches the desired temperature; would you tolerate 9 minutes? If so, we can reduce our costs somewhat."

Similarly, even before September 11, some of the airlines were considering a reduction in certain features in an effort to save costs. Although with less customer involvement than Toyota's air conditioner supplier, Northwest had dropped meal service on flights under

2 hours and 15 minutes and had eliminated special meals for coach-class passengers on all domestic flights. The savings were estimated at $1 million a month.

On the other hand, consider the following text, taken from an advertisement for a Nikon camera:

> Sleek and pocket-sized, with the unique inner-swivel lens design. Lets you take pictures from any angle. Even take one of yourself. 2.0 effective megapixels and exclusive 3× Zoom-Nikkor lens gives you incredibly sharp shots every time. Tons of cool features like 12 selectable Scene Modes, so you can capture the fun wherever you are, in or out, up or down. Plus a built-in One-Touch Upload button sends images to your desktop or to the web so you can send a share with friends and family. Check out the legendary Nikon quality in this metallic-silver and blue digital. Includes rechargeable battery and charger. Awesome, huh?[6]

Now, could any of those features be eliminated without sacrificing the customer's willingness to pay the $379.95 listed price? Did Nikon's customers really ask for (or need or want) an inner-swivel lens design? What does it mean to capture a scene "up or down," and would eliminating that feature require the company to lower the list price? The key, of course, is to think carefully about what features will increase a customer's willingness to pay more, or, alternatively, what features could be eliminated without lowering the customer's willingness to pay.

This idea can be applied to services as well as goods. The owners of Marika, a 10,000-square-foot restaurant in Manhattan, spent $3 million on a renovation that included a variety of features designed to reduce the decibel level. Other restaurants have been known to install acoustical ceiling tiles and carpeting in an effort to reduce sound levels. But some restaurants take the opposite approach. Maxie's steak house in New York is known as one of the city's loudest. According to the owner, "As the night goes on, it gets louder. We turn up the music. We don't get a lot of complaints. It's a happy feeling."[7] In addition, it costs much less. (And it's good business for the local otolaryngologists!)

 But Beware! Be sure you don't make cost-reduction decisions based on your perception of customer needs without paying attention to their wants. One could argue that the purchasers of Mont Blanc pens don't *need* the tiny white glacier on the pen's cap, but they sure want it!

Technique No. 38. Improve Quality

You've also heard this before—the cost of quality—but it really can work. Not only can quality improvements make your customers happier (one would hope), but they can save you money to boot. Under Jack Welch's leadership, General Electric achieved significant cost savings with its "six sigma" approach (1 mistake per million) to quality.

And this idea has legs. In his plan to rescue Conseco—first from bankruptcy and then from low profitability—Gary Wendt initiated a six sigma quality improvement process. Based no doubt on his experience as head of GE Capital Services, Wendt expected the process to save Conseco $100 million.[8]

How does all this get measured? Well consider this: Warranty costs are pretty directly related to product quality. If you improve quality, your warranty costs will decline. Of course, quality improvements may cost something, so there's a trade-off. How do you decide whether to just accept the warranty costs or make improvements that will lower them?

The economics are not that tough, especially when there are industry standards that you can use for benchmarking. For example, Deutsche Bank estimated that Ford Motor Company's average warranty cost per vehicle was $650, versus $550 at General Motors and only $400 at Toyota.[9] With annual warranty costs totaling $2.6 billion, a reduction to even GM's level would result in savings to Ford of over $400 million a year. Bringing warranty costs down to Toyota's level would save about $1 billion. On top of that, there is the likelihood that sales and customer satisfaction would increase as a result of the decline in warranty work.

So, could Ford bring its warranty costs to GM's level by spending $400 million for quality improvements? Would spending $1 billion on improvements bring its warranty costs to Toyota's level? If so, it's probably worth *really* making quality "job 1."

Technique No. 39. Reduce Errors

This is a bit like improving quality, but it spills over into some other areas. Clearly, if you make a mistake and fix it before anyone finds out, quality has not worsened. But it took you some time to fix your mistake, and you could have spent that time doing something else. So, errors can be costly. Consider this from the perspective of Medicare, the federal government's health insurance plan for the elderly. According to an editorial in *Business Week,* "For every dollar the country spends on drugs, it wastes another dollar fixing medical problems caused by those same drugs. Doctors and hospitals are prescribing the wrong drugs to many, and too many drugs to others. Harmful side effects and drug interactions cost $150 billion each year to cure—enough to pay for a Medicare drug benefit."[10] And, if this is a problem that costs Medicare billions of dollars, it quite likely is a problem that costs private insurers and managed-care plans millions of dollars as well.

Technique No. 40. Get Some Sleep

This is a variation on the error-reduction theme, and it's still in the health-care area, but its implications are much more pernicious. We all have heard about the medical residents whose time in the "trenches" seems to be equated with sleep deprivation. And many of us have heard one anecdote or another about residents falling asleep standing up or at a dinner party. But this is not a book about healthy lifestyles—it's a book about cost cutting. What does all of this have to do with cost cutting?

Well, it turns out that after 24 hours of sleeplessness, a person's motor performance is comparable to that of someone who is legally intoxicated. Would you want someone like that performing surgery on you? One surgical resident, who was operating after having been awake for over 36 hours straight, confessed that he fell asleep during the procedure and that his head nearly fell into the incision in the patient's body.[11]

So what does this have to do with costs?, you ask. Well, let's see. First, if the surgeon is asleep with his or her head inside the patient, the operation probably will take longer, so more OR time is used, and with it additional expense for surgical nurses, other personnel, and maybe blood plasma. Second, there is an increased possibility of post-surgical infections (are those funny little hats as well sterilized as the gloves and instruments?) and the resulting need for longer stays in the hospital, plus whatever additional treatment costs are incurred. Then there's the possibility of collateral damage to the patient or one of the other members of the operating team (what did happen to that scalpel when you fell asleep, doctor?) and the costs related to that. And, finally, a malpractice lawsuit is not out of the question.

And here's the real rub. Legislation has been proposed to limit (limit?) residents to an 80-hour workweek and 24-hour shifts, but many doctors apparently resist such interference in their clinical decision making. Maybe if the idea were seen as a cost-control measure, it might gain greater acceptance.

Okay, so you've worked with your customers; you've eliminated unneeded features, improved quality, and reduced transportation costs. Now what? Well, the next obvious group to look at is your suppliers. Here, there is a remarkable range of possibilities, not all of which require getting tough.

✂ Technique No. 41. Think Small

Here's one that's almost a no-brainer. How big are the cars in your company's fleet? What mileage do your salespeople get as they drive around town, or back and forth across some part of the state? Think subcompact. Think really small. The Japanese now offer several choices (four of the ten best-selling cars in Japan in 2001 were subcompacts), with prices ranging from just over $5000 to about $8000 (that's right, four digits). Not all subcompact cars require serious compromises. Some are large enough to store two bicycles in the rear, and some have on-board email so that salespeople can easily keep in touch with the home office. Okay, the color choices (which include paprika orange and lima-bean green) aren't great, but the price (and the mileage) is right.[12]

Mitt Romney had similar success in keeping costs under control for the 2002 Winter Olympics. When asked how he was able to find $200 million in cost savings, his reply was akin to thinking small: "When an organization has to make cuts, the worst thing you can do is to make everyone bleed equally. Instead, we identified our top priority as providing superb sport facilities, and we didn't take one dollar out of that category. We took the savings out of nice-to-have appendages like decorations and celebrations."[13]

✂ Technique No. 42. Share

What was good on the playground may also be good in business. Do you really need distinct parts and components for each of your products? Apparently not in the automobile industry. At Ford Motor Company, one observer opined that Ford "could save a bundle . . . by sharing mundane parts—everything from fuel pumps to steering columns—among its vehicles."[14] Similarly, while he was at Chrysler, Robert Lutz was described as "a master at making cheap winners. The PT Cruiser, for example, was cobbled together using Dodge Neon parts and cost just $600 million, far less than the minimum $1 billion for development that new-car programs typically run."[15]

Chrysler's new president, Wolfgang Bernhard, has continued the tradition. Indeed, component sharing appears to have become a way of life at Daimler-Chrysler. Cloning Mercedes gearboxes for Chrysler family sedans may save as much as $100 million. And, in the ultimate in resurrecting the Six Million Dollar Man, some 40 percent of the content of Chrysler's new Crossfire is from Mercedes, including the engine, transmission, axles, seat frames, and radio controls.[16]

Why should this be limited to the automobile industry? The same kinds of savings may be available to other manufacturers who make similar products, so that components might be shared from one to the next.

Technique No. 43. Plan Ahead

Of course, all this sharing assumes that you get it right and don't end up with the proverbial horse designed by a committee. So, before you start to make the product, be sure that all the parts fit together. Sounds simple, doesn't it? Nevertheless, at many U.S. automobile assembly plants, when production is started, managers find that the components don't fit together, and costly last-minute design changes are required. Japanese auto manufacturers, by contrast, begin at the manufacturing phase; they make sure the parts fit, then back up to make the necessary adjustments in the parts before production actually begins. When production does begin, it proceeds smoothly.[17]

Technique No. 44. Change Your Inputs

Changing the kinds of cars you use is only one example of changing inputs. Before you start to lean on your suppliers to lower their prices, be sure you really need their products. What if you buy something different? Granted, for a diamond ring, you need a diamond, but not all of life is that way. Consider the cost of china in a retail store. If you buy a hand-painted dinner plate, you pay a pretty hefty price. But what if you get a painter to develop, say, a sponge cut in the shape of the design you need, and you use that rather than painting the design stroke by stroke? Does that sound crazy? Well, it's not an idea for everyone, but Marvin Gerouard of Pier 1 Imports found that it worked for him. He was able to save 30 percent of the cost of a Mediterranean hand-painted dinner plate (well, it's still hand-painted even if the artist uses a sponge, right?). When china is 30 percent of your merchandise, the savings are not insignificant.[18]

✂ Technique No. 45. Reduce Waste

This is a variation on changing inputs. Of course, it's easy to say that you should reduce waste, but it's often harder to do. However, waste is rampant in many companies. There's no need to get completely anal or to become a recycling fanatic, but there are some pretty obvious—and some not so obvious—possibilities. Do you really need to ship an unbreakable popsicle-stick-sized item in a 3- × 4- × 10-inch box, filled with Styrofoam pellets? These kinds of decisions, when corrected, can lead to a lot of savings. Way back in 1984, the President's Private Sector Survey on Cost Control (better known as the Grace Commission) identified some $424.6 billion in federal government costs that could be eliminated over 5 years by improving management and eliminating waste.[19]

And there's waste in your own backyard, too. How many napkins do you, as a customer, pull out of the dispenser at the restaurant? How many do you use? A simple new device can fix that. Kimberly-Clark has invented the Megacartridge—a dispenser that limits customers to one napkin at a time. The result is that restaurants use about 30 percent fewer napkins. The dollar impact? Well, the away-from-home napkin market is about $1.5 billion per year. The savings look to be about 30 percent of that, or about $450,000. That's not much for the average restaurant, but every little bit helps, and early reports indicate that the customers don't mind it at all.[20]

Technique No. 46. Fill Up the Trucks

This is a variation on waste reduction. When it comes to shipping and delivery, empty or half-empty trucks can cost a lot. Can you find ways to keep your trucks full, perhaps by consolidating loads? Sometimes it's not all that hard. At Olin Brass, for example, an effort is being made to ship more products in full truckloads. According to the company's transportation manager, "We have combined loads and made stop-offs and sometimes hold metal for a day or so to see if more orders come in."[21] As long as it meets the customers' delivery expectations, why not?

Wal-Mart has taken this idea even further, focusing not just on the trucks going out but on those coming back as well. The retailer's logistical system not only ensures that trucks leave the distribution centers with full loads, but also helps to fill up the trucks on the back haul rather than having them return empty, as is the case for some of its competitors. As a result of this and other techniques, Wal-Mart's transportation costs as a percent of revenue are well below the industry average.[22]

Technique No. 47. Cap Some Fringe Benefits

In a potentially pernicious variation on the theme of changing inputs, some companies are considering instituting caps on certain employee benefits. Stephen Gambale, a consultant on human resource costs, has suggested a cap of $50,000 on company-paid life insurance, and perhaps the elimination of long-term disability insurance.[23] In effect, this is not just changing an input, it's *eliminating* an input.

But Beware! It is possible that eliminating inputs like life insurance or long-term disability may have morale effects in the short term, turnover effects in the medium term, and union contracting issues in the longer term. A company might consider alternatives, such as cafeteria benefits or premium sharing for certain benefits, before eliminating or curtailing a benefit.

Technique No. 48. Look for Substitute Materials

This is like changing inputs, but a little different. Sometimes a substitute material can not only cost less but improve the product's quality. At Stocker Yale, a producer of fiber optics components, for example, one of the products offered by the company's illumination department was an assembly-line illuminator that helped to provide light to employees working with small parts. The product was a heavy box with a small lamp that was attached to it by a very flexible tube. The illuminator case was made of metal and cost about $30. When the firm switched to a plastic casing, which costs only $6, the illuminator became much lighter and easier to use and relocate. Best of all, customers saw it as a better product.[24]

Technique No. 49. Mail Smart

Whoever delivers your products is a supplier, and that includes the Postal Service. Do you really need to send out all that mail? In the catalog industry, for example, approximately 40 percent of the 16 billion catalogs mailed each year in the United States are sent to prospective new customers. The payoff rate is low. Many catalog retailers, including Lillian Vernon and Spiegel, are now mailing smarter: targeting customers who are likely to buy. Other companies are shifting their focus to online sales.[25]

Similarly, Bass Hotels & Resorts, the owner of Holiday Inn and Intercontinental Hotels, knows so much about the individual response rates to its promotions that it no longer bothers sending offers to people who have not responded in the past. As a result, it cut its mailing costs by 50 percent and improved its response rate by 20 percent.[26]

✄ Technique No. 50. Go Postal

Sure, it's terrific that what you are sending will absolutely, positively get there on time. But is it worth it? Do you need it there that quickly? For some items, the answer is yes. For others, maybe the second or third day will do. In case you haven't noticed, the U.S. Postal Service has become—or at least is *trying* to become—a good alternative, and at a much lower cost. The Postal Service now has tracking and confirmation tools, and it offers expedited shipping options—next day, second day, and priority—at a much lower cost than the overnight carriers. Soar like an eagle? Probably not, but no longer snail mail either.

✄ Technique No. 51. Turn Down the Thermostat!

What's a degree worth to you? No, not a college degree—a Btu-type degree. Since your utility companies are suppliers, too, you might as well look to them for some savings. Separate zones are one possibility. A degree or two lower in the office might work, too.

The Findley Lake Inn in New York has taken this to an interesting extreme. Findley Lake is a five-room, two-apartment bed-and-breakfast that does all its business on weekends. The inn's owners have decided to turn off the heat completely on weekdays and typically don't open up rooms until 2 P.M. on Fridays. According to the owner, "It's been very cold this winter, but in some respects this has helped us."[27] (On the other hand, if the pipes freeze, . . .)

Of course, this idea can be extended to lots of other utilities, and sometimes it's the simplest things that can help. Make sure the office lights are out at night; radios, TVs, and computers are turned off; and so on. Maybe Mom was right after all. (Did LBJ really walk around the White House at night turning off the lights?)

So far, we've been talking about cutting supply costs without necessarily getting tough with suppliers. But sooner or later, the day will come when you'll have to get tough. How might you best approach this? Here are a few thoughts.

✂ Technique No. 52. Share Fringe-Benefit Costs with Employees

Remember, your health plan is a supplier. With this in mind, many companies have begun to ask their employees to share some of their health-care costs. These range from additional premiums for drug pre-scriptions to asking employees to pay more of their medical expenses out of pretax medical spending accounts. With health-care premiums increasing at double-digit rates, this can amount to a big saving for some companies. A recent survey by the National Association of Health Underwriters indicated that (1) the average increase in health insurance premiums in 2000 was 15 percent, (2) 12 percent of com-panies are considering dropping health insurance because of price increases, (3) 45 percent of small business employees contribute to health-plan premiums, and (4) 42 percent of total premium costs are borne by employees in small businesses.[28]

Unfortunately, this is not really cost cutting per se. The health premiums continue unabated. However, the *company's* costs are reduced, since employees now pay part of the tab. In contrast, con-sider the following technique.

✂ Technique No. 53. Collaborate with Your Suppliers

Maybe you can share in some cost-cutting efforts at your suppliers' end, with the idea that everyone can win. Some employers have found that this works with health insurance premiums. With double-digit increases forecast, some employers have begun to look for ways to collaborate with their insurance carriers in cost-reduction programs. A group of California schools found a way to do this. Although some California companies were seeing health-care premium increases of

50 to 100 percent, 550 California schools collectively obtained a 3-year rate guarantee without a premium increase. How? They agreed to contribute an amount equal to 2 percent of their premium to loss-control efforts.[29] Everyone won. The rate increase was abated, and the health plan had both an incentive and some needed financing to support its cost-control activities.

Technique No. 54. Consolidate Suppliers to Obtain Lower Prices

Do you need multiple suppliers for the components of your products? Can the same supplier provide components for multiple products? Can you consolidate your purchases from two suppliers so that they all come from just one? Presumably, if you promise greater volume, you may be able to convince your suppliers to lower their prices. That was the experience of Valeo, France's largest maker of automobile components (mechanical and thermal systems and electrical and electronic systems). Valeo was under pressure to eliminate its losses (which had totaled 185 million euros during the first six months of 2001). In an effort to reduce its raw material costs, Valeo severed links with 509 of 4485 suppliers. The goal was to increase the size of the orders with the remaining suppliers, improve their productivity, and therefore obtain lower prices.[30]

Technique No. 55. Lean on Your Suppliers for Lower Prices

How much can you push your suppliers? It depends on how badly they need your business and how much slack they have in their own cost structures. When you're a big buyer, you can exert a fair amount of clout. Sometimes it's easier when you're the new kid on the block. For example, 3 weeks into his job as CEO of Chrysler, Dieter Zetsche demanded that suppliers cut their prices by 5 percent—a cut that would have a $2 billion impact on Chrysler's bottom line. He also informed them that they needed to cut their prices an additional 10 percent by 2003. About 10 percent of the suppliers walked away, but the rest are now seeking ways to cut their costs.[31]

Taking a page from the auto industry, the pharmaceutical industry has begun to lean on its suppliers as well. Hansjurg Wetter of Novartis has no hesitation about doing this. He was quoted as saying, "We are trying to emulate the example of the automotive industry, where encouraging heavy competition among suppliers has yielded substantial cost cuts. We hope to successfully apply the strategy to pharmaceuticals."[32]

✂ Technique No. 56. Target Certain Suppliers for Big Cuts

It isn't necessary to ask each supplier to make the same level of price cuts. Some suppliers presumably have more slack than others and can be targeted for larger cuts, while others may not be able to achieve significant reductions. At Nissan Motor Company, for instance, suppliers worldwide were asked to help the company achieve a 20 percent reduction in costs by 2003. The program did not require each supplier to cut its costs by the same amount, however: Each had a different goal assigned by Nissan. One result was the elimination of about 10 percent of the company's 300 North American suppliers. According to Nissan's senior vice president for North America, these cost-cutting efforts saved the company $700 million in 2000, an average savings of over $1000 for every car the U.S. and Mexican operations built during the year.[33]

So, you're running out of options in the direct nonpersonnel area. You've checked in with customers, adjusted some of your product characteristics to fit their needs and wants, gotten them involved in helping you save costs, and focused on your raw materials and suppliers. What next? How about getting your employees involved in identifying activities that may not be needed or that might be changed so that you operate at lower cost? Here are a few ideas that you might consider in this arena.

Technique No. 57. Push Thinking Down into the Organization

Your employees can be a wonderful source of cost-cutting ideas. Sometimes just asking can work, although some companies have found that techniques such as offering cash bonuses or time off for accepted suggestions or giving bonus vacation days for savings that exceed some threshold can lead to some especially creative ideas for cost reductions.[34] At Chrysler, for example, plant managers were asked to think creatively about cost-cutting measures. One plant manager discovered that shutting down the escalators in the factory would save $80,000 a year.[35] Who used those escalators, anyway, and for what? And, who knows? Maybe the extra exercise can help to reduce health-care costs.

Technique No. 58. Find the Slack

Slack consists of those resources you have available, or those expenses you incur, that add no easily discernible value. Plush carpets and executive washrooms, or plush carpets *in* executive washrooms, might be thought of as slack. Of course, what is slack for one company is not necessarily slack for another. Plush carpets and mahogany tables in the purchasing department at Wal-Mart would be considered slack. On the other hand, the same features in a law firm's conference room may be needed to convince potential clients that the firm's hourly rate is justified.

Sometimes finding slack can substitute for choices that might have dire consequences. For example, when he took over as budget director of Illinois, Leonard Schaeffer faced a difficult choice: raise taxes or reduce spending. With voters likely to be opposed to a tax increase, spending cuts seemed the obvious route. But where? Some spending cuts would affect needed services for the state's most vulnerable citizens. Some other expenditures reflected legitimate resource needs or were mandated by legislation. So Schaeffer began to look for places where he could reduce spending without making sacrifices in the state's core programs—that is, looking for slack. And he found it. Indeed, as he put it, "I cut all kinds of unnecessary crap—cars, airplanes. The state of Illinois had nearly as large an air force as Israel."[36]

✂ Technique No. 59. Purchase on the Basis of Value Rather Than Cost

Uses of this technique can range from the sublime to the not so sublime. In the latter category we might include a decision to purchase $300 personal computers because they are cheap. Most companies would not do this, but why not? Clearly, these companies are considering benefits as well as costs, or value (the ratio of benefits to costs). We do this all the time when we make purchases. We don't purchase the cheapest automobile, refrigerator, television, and so forth. In all of our purchase decisions—whether consciously or subconsciously—we are thinking of the relationship between benefits and costs.

How far can you extend this idea? If it works for cars, refrigerators, and personal computers, maybe it can work for other nonpersonnel items as well. For example, some years ago, General Electric began to shift its health-care purchasing strategy toward value. Once the company had completed the restructuring of its criteria, the per-member-per-month cost accounted for only 20 percent of the total—the same percentage as employee satisfaction. GE also used a variety of other criteria in its health plan selection decision, such as the kinds of information and services the plan would provide to the company's benefit managers on a regular basis.[37] GE felt that this improved information would help it not only to manage its health-care costs better, but also to increase employee satisfaction in a way that would reduce turnover.

With the GE example in mind, imagine the following scenario: A health plan sees an opportunity to deliver some new services to meet the currently unmet needs of a group of consumers in a community (perhaps diabetics or patients at risk for diabetes). It proposes a premium *increase* to a large employer (one of its customers) to help it meet this need.

Most employers would be aghast at the idea of a premium increase, but assume for the moment that an employer accepts the proposal. The plan then uses the incremental revenue to provide additional compensation to providers (mainly physicians and hospitals) for new forms of care and possibly new services (such as screening and prevention). As a result, the patients' (employees') condition is managed better, and their health is improved. With improved health comes an increase in on-the-job productivity and a reduction in absenteeism. The improved productivity and reduced absenteeism benefit the employer financially, thereby completing the cycle.

Overall, if the cost savings from the increased productivity are greater than the incremental premiums, the employer has reduced its total costs. Likewise, if the increased premiums to the health plan are greater than the incremental payments it makes to providers, its profitability has increased. And if providers find that the increased payments are sufficient to cover the new or reconfigured services they deliver to their patients, their incomes or profits have increased. Finally, if patients (employees) are healthier and more productive, they presumably are happier. In short, everyone wins, even though there is an *increase* in the employer's premium. This is a decided contrast to the intense— almost maniacal—focus on premium cost that continues to characterize most contracting efforts between health plans and employers.[38]

Make Sure You Avoid These YGBKs

YGBK No. 3. Quality Cuts

As Ford Motor Company has demonstrated, lower quality can lead not only to higher warranty costs, but also to far more serious problems. Ford and Firestone found out that the consequence of really low-quality tires on certain vehicles could be class-action lawsuits.

(continued)

(Of course, the manufacturers of *high-quality* cigarettes have also faced class-action lawsuits.) Indeed, it's hard to read the local newspaper without learning of another lawsuit resulting from a quality problem with a company's product, whether it be poorly refrigerated food products or failed airport security checks.

Sometimes even minor reductions in quality can have serious repercussions. Consider the case of Webvan Group, Inc., one of many companies providing online ordering of groceries. Webvan placed enormous emphasis on its technology and infrastructure, but it didn't spend much time on the basics of the grocery industry. The company required about 4000 orders a day to break even, compared to just 1500 for HomeGrocer, a competitor. To cut costs, Webvan switched to lower-quality produce suppliers, resulting in products that many customers found unacceptable. In 2001, after operating losses that had increased in each of the three prior years, the company closed its doors.[39]

YGBK No. 4. Penny-Wise, Pound-Foolish Cuts

Sometimes, it's wise to look at the whole picture before instituting spending cuts. Chevron Oil, admittedly a biased observer, suggests that lower-grade lubricants don't protect machine components as well as the more expensive stuff. When companies use lower-grade lubricants, equipment may experience more downtime or need replacement sooner.[40]

But Milton Roemer, a health economist, provided perhaps the best example. Roemer studied a decision by MediCal (California's health-care program for the indigent) to institute a $1 copayment for patients who saw a physician for primary care. The policy had its intended effect: Primary-care visits declined, and with the decline there was a reduction in MediCal's costs. Then, some months later, many of those same patients were hospitalized for conditions that could have been prevented with timely primary-care treatment. Overall, the effect of MediCal's new policy was an increase in costs.[41]

3

OFF WITH ITS (OVER)HEAD!
THE RED QUEEN STRIKES BACK

Here's where the fun starts. The words *overhead* and *bureaucracy* are perhaps the two most pejorative in business. (Well, at least they were until Arthur Andersen moved the term *shredder* out of the world of the Teenage Mutant Ninja Turtles and into the world of business, while simultaneously converting the term *independent auditor* into an oxymoron.)

For some companies, some of the areas discussed in this chapter may be considered direct costs rather than overhead costs, just as other companies might consider some of the costs in Chapter 2 to be overhead costs. The key, of course, is not where a cost is classified but the idea that there are ways to reduce it. In all instances the techniques in this chapter offer the opportunity to eliminate some potentially unneeded activities, with corresponding cost reductions, and possibly to cut costs without the need for personnel reductions.

Oppenheimer Funds is a nice example of a firm that is committed to cutting costs without reducing personnel. In the face of the late 2001 economic slowdown, Oppenheimer asked every department to cut back its expenses by at least 10 percent. According to Jim Ruff, president of Oppenheimer Funds Distributors, the firm was intent on avoiding even a discussion of layoffs. Instead, departments were asked, among other things, to assess how much was being spent on first-class travel, rental cars, and accommodations. "If we dig deep enough and really look into our budget, we won't even have to have a discussion on people," Ruff said.[1]

That's one good example, but there are many more. Let's look at what some other companies have done.

✂ Technique No. 60. Reclassify Some Overhead Costs as Direct Costs

This sounds like an accounting gimmick, but it need not be. Several years ago, General Electric was faced with health-care costs in excess of $1 billion. The costs represented 30 percent of after-tax corporate profits and exceeded the income of any of the company's 12 business units. To address the problem, the company decided that its health insurance plans were, in effect, suppliers—and needed to be managed just like the company's other suppliers. Thus, instead of keeping health-care premiums as part of corporate overhead, GE made them a direct expense for each of its business units. Jack Welch then challenged the leader of each business unit to keep health-care costs flat in his or her business plan and to manage them more aggressively.[2]

In effect, Welch had shifted GE's health insurance costs from overhead to direct expenses. The result: Whereas in the past the CEOs of the business units had been largely unconcerned about health-care costs, they now were quite concerned about them. Those costs now directly affected each business unit's bottom line and, with it, the CEO's bonus.

Results like this, but extending beyond health care, can be achieved in other companies through, say, a creative use of transfer prices that results in the various business units "purchasing" overhead resources rather than having the costs allocated to them. When the leaders of the business units purchase the resources and when those costs affect their bottom-line performance, they are motivated to consider their use of corporate overhead.

But let's look at ways in which the corporate office itself can begin to think about reducing overhead. There are lots of possibilities here.

✂ Technique No. 61. Reconfigure Travel

This technique includes the usual suspect, coach instead of first-class travel, but it can include much more. What about shifting the timing of travel? If you pay for a Friday and Saturday night hotel stay (or a Saturday and Sunday night stay), can you reduce your airfare by a larger amount? Maybe, if the destination is reasonably attractive, an employee could bring a spouse for the weekend at little incremental cost.

Similarly, what about consolidating some travel—say, purchasing books of tickets with 14- or 21-day advance notice? What about having the travel department work to configure trips in such a way that the total airfare is lower than it might otherwise be?

Remember that travel includes more than just airfare. Ground transportation, hotel and meals, and various other on-ground expenses are also candidates for reduction. In addition, with Internet sites offering opportunities for discounts, travel increasingly is being viewed as a commodity. There are many opportunities for cost savings.

✂ Technique No. 62. Negotiate Better Hotel Rates

During an economic slowdown, travel is reduced and the travel industry suffers. Between April 2000 and April 2001, hotel occupancy rates fell by over 17 percent in San Francisco and Silicon Valley, 11.8 percent in New York, 10.1 percent in Chicago, and 7.1 percent in Boston.[3] What does this mean for your travel department? If you do a lot of traveling to certain cities, you probably can negotiate better hotel rates. With the variable cost of a room at about $15, hotels can afford to go pretty low on rates in exchange for substantial volume.

✂ Technique No. 63. Reduce Travel

Do you really need to travel at all? Teleconferencing is on the rise and can work, especially for internal company meetings, such as national sales meetings. It may turn out that many people are happier when they do not have to travel, and much more work is likely to get done when you eliminate the need to travel. This is what Siebel Systems did. The company halved its travel budget by instructing employees not to travel anywhere except to see a customer. Gillette's employees fly coach instead of business class to Europe. Staples is using more teleconferencing than it did a few years ago.[4] Similarly, faced with declining revenues in the early 2000s, Brobeck, Phleger & Harrison, a prestigious San Francisco law firm with a no-layoff policy, told its employees to stop using Town Cars. It also eliminated expense accounts and travel.[5]

Stretching this idea to perhaps its ultimate limit, the CEO of a fledgling start-up, with no venture capital and little owner-invested capital, reported that his one perk was going to and from work in a chauffeur-driven vehicle. The fact that he needed to share this vehicle with some 30 or 40 other passengers was of little consequence to him![6]

Might you ask your employees to take the bus or subway when traveling around town? Is train travel a possibility for medium-length trips? While many train fares are the same as comparable airline fares, there are some significant savings: reduced check-in and waiting time, improved on-time performance (sometimes), and the opportunity to engage in relatively uninterrupted work, since a laptop can remain on and a cell phone can be used for the entire trip. These savings may compensate for the longer travel time between the two points, especially in some busy corridors like Boston-New York-Washington, and San Diego-Los Angeles-San Francisco.

✂ Technique No. 64. Retreat from the Retreat

What are those retreats all about, anyway? Could you hold an all-day meeting in the office, send out for sandwiches, and have the receptionist tell all callers that you're "away" at a retreat? Some companies, questioning the value of their retreats, have canceled them entirely. This was the case with Brobeck, Phleger & Harrison. Faced with declining revenues in the early 2000s, the firm canceled partner retreats.[7] Other organizations have looked at ways to reduce their meeting or retreat costs. They use hotels instead of resorts, dine in the hotel instead of at an off-site restaurant, and insist that participants do some premeeting reading so as to cut down on presentation time and shorten the overall length of the meeting.[8]

Technique No. 65. Prune the Perks

What are your corporate perks? How much do they cost you? When was the last time you did a cost-benefit analysis on them? Could you eliminate some? For example, corporate boxes at sporting events are expensive. Why not think small? The minor leagues are on the rise, and the prices are right. As a result, attendance is way up. Luxury boxes, party decks, and even conference centers are available at a fraction of the cost for the big leagues. As a comparison, a family of four can buy tickets, drinks, hot dogs, and programs for about $45 at a AAA game, compared to about $120 for the major league equivalent.[9] It's also likely that the players' skills and egos are more closely aligned in the AAA than in the majors.

Technique No. 66. Assess Administrative Activities

Some administrative activities may not be worth the time they take, even if they bring in some additional revenue. Sometimes an analysis of these activities can lead to extremely counterintuitive results. Consider the case of 3M Company. 3M redesigned its reporting system so that each operating unit received statements that separated direct production activities from activities devoted to production support. The company applied activity-based costing (ABC) to the analysis of corporate logistics costs, particularly the analysis of the cost of processing customer orders and making credit adjustment decisions. It discovered that the cost of *processing* small credit claims was almost as great as the cost of *settling* them. As a result, it established a new policy that allowed sales representatives to approve on-site credit adjustments for small complaints.[10]

✂ Technique No. 67. Reduce the Reports

How long has it been since you checked with report recipients to make sure they actually use those beasts? In some companies, once the accounting or IS department develops a report, no one questions its utility. Yet it may have become unneeded, redundant, or, even worse, misleading. An operational audit might pick this up, or it may just take a short questionnaire to find this. In some organizations, there are regular meetings that focus on finding and eliminating unnecessary procedures, forms, and layers of oversight. The meetings attempt to identify studies, reports, analyses, investigations, and approvals that have become routine and repetitive, and to stop them if they're no longer needed. At one airline, meetings of this sort eliminated a 300-page report when the managers receiving the report discovered that the same information was available elsewhere.[11]

✂ Technique No. 68. Bust the Bureaucracy

Stale and outdated reports are only one example of how procedures can just keep going on and on, sometimes—usually—resulting in an unnecessary expenditure of resources. What about the weekly or monthly update meetings? Could you do this via email instead? Or could you perhaps distribute the basic information via email and limit the meeting to Q&A? Are all those supply and material requisitions really needed, or could you automate them via the use of bar codes? Wal-Mart has done this for inventory restocking in its stores. Why not extend the idea to supplies in general? Not only might you save some time, but it might turn out that the system will enable you to consolidate purchases from several departments, permitting you to negotiate lower prices.

How far can you extend all this? It depends in large measure on what business you're in, what activities are repetitive, and whether oversight is really needed. In one university, for example, every time a department chair hired a part-time faculty member to teach one course, he or she needed to send a special request to the university's provost, accompanied by a résumé and three letters of recommendation. Really, now!

✂ Technique No. 69. Cut Recruiting Costs

Let's face it. In a recession, it's a buyers' market for employees: They want you more than you want them. In fact, if you're laying off people, you may not need to do any recruiting, and you'll certainly need to do far less. That should allow you to decrease your recruiting expenses. At Siebel Systems, for instance, the slackening economy had reduced sales forecasts. The annual growth of the company's market was shrinking from 50 percent to 25 percent, and sales were expected to fall by 60 percent from the forecast level. The company slashed its recruiting budget from $8 million to $1 million.[12] Other companies have found that they can do at least some preliminary screening with teleconferencing rather than on-site interviews.

✂ Technique No. 70. Go Paperless

We keep hearing about the paperless society, but who's in charge of making it happen? It's not enough to send a document as an attachment to an email rather than in paper form if everyone then prints it out; in fact, it probably costs *more* that way. Instead, you have to find a way to keep the document stored electronically. General Electric is doing just that. The company has declared war on employee desktop printers, individual fax machines, and individual copiers. In all, the company returned, donated, or threw out 30,000 machines. If you haven't got a printer, it's hard to print. As a result, paper consumption was down by 28 percent in 6 months, and annual savings of $18 million were anticipated. The employees seemed quite content (well ... maybe) to store data in laptops and on smart phones.[13] (Let's hope GE is investing some of those savings in data backup systems.)

Technique No. 71. Go Nomad

How many of your people are in the office each day? Is a reasonably high percentage on the road? If so, does it make sense for each of them to have a separate office, or could they do some sharing? Boston Equity Office Properties, which, ironically, owns more office space than any other publicly held real estate company in the country, did some research and discovered that, on average, its employees were out of the office 70 percent of the time. The company decided that it could get by with less space. It eliminated 15,000 square feet, which it then leased to paying customers. How? By asking its employees to share space. When an employee arrives in the morning, a computer system determines the office that he or she will occupy for the day— and just that day. (Why not just first come, first served?) The nomadic approach not only allowed the company to reduce the space that it occupied, but also allowed it to bring its management teams from 19 separate buildings into just one, thereby speeding decision making and information sharing. It also discovered that it had multiple copies of many lease contracts that could be consolidated.

Upon arriving in the morning, each employee receives his or her "puppy"—a small file cabinet on wheels that contains files and usually also a bag with personal items, such as family pictures that go on the desk for the day. Employees use laptop computers, and each desk is equipped with all the high-tech connections needed to get up and going quickly. (Now the company just has to be sure that its clients don't learn about this technique.)

✂ Technique No. 72. Go Cash and Carry

Not only do some bills not get paid, but a billing system costs you money. If people are there and they're willing to pay right away, let 'em! What's wrong with a little old-fashioned cash? In fact, sometimes the cost of sending out the bill can exceed the amount of the payment. Most health insurance companies, for example, require patients to make a copayment of $5 or $10 for every visit to a physician, and $25 or more for a visit to an emergency room. Some physicians and some emergency rooms do not collect the money at the time of the visit. Instead, they send out a bill. Given the cost of stationery, labor, postage, and accounting, it is hard to imagine that a physician makes much on a $10 bill to a patient, and she or he may even lose money on a $5 bill. Why not just ask the patient to pay? In fact, in the case of an emergency room visit, patients may be much less willing to pay for the visit when there's no longer an emergency. Since relatives and friends usually stand around for a considerable amount of time anyway, why not ask them to make the copayment and be done with it?

✂ Technique No. 73. Consolidate Shipments

The price of an overnight shipment is not a linear function of its size or weight. Consolidating shipments to major customers may have a significant payoff if you are in a business where shipping costs are a large share of your overhead. The Walt Disney Company, for example, spends some $9 billion a year on shipping and other supply-related overhead activities. By consolidating its express mail shipments, the company expects to save a sizable portion of that $9 billion.[14]

✂ Technique No. 74. Incur Overhead Strategically

The goal is to figure out where you want to add overhead and why. Sometimes it makes sense to add to overhead. Wal-Mart, for example, has higher information-technology overhead than its competitors, not because it is sloppy in its use of this resource, but because it has decided that a sophisticated IT system can allow it to keep inventories low, work more effectively with suppliers, and carry out a host of other activities.

Cisco Systems is similar. At Cisco, overhead exceeds the median for companies in its industry, but Cisco's cost of goods sold is just 30.9 percent of operating revenue, well below the median of 51.8 percent. Could it be that Cisco is doing something in the central office that keeps its cost of goods sold down? It turns out that Cisco spends money on Web-based systems to improve its outsourced-manufacturing model. The company also spends a high percentage of its overhead on sales to help ensure a high level of customer satisfaction.[15]

✂ Technique No. 75. Use Competitive Intelligence

Here's a variation on a theme that will test your ethical principles. Some companies are using competitive intelligence, a euphemism for corporate espionage, to help avoid costs, but not in the way you might imagine. According to a story in *Business Week,* Avnet, Inc., a Phoenix-based electronics distributor, relying on the predictions of its in-house analysts, avoided a price war. The analysts had predicted that two of Avnet's competitors soon would be out of business and were engaging in desperate price cutting to gain market share. By avoiding the battle, Avnet was able to compete more forcefully with the rivals that remained after the bloodbath.[16] As a military strategist once said, "Wars are won as much by the battles you choose not to fight as by those you fight and win."

✂ Technique No. 76. Think about the Little Stuff

The little stuff can add up. Call it penny-jar syndrome if you wish, but for many companies it not only translates into significant savings, but it sends a clear message that management is serious about cost cutting.

To illustrate, an article in *Air Conditioning, Heating, & Refrigeration News* suggests using decals instead of special paint for logos on autos and trucks, paying employees mileage to use their own vehicles rather than buying company vehicles, removing or reducing the number of cellular phones, centralizing tool storage, using identifying marks on tools, and keeping records of who checked tools out. These and a variety of other relatively small-ticket items are designed to attack the "blob" of overhead.[17] Similarly, Apache Corp., while engaging in some creative and significant cost-reducing activities, also eliminated company-supplied Styrofoam coffee cups.[18] Presumably, the company asked everyone to bring in a china cup (either that or a long straw).

An article in *Food Management* suggested some little stuff for restaurants, such as purchasing walk-in coolers with extra-wide doors to allow the delivery of a full pallet of food at once, using automatic slicers for some prep work, using "combi ovens" to cook food faster than a conventional oven, recycling fat from fryolators, purchasing trash compactors, purchasing hi-tech knife sharpeners, and a host of other ideas.[19] A piece in *Nation's Restaurant News* suggested using the restaurant's bulletin board to post monthly invoices for electricity, water, heat, gas, food, beverages, insurance, and the lease. Doing so, the article argued, allows employees to review these "invisible costs" of doing business and compare them with their home expenses.[20] Presumably this will make them a bit more compulsive about turning out the lights.

Technique No. 77. Manage Your Training Costs

When new technology is introduced, employees must often be trained to use it, but who should do the training? Must it be done by your IT department, or are there alternatives that could save both time and money? Could you negotiate training by the vendor as part of the purchase deal for the new technology? Could you have employees train one another rather than using the more expensive IT staff? Could you make employees responsible for their own training?[21]

But Beware! Focusing on the banking industry, Andrew Hubbard (a trainer) argued that professional trainers are much more cost-effective than in-house people. They create user-friendly manuals, pace the material properly, and train participants to use the manual properly. He also argues that an appropriate site (not the employee lunchroom), dedicated laptop computers, and catered lunches, while appearing to raise costs, actually are more cost-effective when the cost of downtime is considered.[22]

✂ Technique No. 78. Manage Your Growth

Sometimes when you're growing fast, you lose sight of the systems and procedures that need to be in place to support this growth. When this happens, costs can get out of hand. Home Depot provides a good case in point. At Home Depot, total square footage increased by 25 percent a year during the 1990s. Senior management was so focused on store growth that it failed to pay enough attention to controlling the company's operations. Because its basic systems—purchasing, accounting, and logistics—were not updated, there were redundancies in the supply chain, loose inventory controls, and a lack of a uniform system to assess employee performance.[23] As a result, while the company was growing, it was not getting the economies of scale, and the resulting profits, from its growth that it otherwise might have. (And why, by the way, do the members of the orange-apron army never ask me if I need help?)

✂ Technique No. 79. Reduce Moving Costs

Have you looked at your moving policy recently? Do you need to move your employees as often as you have been doing? If so, must they have their own furniture, or would it be acceptable (and perhaps less costly) to rent furniture for them or to have them rent a furnished house? Maybe the company should purchase and even furnish houses in areas where there's a lot of turnover.

But that's only part of the story. For some companies, moving employees is more costly than necessary because of the routes that are chosen. A transportation manager at Belmore Furniture Co. doesn't accept the conventional wisdom that you should minimize the total number of miles traveled in a move. He has achieved some savings by planning routes that, while longer in terms of distance, avoid mountain travel and thus use less fuel and take fewer hours.[24] Don't be afraid to let those creative juices flow!

Technique No. 80. Eliminate Requisitions and Purchase Orders for Small Items

This is not something the purchasing manager will support, but it will make the CFO happy. Consider the experience of Superior Products, a consumer goods distributor. Superior eliminated requisitions and purchase orders on items under $100. For these orders, the department head or supervisor telephones a purchasing agent, who telephones the supplier, who ships the item. It takes half the time to get the items, and reductions in labor and forms cost in the purchasing department amount to about $18,000 a year.[25]

Technique No. 81. Cut the Frivolity

Free massages, free lunches, snacks, happy hours, nights on the town, Caribbean cruises, concierge service—maybe not for a while. Living. com, for example, eliminated its kitchen cupboard, which was once stocked with foodstuffs to help programmers work 80-hour weeks. The online furniture retailer also eliminated free massages and its weekly happy hour. Aetna is saving $400,000 by making employees at its Blue Bell, Pennsylvania, office buy their own coffee and tea. Excite@Home now requires employees to pay a quarter a can for soda that used to be free. With over 600,000 cans consumed annually, the savings totaled some $165,000. When you're losing money, that can help a lot. Similarly, one year of concierge service—which helps employees with such chores as planning a vacation or buying theater tickets—can cost a large company $100,000.[26]

 But Beware! Once given, some of these perks are hard to take away without affecting morale. Moreover, if companies eliminate them with little or no employee input, the lower morale or reduced commitment to the company's success can outweigh the savings.

Make Sure You Avoid These YGBKs

YGBK No. 5. The Pension Fund Trap

If you're trying to save on labor costs, beware of the pension fund trap. The result—a pension fund with insufficient resources to pay the pensions that retirees have earned—can be unpleasant at best. The situation of Polaroid Corporation is illustrative. In October 2001, Polaroid's senior management sent a memo to the company's employees informing them that the pension plan had enough money to pay only about 90 percent of all the benefits that the employees had accrued. The memo said that the plan's decline from $1.3 billion in 1998 to $900 million in 2001 was due in part to the poor performance of the stock market and in part to layoffs, which increased the plan's "payoff volume." The decline, however, was greater percentagewise than that for other large companies.[27]

The lesson: While swings in the stock market can cause fluctuations in the value of a pension plan, a frequently unanticipated impact of employee layoffs is that the departing employees will decide to "retire" and begin to withdraw their holdings. While the impact can be short term until the pension plan regains value, the decline can have negative publicity effects, making it difficult for the company to rehire when its business turns up. It also can create problems in selling or merging the company, since the surplus or deficit in the pension fund will be factored into the company's value to potential purchasers. In Polaroid's case, the relatively large number of laid-off people who decided to retire, coupled with the stock-market decline, produced a double whammy.

YGBK No. 6. The Silly Stuff
In a quite clever advertisement for its high-speed Internet access service, Covad Communications Company included the following facetious (but too close for comfort) email that a hypothetical accounting department sent to all staff:

From: Accounting
To: ALL STAFF
Subject: muffins
Message: As of today, meeting muffins will be for client consumption only. And when possible, encourage them to go "halfsies" with one another.
Onward and upward
-the Mgt.

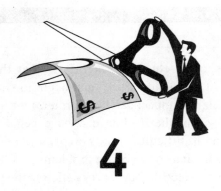

4

FIXED ASSETS ARE NOT SMALL GELDED DONKEYS
NIPPING DEPRECIATION IN THE BUD
WITH STRATEGIC INVESTMENTS

Sometimes it makes sense to think about the longish run, not just in terms of cost-cutting strategies per se (which are discussed in Chapter 7), but also in terms of fixed assets. We always refer to depreciation as a *sunk cost*; there's nothing you can do about it, since it is the result of decisions made in the past. But at the time you decide to acquire a fixed asset, depreciation is anything but a sunk cost—it's an expense waiting to happen. The resulting question, of course, is how do you think strategically about your investment in fixed assets?

In the first place, there are the usual suspects. If you're not doing a present-value or internal-rate-of-return analysis, or at least a simple payback period analysis, you probably should be. Appendix A discusses some of the techniques and frameworks needed to perform these sorts of analysis.

Some returns are difficult to quantify, but others are pretty easy. Moreover, proposals in which the advocate is suggesting some type of cost saving can usually be assessed more easily than proposals in which the advocate is suggesting a new program or product line that will lead to greater profitability. Indeed, it's doubtful that the annals of business contain even one example of a proposal for an investment in a new product or product line that forecast a loss, or even a low internal rate of return. Advocates of new programs are always optimistic.

So what's a CEO to do? Here are some techniques that may perhaps be helpful.

Technique No. 82. Relate Capital Budgeting to Strategy

Companies have been known to slip into new lines of business that are marginal at best. One solution (discussed later) is to sell off or otherwise eliminate those lines of business. A better solution is not to get into it in the first place. In part, this means that proposals need to be assessed in terms of their strategic fit as well as their cash flows. For example, Emerson Electric does not enter all electrical products markets; it limits itself to markets for electrical products with moderate rates of technological change and medium capital intensity that are sold to industrial customers. Cooper Industries limits its acquisitions to manufacturing industries with mature technologies, moderate capital intensity, and customers that value brand names. At E.G.&G., Inc., the capital budgeting *process* is designed to ensure a fit. Each division prepares a strategic plan in the spring. The plan defines such things as its business elements, competitors, and competitive advantages and disadvantages. In the fall, the firm develops a plan that looks ahead into the next calendar year. This establishes the framework for capital budgeting activities.[1]

Contrast this way of thinking with the proposal of Zapata, a Texas-based group with holdings in marine protein and food packaging companies, to purchase Excite, one of the leading Internet service companies. Avram Glazer, Zapata's chief executive officer, cited Excite's "excellent fit with Zapata's new strategic direction," saying that the proposed transaction "makes sense for Excite's shareholders because of the capital resources that Zapata can bring to Excite." Excite rejected Zapata's takeover offer.[2]

✂ Technique No. 83. Carefully Assess Investments in Strategic Alliances

Investments in assets that support a strategic alliance can be extremely powerful: Both companies can win big. But these sorts of investments also create vulnerability to a holdup if your partner company decides not to play by the old rules. One example of a strategic alliance that has the potential to become an *entangling* alliance is baseball owners' investment in minor-league players. What happens when a player—who has developed his skills in the minor leagues after several years of support, including a signing bonus—reaches the big leagues? The player has developed some skills, but he has also given up the opportunity to engage in some other income-earning activity, such that his next best income-earning opportunity may now be as a cabdriver. Similarly, the owner has made an investment. Will the player try to hold up the owner for a high salary by threatening to move to another team at free agency time? How will the owner respond? If an attempted holdup takes place on a massive scale and if the owners refuse to pay, the result can be a strike in which there are no winners, as happened a few years ago, and almost again in 2002.

Or what about Wal-Mart's investment in shared information technology with Procter & Gamble, Airborne Express's investment in warehouse space and information tracking for small parts for Xerox, or Dell's investment in complementary logistical systems with Sony, so that the Sony monitor arrives at the customer's office at the same time as the Dell computer, even though the two were sent from different plants? Each of these shared investments created value and deterred imitation, but it also reduced each firm's bargaining power vis-à-vis its partner, thereby creating the potential for a holdup.[3]

Technique No. 84. Site Your Facilities Strategically

To get even more fundamental, consider the case of Crown Cork and Seal, a bottle and can manufacturer. John Connelly was faced with an intense competitive environment when he took over as CEO in the 1980s. As part of a series of strategic moves designed to strengthen Crown's competitive position, Connelly began to site the company's plants strategically. Since shipping costs are a high percentage of the cost of a bottle or can, and since the company's products were essentially commodities, Connelly's siting strategy gave Crown a significant cost advantage over many of its competitors.[4]

Hyundai no doubt had a similar idea. Following a 41.7 percent gain in U.S. sales in 2001, it decided to build a $1 billion plant in Alabama. Kim Dong Jin, Hyundai's president, was quoted as saying that he hoped the plant would be profitable during its second year of operation.[5] That sounds like pretty strategic siting of a plant.

Technique No. 85. Make Sure Your Analysts Ask the Tough Questions

What do you say to the marketing manager who proposes investing in a new product line and claims that the product line will achieve breakeven within just a few months? Could it be true? Maybe, but somewhere there also may be pigs that can fly. What you really need are some analysts outside the marketing department, perhaps in the CFO's office, who will ask the tough questions: What kind of market research was done? What has been the experience of other companies in this market? If this is such a good idea, why hasn't a competitor done it already? If it turns out to be a good idea, who else will want to come into the market, what are the barriers to entry, and what are competitors' chances of taking share from us if they get in?

What's the worst-case scenario? Have you received a sign-off from manufacturing on production costs? What kind of analysis did manufacturing do? And so on.

✂ Technique No. 86. Be Sure There's Causality

One of the trickiest tasks for the analyst staff is to determine whether there is a causal link between a proposed investment and the anticipated payoff. For example, a federal agency proposed investing in a personnel training program, arguing that it would result in program participants getting new jobs and that the new jobs would increase the participants' annual earnings by an average of $25,000 per person. Since the training cost an average of $5000 per person, the proponents argued, the investment was well justified. However, there was no evidence that the training would indeed generate the increased earnings.[6]

A similar story is told of the idea that TV commercials would convince motorcyclists to wear helmets and that therefore helmet laws were not needed. However, only about $1 million was made available for an advertising campaign, a trivial amount given the cost per minute. More important, there was no evidence to suggest that a causal linkage existed between that amount of advertising and a change in the behavior of motorcyclists.[7]

✂ Technique No. 87. Check the Data

An absence of underlying causality may not be as readily apparent as it was in the previous two examples unless the analyst (or the advocate) does some background research. Without some sort of research, the advocate of an investment proposal may be relying on inaccurate intuition. This was illustrated quite dramatically in the late 1980s, when locusts were attacking the crops of many African nations. The U.S. Agency for International Development and other international aid agencies responded with $275 million and a fleet of aircraft that sprayed crops with millions of liters of pesticides. A few years later, a report by the Office of Technology Assessment (OTA) said that the campaign may have been a wasted effort. The OTA concluded that "Massive insecticide spraying . . . tends to be inefficient in the short term, ineffective in the medium term, and misses the roots of the problem in the longer term." Moreover, the study suggested that the justification for the entire operation may have been flawed because locusts aren't as big a threat as had been thought.[8]

What does this have to do with you, the manager? Well, if you're a farmer with a locust problem, a lot. But what if you're not? You can still assess an investment proposal with a keen eye and a cold heart and ask, "Why?" In one restaurant, for example, the manager spent a considerable amount of money to repaint a large wall with intricate and detailed murals three times over an 8-year period. To what end? Was there any indication that customers were becoming tired of the wall and were eating elsewhere as a result? Was the wall offensive to some customers? Apparently, the only person who had become bored with the wall was the manager.

Technique No. 88. Look for the Hidden Causality

While we're on the subject of causality, let's look at the other side of the coin, keeping in mind that the ultimate goal of any asset acquisition is an improvement in the bottom line. Sometimes that improvement may be somewhat small compared to the investment itself, but it will continue over several years. Under these circumstances, which are the normal ones, the future cash flows from the investment, when discounted to their present value, should be at least equal to the amount of the investment. In addition, and of considerable importance, those future cash flows need to be *caused* by the investment. That is, without the investment they would not exist.

But there's the rub. Sometimes the relationship between the investment and the cash flows can be somewhat circuitous. Here's where the clever analyst needs to find the hidden causality. Apache

Corp., a Houston-based oil and gas exploration and production company, is a case in point. Apache incurred some additional capital costs to install alarms on its oil wells. The alarms alerted company technicians 24 hours a day to any technical problems that shut the wells down. The result was that the technicians could repair the wells immediately, rather than allowing a well to stay offline overnight.[9] There were no cost savings as such: The repairs would have been made anyway. But when the wells stayed offline, there was a high opportunity cost in terms of lost production, and this was avoided with the installation of the alarms.

East Iowa Plastics provides another example that is even more tenuous and yet just as powerful. The company's four thermoforming machines were underused, and its two shifts of production workers overlapped by 4 hours. To fix the problem, the company added some automated accessories so that some equipment could run 24 hours a day, and it added a gas pipe that tied two older compressors together, thereby avoiding the need to replace them. Machine utilization rose to close to 100 percent. More important, although sales fell from $2.4 million annually in 1998 to an expected $1.3 million in 2001, the plant reversed its losses and began earning a profit.[10]

✂ Technique No. 89. Look for a Double Whammy

How about an investment that not only leads to lower operating costs but has a secondary impact on, say, employee productivity? This is what Pennsylvania Power & Light Company found to be the case when it installed a new lighting system that was oriented toward employee workstations. The system replaced an old fluorescent system that was expensive to maintain and created eyestrain, with a resulting negative impact on productivity. The new system, which cost less than $50,000, generated a return on investment of 501 percent. On top of that, employee productivity increased and sick leave declined.[11]

Technique No. 90. Look for Investments with Legs

This is a bit like the double whammy, but with a slightly different spin. If you can spread an investment over a larger volume of production than was originally intended, and if that larger output provides you with additional revenue, the per-unit cost of the investment has fallen. Is this accounting gimmickry? Not really. In fact, the accounting system may obscure the benefits, especially if depreciation is computed on a per-unit basis using the originally anticipated volume of production.

To see the advantage of this technique, keep in mind that the initial cost of whatever asset you invested in is unchanged, but that when you assess profitability, you need to determine how the expenses you incur are matched to the revenue you earn. If you earn more revenue from a particular fixed asset as a result of additional sales volume, you've just lowered the unit cost of the investment, regardless of what the depreciation figure may show.

To see how this works, consider television programs developed by the broadcast networks. The development of a program is a fixed cost—you incur it one time and that's it. Think of it as an investment. Now, what if you can earn some additional revenue from a given program by replaying it, say, on cable? In fact, some networks do this within just a few days of the original broadcasts.[12]

So we're not really talking about what the accounting system shows, since it quite likely is biased by the initial estimates of output volume. Instead, we're talking about whether a given investment has legs, and what sort of differential costs we will incur when we extend its use to provide additional volume. This idea has applicability well beyond the broadcast networks. Consider, for example, the cost of designing a new-model automobile. Can some design features be used for other models? If so, the investment has legs. Can certain technologies that have outlived their advantage in the United States be used in countries where the state of the art is lower? This was Crown Cork and Seal's approach to investing in Crown manufacturing in developing countries, where Crown technology had been introduced but where there was no need for high-technology production facilities. In effect, the company's R&D investment in the United States had legs.

Technique No. 91. Include Opportunity Costs in Net-Present-Value Computations

Frequently, a potential new asset is assessed in terms of either the cost savings it can realize or the additional contribution it can make to the bottom line. But sometimes, as the Apache example demonstrates, opportunity costs are also relevant. United Architects provides an interesting example. Managers at United were unable to justify to senior management or the CFO the several hundred thousand dollars required to purchase a computer-aided design and drafting (CADD) system. After losing several bids to competitors because of unsophisticated drawings and presentations, however, the affected managers computed the amount of contribution margin that the company *would have* received had it won its reasonable share of those competitions. This resulted in a positive net present value and tipped the balance in favor of purchasing the CADD system.[13]

Technique No. 92. Keep the End Goal in Mind

A capital investment may not be all that its cracked up to be, especially when compared to alternative ways of solving the problem. For example, several years ago, the federal government began to support local transportation for people with handicaps. Since the U.S. Department of Transportation subsidized bus and subway lines, its natural inclination was to finance the modification of buses to include lifts that would permit easy access for wheelchairs. The extra capital and maintenance costs of this equipment turned out to be huge, and usage was not high because people with handicaps had no way of getting from their homes to the bus stops. As a result, the cost per passenger was high—$1283 per trip in Detroit, for example.

Subsequently, transportation was provided by vans that picked people up at their homes and took them directly to their destinations. This was both more convenient for people with handicaps and less expensive to operate—it cost between $5 and $14 per passenger trip in most cities that tried it. Although it may now seem obvious, a focus on the goal of transporting people with handicaps, rather than on modifying existing modes of transportation, would probably have avoided the costly installation of passenger lifts in buses.[14]

Technique No. 93. Consider Alternatives with Higher Payoffs

Since resources are scarce and have alternative uses, any capital investment needs to be considered in light of other potential uses of the funds. Sometimes emotions cloud the issue, however. This is particularly true when lives are at stake, as they are any time disease and disease prevention issues are put on the table. At one time, for example, the standard for exposure to benzene was 10 parts per million (10 ppm), averaged over an 8-hour working day. At this rate, one benzene worker would die of benzene-related cancer every third year. According to the Occupational Safety and Health Administration (OSHA), a standard of 1 ppm would eliminate the risk, but would cost $100 million annually for the 30,000 workers who were exposed. Was this worth it? In part, the answer depends on the value you place on a human life. If, however, you are willing to place a dollar value on a human life, would you put that same amount on other human lives? This is the question that arose in the benzene case. In particular, one analyst asked the following question: Would each of the 30,000 benzene workers be willing to pay $3333 a year (his or her share of the $100 million) to eliminate the risk? If not, would the $100 million be better spent for, say, a cancer screening program that could save more than one life every third year?[15]

Similarly, in one school of management, the administration spent a considerable amount on paintings for the walls and sculptures on pedestals throughout the building. However, students had to sit on the hallway floors while waiting to see their professors during office hours because the school hadn't purchased any chairs for them. Maybe an investment in chairs would have had a higher payoff in terms of student morale and downstream alumni contributions.

✂ Technique No. 94. Don't Buy More Power and Features Than You Need

Let's be clear here. We're not talking about eliminating air conditioning from the automobiles of traveling sales representatives. We might be talking about purchasing smaller cars or cars with smaller engines, though. The key question is, what power and features do you need to do the job? One area in which this question might be asked—but in many instances is not—is the acquisition of new computers. What are you going to use the computer for? How much power do you need? For example, a value engineering manager for a textile manufacturing company found that computers whose unit costs were between $4000 and $7000 were being used 80 percent of the time as word processors and only 20 percent of the time as computers. The high-end PCs were phased out and replaced with low-end models. Nationally, statistics indicate that 77 percent of computer owners use their machines mainly for word processing and spreadsheets.[16] Do you need a 500-plus-megahertz processor and 512 megabytes of RAM for that? It's doubtful.

✂ Technique No. 95. Relate Capital *Debudgeting* to Strategy

And speaking of unneeded features, let's look at unneeded capital in general. Sometimes it can help the bottom line to simply jettison unproductive or money-losing programs, product lines, and even entire businesses. Some companies do this without emotion; others tend to have some difficulty letting go. For each such investment, the key is to be prepared to accept it, fix it, or sell it. Accepting it means that you will consider it a loss leader, keeping in mind that a company with some loss leaders also needs some gain trailers. Fixing it means digging in and either reducing costs or increasing revenues without a corresponding increase in costs. Selling it means just that: You forget the sunk costs, get whatever you can for it, and move on.

As an example of this idea taken to its extreme, consider the approach of William Ford when he took over the struggling Ford Motor Company in late 2001. He was quoted as saying, "Everything is up for review—every asset, every piece of geography. We'll continue to review our mix of businesses." On the potential hit list were some downstream auto-related ventures acquired by Ford's predecessor: a repair chain, a junkyard business in Florida, and several e-business start-ups that the company had financed.[17]

James Kilts had a similar problem when he took over at Gillette. Like Ford, he was considering getting out of some businesses, such as the Braun household appliance division.[18] In effect, both Ford and Kilts were questioning whether their company's strategy was being compromised by a variety of ventures, some which were marginal and all which were detracting managers from the company's main business.

Technique No. 96. Close a Division

As Ford and Kilts have suggested, maybe a whole division needs to be closed down or sold. Some computer industry analysts thought that this was what Samuel J. Palmisano (Lou Gerstner's replacement at IBM) should do with IBM's hard-drive operation. They reasoned that not only were hard drives a commodity in a shrinking market, but IBM's strategy of being a service provider did not fit with a hard-drive business.[19]

Technique No. 97. Close a Plant

Okay, closing or selling a whole division is pretty radical. What if you like a division, it fits with your strategy, and it has potential, but business is down and you don't expect it to recover, or at least not very soon?

Maybe it's time to bite the bullet and shut down a plant, or perhaps even sell a plant. Bill Ford wanted to do this shortly after he took over at Ford, but he could not. His challenge was to eliminate the cost of excess factory capacity, and industry analysts believed that to do this, he needed to close two or three assembly plants. Unfortunately, he was unable to do so because in the union contract, the company had specifically agreed not to close or sell any plants. Therefore, instead of closing plants, Ford needed to find another approach. One option that was considered was eliminating some work shifts and slowing down the assembly lines at all Ford's North American factories. This would serve the purpose of reducing output, but it also would minimize job reductions.[20] Thus, Ford was forced to look elsewhere for significant cost savings.

Mattel, by contrast, was somewhat more successful. By closing a factory (and also cutting its workforce and taking steps to reduce product development time), the company was able to report a 19 percent increase in earnings, despite a sales increase of only 2 percent.[21]

✂ Technique No. 98. Delay the Opening of a Plant

All right, so you're not going to close a plant. Do you have new plants coming on line, and, if so, can you delay the opening date? This can be especially effective if you are in an industry with slumping sales and the plant is a new one (as opposed to a replacement) that will give you additional capacity. This is exactly what Park Place Entertainment did. It postponed construction of a $475 million tower at Caesar's Palace in Las Vegas. Similarly, Starwood Hotels postponed a $100 million renovation of the St. Regis in San Francisco.[22] Both companies had the same rationale: With the post-September 11 reduction in travel, these facilities would not be as fully occupied as initial plans had forecast.

✂ Technique No. 99. Make Your Plant More Flexible

Who says that everything in a plant except the raw materials needs to be affixed permanently? Consider Igus, Inc., in Cologne, Germany.

Igus invested in a flexible design for its manufacturing plant (which is about the size of three football fields). Very few things on the plant floor are welded down, so machines and modular furniture can be rearranged almost overnight. The overhead electric wiring is exposed for easy access, and there are few support columns. Igus can expand, shrink, or relocate entire departments on a moment's notice.

In part, this approach is due to Igus's strategy, which involves highly customized and innovative production to meet customer specifications, sometimes for a one-of-a-kind product. Products range from assembly lines (for someone else) to movable stages for a theater.

But Igus has taken its flexibility one step further, which has nothing to do with its manufacturing strategy per se. Workers on the floor have motorized scooters and mobile phones, giving them the ability to minimize downtime between activities. Even the office staff has scooters (although not motorized ones).[23]

Technique No. 100. Move Your Company

And while we're on the subject, let's look at some other options. Sure, it costs money to move, but maybe the cost of the move should be looked at as an investment that will have a quick payback in terms of cost savings. Can you find a place that makes sense from the standpoint of your raw material sources and your shipping destinations? Can you find a place where the annual rent would be so much lower than what you're now paying that the cost of moving would be repaid in only a year or two? If so, why not move? This is what happened in Silicon Valley. In September 2001, the asking price for Silicon Valley office space was down 40 percent from its high in the final quarter of 2000. As a result, some companies were for the first time considering a move there. For example, by moving its headquarters to the Valley in early 2002, Notiva Corporation, a software start-up based at the time in Rochester, New York, was looking at not only better facilities for the money but a sizable venture capital community, a wide array of needed services, and a large pool of talent.[24]

Technique No. 101. Move Your Office

Here's a strange spin on the previous idea: The company stays put, but the CEO moves his or her office. Why? To save time. Sure you lose some perks, but do you really need them? What happens when you run the numbers? The little things may add up to a lot. Consider the case of Richard Priory, CEO of Duke Energy. Priory traded his penthouse office for a modest space located on the third floor of the company's building. Priory was quoted as saying that the move saves him 5 minutes of travel time each day.[25] That translates into roughly three 8-hour days a year—not bad, given the precious nature of a CEO's time.

Technique No. 102. Keep Your Old Equipment

Finding itself cash-strapped, the U.S. Navy was considering installing some new technology on existing ships, rather than building new ships. What would the cost savings be? The answer was unclear, but it was reportedly in the double-digit billions.[26] If it's good enough for the Navy, why not for you?

Well, the decision to keep old equipment instead of upgrading can be a tricky one. New equipment may be more efficient, offer new capabilities, and have a lower need for repairs and maintenance, all of which are arguments for replacement. But what if the new equipment does not provide those benefits? Even if it does, can you quantify them in some way? Increased efficiency can be quantified in terms of increased output per machine hour, but that's useful only if you're capacity-constrained. If you're not, what's the point? Can you quantify maintenance in such a way that you do not fall into some accounting trap? Suppose, for example, you get the new equipment, but maintenance is largely a fixed cost and therefore doesn't fall but is just reallocated to another cost center. If you are not able to actually *reduce* maintenance in some way, then what's the point?

✂ Technique No. 103. Get Rid of Your Old Equipment

This is the flip side of the coin. Can both be right? Absolutely. It all depends on the circumstances. Suppose, for example, that repair and maintenance costs are mounting fast. In the construction industry, and in other industries where equipment is subjected to a great deal of wear and tear, the issue is not just repair and maintenance costs, but also the opportunity cost of equipment that is idle while it's being repaired. Indeed, one of the hidden costs of a machine that is idled because it needs repair is the opportunity cost of other machines that depend on it that are also idled. At some point, the opportunity cost is so high that it makes sense to scrap the old machine and bring in the new.[27] The key is to make sure that these costs really exist and that they are *differential,* i.e., that they will change if you get some new equipment. And watch out for those allocated costs. They probably won't change at all, yet the accounting system may lead you to believe that they will.

Make Sure You Avoid These YGBKs

YGBK No. 7. Extend the Estimated Economic Life of Your Assets

Depreciation is a legitimate accounting technique that allows a company to expense its fixed assets (mainly plant and equipment) over their useful lives. But depreciation is an estimate. Who knows how long the equipment will actually last? Who knows what it will be worth at the end of its so-called economic life? The shorter the economic life and the smaller the residual value, the higher the annual depreciation and the lower a company's operating income. Therefore, by lengthening an asset's estimated economic life and increasing its estimated residual value, a company can lower its annual depreciation expense and increase its operating income. By taking this to an extreme, a company could bring its depreciation expense down to next to nothing.

But beware. This was the approach used by Chambers Development Company to improve its net income. Chambers operated landfills, and it depreciated them over a much longer period than their usual lives. What was the justification? Uncertainty. "Nobody is certain ... how long a landfill takes to fill up with trash. That gives accountants plenty of wiggle room in deciding how long to allow a company to depreciate landfills. The longer the period, the smaller the hit to annual earnings."[28]

And as with Enron, but on a smaller scale, the scam couldn't go on forever. When Chambers finally recomputed its annual earnings using a more realistic estimated economic life for landfills and making some other changes to its "aggressive interpretations of accounting rules," its 1991 earnings dropped from 83¢ per share to only 3¢. The company's stock price fell by more than half in a single day.[29]

YGBK No. 8. Make an Expense into an Asset

Here's another aggressive accounting technique (and you thought Enron was the first to do this?). Who's to decide whether a cash outflow is for an expense or an asset? If you make it into an asset, there's no hit to earnings. That's what a company called Pre-Paid Legal Services (PPL) did. PPL decided to treat commission payments to its sales force as assets, arguing that by doing so it was complying with GAAP's matching principle. That is, since the company would be earning revenue from these sales in future accounting periods, it should write off its commissions over the same periods. Unfortunately, the SEC is not especially supportive of the idea of deferring expenses by capitalizing them. Prepaid insurance is one thing, but prepaid commissions? Nope! Expensing the commissions erased half the earnings that PPL had reported in the previous 2 years and three-fourths of the company's net worth.

PART II

BEYOND THE BASICS

Once you've attacked the basic items on the income statement, where do you go next? Happily, there are many other options. For one thing, thinking more carefully about some of the financing choices you made, including how you manage the items that make up your working capital, can be very helpful. Shortening inventory holding time by just a few days can reap quite serious rewards if inventory represents a sizable portion of your assets. These matters are the subject of Chapter 5. Similarly, some of the emerging (or, by now, pretty basic) technologies can be helpful. Many companies are using the Internet in some extremely creative ways. Others have adopted some of the new manufacturing technologies, such as reengineering. There is lots of potential here, which is discussed in Chapter 6. Finally, sometimes you have to spend money to save money. Chapter 7 looks at where some of the high potential for this exists. It includes a discussion of outsourcing, which frequently is seen as a panacea, and sometimes is. But a company can rush into it blindly without really thinking about what it's getting itself into. Some of the ideas in this chapter can help you think more clearly about when, with whom, and how to outsource.

5

SHOW ME THE MONEY
THOSE INTEREST BUCKS CAN
BE A LITTLE DEAR

Think of cash as a product: The more you use, the more it costs. You can use it to buy inventory or to finance your customers' purchases (via your accounts receivable). The cost can be either the opportunity cost of not being able to put your cash into, say, some marketable securities, or it can be a direct cost, such as when you borrow cash and pay interest. So, if you want to cut costs, reduce your use of cash for those things that give you no return or reduce your borrowing.

That's easy to say, but actually pulling off a reduction in your use of cash can be a little tricky. Here are some techniques that some companies have found to be quite workable.

✂ Technique No. 104. Reduce Your Inventory Holding Time

Holding onto inventory is costly. Every dollar invested in inventory is a dollar that's not in cash, and every day you hold inventory is a day without some cash that you otherwise would have had. As far back as the early 1900s, Pierre du Pont was seeking ways to reduce the number of days' inventory held. More recently, many companies have moved to just-in-time production, which has reduced inventory holding time not just to a few days but frequently to a few hours.

Just-in-time, or JIT, as it's called, has been around for a couple of decades and is used mainly in manufacturing. Sometimes the timing is so tight that if a raw material shipment does not arrive at a certain time, the plant will not be able to operate. JIT has also been used in merchandising, however. Sometimes it can be quite simple, such as at Gillette, where the company wanted to eliminate marginal products that took up shelf space and extended days' inventory. The goal was to cut inventories from 120 days to 90.[1]

Whether Gillette achieved its goal or not, its approach was pretty simplistic. Much more sophisticated systems have been developed. At the Haggar Apparel Company, for example, the *Haggar Order Transmission (HOT) Quick Response System* assisted some 100 major merchants, representing about 26,000 stores, to reduce the amount of inventory they needed to carry. The system allowed a retailer to use a PC software package to scan its inventory and produce orders in a relatively inexpensive way. This helped the retailer to order the merchandise it needed quickly and to keep inventories down.[2]

Wal-Mart has taken this idea even further. Installation of the company's electronic data interchange (EDI) system enabled some 3600 vendors (representing about 90 percent of Wal-Mart's dollar volume) to be networked into the company's bar code system. When a store's inventory of a particular item falls to a preset level, the vendor automatically sends a predetermined supply of the item to Wal-Mart's distribution center for shipment to the store. As a result, Wal-Mart's square footage devoted to inventory storage is only 10 percent, compared to the industry average of 25 percent. Sales per square foot are about $300, compared to $209 for Target and $147 for Kmart.[3]

Technique No. 105. Shorten Your Accounts Receivable Collection Period

Just as holding onto inventory is costly, so too is holding onto accounts receivable. The more days it takes the average customer to pay, the longer you have cash tied up in a non-interest-earning status, or the more borrowed cash you must use. Either is costly.

So, how do you fix this? Well, one possibility is to get people to pay cash on the spot, rather than charging their purchases. Sometimes this can be as simple as asking, as is done by some health-care providers who are due a copayment at the time of the patient's visit. Remarkably, some of these providers actually send out a bill for $5 or $10. Not only are the accounts receivable a use of cash, but the cost of the billing function alone can eat up most of what is due.

In other instances, a discount for prepayment can encourage a customer to pay quickly. You may be familiar with the payment terms of 2/10, n/30, a fairly common discount. A company that pays its bill within 10 days is entitled to deduct 2 percent from the invoice amount.

 But Beware! Be sure to run the numbers, though. How much have you paid to shorten your accounts receivable collection period? A discount of 2 percent for 10 days translates to over 70 percent a year. Unless you think there's a chance the bill won't be paid in 30 days, but would be paid in 10 days with the discount or unless industry practice dictates these sorts of terms, you're probably better off borrowing for the extra 20 days—unless, of course, your bank will charge you 70 percent interest!

What if you don't want to give a discount of that sort and you can't collect at the time of purchase? What other options are available? One possibility is to see how your collection period compares to the average in your industry. If you're about on target, there may be nothing you can do, but if it's taking you longer to collect the average account receivable than it's taking others in the industry, you may need to examine your payment policies and the way you communicate them to customers.

Or it may be that you're just not following up at the right time. There is strong evidence to suggest that the older an account receivable is, the less likely it is to be collected. This argues for some fairly aggressive efforts to collect receivables before they become too old. Not only will your cash flow improve, but you may avoid bad debts. Run the numbers. What would it cost to have people make phone calls to all accounts as soon as they reached some predetermined date and hadn't paid? What would that do to collections and bad debts?

Technique No. 106. Lengthen Your Accounts Payable Period

This, of course, is the flip side of inventory and accounts receivable. Now you're on the other end. Whereas holding either inventory or accounts receivable can be considered a *use* of cash, purchasing on account is often seen as a *source* of cash, one that is usually interest-free as long as you pay within some reasonable period, such as 30 days. Indeed, in some instances, your creditors will allow you to extend your payment period much longer. For example, Jimmy Hourihan of Dublin, Ireland, a manufacturer of women's apparel, extends credit to U.S. retail stores for several months. At the end of each season, the stores return the clothing that did not sell and pay for those items that did sell. Extending credit of this sort is the only way that Hourihan can get his apparel into the U.S. retail stores of choice.

Similarly, J. Herbert Hall, a jewelry store in Pasadena, California, hired a manager of accounts payable. The person's job was to stall creditors as long as possible. With expensive items of jewelry sitting on the showroom floor for months at a time, the company would have needed to borrow large sums of cash if it paid its vendors in just 30 days.

Sometimes, the solution to lengthening the accounts payable period is just making sure that you pay on time and not a day earlier. For example, the cash manager at Occidental Petroleum, with annual check disbursements in excess of $10 billion, learned that some suppliers were being paid early. He developed a series of measures to better monitor payments, and discovered that some payments for large invoices were being mailed out 10 to 12 days in advance of the due date. By changing the system to make payments on the due date by wire or with an automated clearinghouse (ACH) credit transaction, he was able to realize substantial savings in interest expense.[4]

Technique No. 107. Speed Up Your Operating Cycle

The previous three techniques—reducing inventory holding time, shortening the collection period for receivables, and lengthening the accounts payable period—involve the operating cycle. This cycle, which all organizations must manage to ensure that they will have sufficient cash on hand to meet daily needs, is shown in Figure 5-1.

As Figure 5-1 indicates, if we assume for the moment a startup situation, operations begin with the purchase of some inventory. In a manufacturing organization, this ordinarily is raw materials inventory. Inventories differ in merchandising organizations (such as a retail store), where no manufacturing takes place, and in service organizations (such as a law firm), where no goods are sold. Even service organizations typically need an inventory of supplies, however.

Generally, vendors will not require cash on delivery of the materials, and so an account payable is created (or is increased). As a result, the liability accounts payable increases by the same amount as the asset inventory. So far so good; no cash has been used. Eventually, however, the accounts payable must be paid in cash to vendors.

In a manufacturing organization, the raw materials inventory is used up in the course of manufacturing the products, resulting in a finished goods inventory, which subsequently is shipped to customers. This, of course, requires some marketing and sales activities.

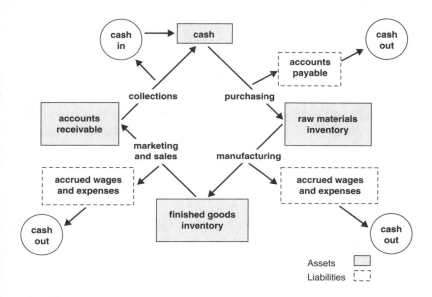

Figure 5-1 The operating cycle.

In carrying out its manufacturing and marketing activities, an organization will incur some expenses, such as salaries and wages for its employees. Since some employees are paid biweekly and others are paid monthly, wages are not paid out immediately in cash, which can give rise to an account called Accrued Wages—the equivalent of an account payable to employees. The manufacturing and marketing activities also give rise to some other expenses that do not result in immediate cash payments, but these too must be paid in cash eventually, usually pretty quickly. Of course, many expenses, such as rent and utilities, are paid in cash at almost the same time they are incurred.

Similar activities take place in merchandising and service organizations. Goods are sold (in a merchandising organization), or services are delivered to customers (in a service organization). Although raw materials inventories are not transformed into finished goods inventories as they are in a manufacturing organization, inventories must nevertheless be purchased, with the associated cash payment typically taking place before the inventories are resold or used. Imagine, for example, how long a couch sits in a furniture showroom, or a ring in a jewelry store, before it is sold.

Once the goods and/or services are sold and delivered to the customer, the organization recognizes revenue. However, in those organizations that sell on credit (as most do), the revenue is not received in cash immediately. Instead, it takes the form of an account receivable. Only when these accounts receivable are collected does the organization actually receive cash. At that point, the operating cycle begins again. This operating cycle must be carefully managed so that the organization not only doesn't run out of cash but also has the minimum amount of cash tied up.

The epitome of a company that manages its operating cycle to the limit is Dell Computer, a company that has an operating cycle of *negative* 6 days. This means that, on average, raw materials are received, the product is manufactured and shipped, and the customer has paid 6 days before Dell pays its raw material vendors. Few companies achieve this kind of cash conversion. In Dell's case, it is a result of the company's unique made-to-order business model.

Not only does Dell save money by not using cash in its operating cycle, but, in an industry where raw material prices decline by an average of about 1 percent a week, Dell also is able to purchase its raw materials at a much lower cost than it would if it had to maintain a sizable inventory. The resulting cost decreases allow Dell to earn significant profits in an industry where most other manufacturers are struggling to break even.[5]

Technique No. 108. Manage Your Financing Cycle

Cash is paid out for activities other than operations. When an organization purchases some equipment, for example, it ordinarily must make the payment in cash. In some instances, organizations will finance these acquisitions with borrowings, such as bank loans or notes. Eventually, however, these borrowings must be repaid, and generally some interest payments are due. These inflows and debt service payments are shown schematically in Figure 5-2.

As Figure 5-2 indicates, borrowing can increase an organization's cash (as can the receipt of contributed capital). Although, as Figure 5-1 indicates, some borrowing takes the form of accounts payable and accrued wages, more formal debt (such as loans, bonds, mortgages, and the like) is usually what is meant by borrowing.

Assume, as is generally the case, that the borrowed cash is used to purchase fixed assets, such as plant and equipment, which are used in manufacturing and/or merchandising the company's products or in delivering its services. Even a small organization that produces, say,

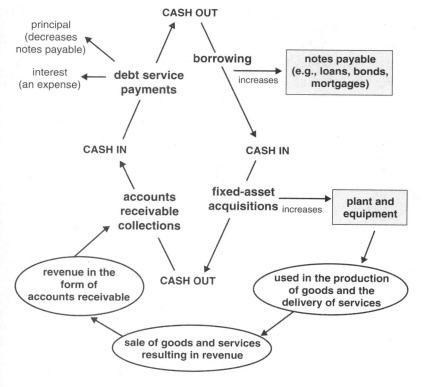

Figure 5-2 The financing cycle.

quarterly newsletters usually needs some fixed assets, such as desks, chairs, a computer, and photocopying equipment.

As Figure 5-2 indicates, the sale of the company's products and services provides revenue, but usually in the form of accounts receivable, which eventually are collected in cash. The cash received from the collection of the company's accounts receivable then can be used to make debt service payments.

Managing this financing cycle is one of the most difficult tasks facing an organization. Senior management must make sure that the organization has enough cash on hand to purchase the fixed assets needed to produce the organization's products or deliver its services. But senior management must also worry about the timing of the cash inflows from the sale of products and services relative to the timing of the required debt-service payments. Having a debt-service payment come due before the cash is available to make the payment can put an organization in serious difficulty with its lenders. To solve this problem by resorting to short-term borrowing can be quite costly.

General Motors provides a useful example. In 1991, after incurring a $6 billion operating loss, GM found that its debt was becoming an increasingly serious issue. The company's poor operating performance, in combination with its debt-service obligations, meant that its credit ratings were in danger of falling, adding an estimated $200 to $300 million a year to its borrowing costs (because of higher interest payments required). An article in *Business Week* discussed the nature of GM's problem by referring to its debt-to-capital ratio, which at the end of 1991 was 70 percent, up from 40 percent in 1989. A Standard & Poor's vice president for corporate finance noted that GM was "aggressively leveraged at this point."[6]

✂ Technique No. 109. Don't Take On Too Much Debt in the First Place

GM is only one of many companies whose experience might lead us to conclude that the easiest technique for managing the financing cycle is not to borrow. How did that debt end up on your balance sheet in the first place? What were you thinking? What should you—or might you—have been thinking? One way to assess the amount of debt that is appropriate for your organization is to look at how your *financial risk* compares to your *business risk*. Financial risk refers to the amount of debt you have on your balance sheet. Other things being equal, higher financial risk means higher debt-service obligations, thereby increasing the risk that you will be unable to meet these obligations.

Business risk, by contrast, refers to the certainty of your annual cash flows. It works inversely: Organizations that have a relatively high business risk have a high degree of *uncertainty* about their cash flows. A good example is a farm, where product availability and cost are greatly influenced by unpredictable climatic conditions. A good example of an organization with a low business risk is a fast food restaurant located in a busy urban shopping center. The farm will probably face a great deal of uncertainty about its annual cash flows from one year to the next, whereas the fast food restaurant will be almost completely certain of its cash flows.

The combined effect of financial and business risk is illustrated in Figure 5-3. As the figure suggests, other things being equal, an organization with low business risk can have a fairly high financial risk. Assuming that the organization doesn't take on more debt-service obligations than its cash flow can support, the relative certainty of its annual cash flows gives it some reasonable assurance that it will be able to meet these obligations from one year to the next.

By contrast, an organization with a high business risk will generally find it unwise to have high financial risk. Since debt-service obligations remain constant each year, the organization could quite easily find itself in a situation where, because of events beyond its control, cash flows are not sufficient to meet these obligations. The result could be detrimental to the organization's continued existence as a financially viable entity.

Zale Corporation provides a good example of the difficulties that can arise when a company with high business risk takes on a lot of

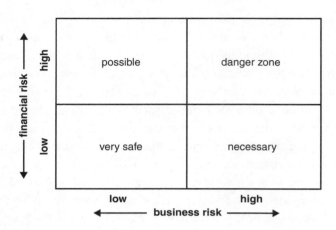

Figure 5-3 Business risk versus financial risk.

debt. In December 1991, following a 1990 operating loss of $54 million on sales of $1.3 billion, Zale, the world's largest retail jewelry chain, was counting on brisk Christmas sales to help it avoid bankruptcy. But the country was in the midst of a severe recession—not a time for jewelry purchases. Zale's operating losses made it difficult for the company to come up with the cash needed to meet its debt-service obligations. This problem was exacerbated by Zale's earlier decision to have a heavy debt load on its balance sheet.

The result? Zale's incurred a second-quarter 1991 loss of $85 million, meaning that it could not pay its bank credit lines and was in default. Then, in early December, with debt totaling $1.2 billion, it missed a $52 million interest payment. The lenders granted Zale a 30-day grace period, but without substantial Christmas sales, it would be unable to make the payment by December 31. Some of its larger institutional bondholders were threatening to put the company into bankruptcy.[7] Zale's is still around, of course, but *despite,* rather than because of, its aggressive financing policies. Maybe it should have hired that accounts payable manager from J. Herbert Hall!

Okay, okay. Not taking on too much debt is a great idea, but it's too late. What is a company that already has a lot of debt to do? There are a few techniques to consider, all of which might make the financing cycle easier to manage.

✂ Technique No. 110. Restructure Your Debt

Some companies wake up one morning to find themselves with a great deal of debt on their balance sheets. The resulting high debt-service obligations affect both profitability and cash flow. Some of these companies have been able to restructure their debt to gain more favorable terms. That may mean converting some short-term borrowing or lines of credit, which typically carry high interest rates, to a longer-term note with a lower interest rate. These sorts of arrangements are pretty commonplace, but they're not the only option. As the following techniques indicate, there are several other possibilities.

✂ Technique No. 111. Trade Debt for Equity

Rather than restructuring existing debt, which may result in more favorable interest rates but will leave the company with a significant debt-service obligation, it may make sense to sell some stock and use the proceeds to pay off the debt. That's what Hospital Corporation of America (HCA) did a few years ago. HCA used $558 million from a U.S. public offering, plus some stock sold overseas, to help repay the large amount of debt it had on its balance sheet from a 1989 leveraged buyout.[8] The result was a significant reduction in the company's debt-service obligations.

More generally, in what has been described as "Wall Street's latest flavor of the month," a debt-equity swap has been linked to a spinoff. The debt is sold to bankers a few weeks before the initial public offering of a spinoff corporation, and the bankers then reswap it for an allotment of shares in the spinoff that was agreed upon beforehand.[9] In effect, the bankers eat the debt in return for some equity—not exactly the business of banking, but better than having bad debt, especially if the spinoff performs well and its share price increases.

✂ Technique No. 112. Reduce Debt by Selling Off Some Assets

It was HCA's good fortune that it was able to issue equity. Not all companies can do so, and even those that can need to hold out some sort of promise to their new shareholders. Few people will buy a company's stock if the only reason to do so is to help the company reduce its debt-service obligations. There has to be a bit more at work.

But what if there isn't? How then do you raise the cash? One possibility is to sell off some assets. That's exactly what Goodyear Tire and Rubber Co. did some years ago. In 1990, after suffering its first loss in half a century, Goodyear reduced its dividend by a total of $80 million. It also began to limit capital expenditures so that its cash flow from operations would be sufficient to handle its basic needs. But, according to an article in *Business Week,* that cash wouldn't "stretch far enough to pay of much of Goodyear's $3.6 billion in debt." Therefore, Goodyear decided to try to negotiate an extension of its $2.24 billion in revolving credit lines (i.e., its short-term borrowings). According to a lender quoted in the article, however, "They have a big chunk of debt. It's out of proportion to the cash flow. You've got to do something about that in a rather short period." As a result, there was a possibility that Goodyear would begin to sell off some of its assets in order to raise cash needed to reduce its debt burden.[10]

✂ Technique No. 113. Reduce Dividends

Goodyear's decision to reduce its dividends was a risky move. Dividends are not an expense, but they are a cash outflow, and if cash is tight, reducing dividends may help. Clearly, in tough times, every little bit helps. There are two big caveats to be considered in this decision, however. First, a reduction in dividends is usually interpreted by Wall Street as a sign of trouble, and it is likely that your stock price will fall. (On the other hand, who on Wall Street didn't know that Goodyear was in trouble before it announced the dividend cut?)

Recent research suggests that there may be another factor—or at least a problem of a different nature—however. According to this research, high current dividend payouts are a good predictor of high earnings growth, and vice versa. One explanation is that companies that retain a smaller share of earnings are likely to choose their investments more carefully than those that decide to forgo dividends. By contrast, low dividend payouts, with a resulting increase in retained earnings, may result in some imprudent or "empire-building" investments.[11]

Technique No. 114. Lease Instead of Buy

Cash-flow considerations such as those previously mentioned may sometimes lead a company to consider leasing, rather than purchasing, at least some of its equipment. This can happen even though (1) both capital and operating leases create payment obligations, (2) most capital leases are treated as debt on a company's balance sheet, and (3) in the middle of the action is a lessor who presumably is not in the game for charitable reasons. Nevertheless, cash flow and other considerations were behind the decision of International Technology, in Torrance, California, to lease rather than buy $780,000 worth of equipment from Gandalf Systems Corp. in Cherry Hill, New Jersey. IT's telecommunications manager was quoted as saying, "Five checks [totaling] $780,000 over a year's implementation was not palatable versus a [smaller] check every month to lease." Even though the lease was a capital lease, the manager expected to be able to upgrade his equipment whenever he wanted to at a minimal cost.[12]

Similar reasons presumably underlay the decision by Technology Investment Strategies, Inc., to lease its voice-response equipment for PBXs and its videoconferencing equipment. Indeed, the phenomenon appears to be industrywide, with "most of the big router deals involving leasing." For the two major lessors of communications equipment, business was growing at about 15 percent annually.[13]

Why all this growth in leasing? Well, it has a lot to do with costs. The reasons given for using operating leases include the need to conserve capital, the ability to easily upgrade equipment, the fact that payments can be scheduled to coincide with a lessee's cash flow, and a desire for off-balance-sheet financing. Only the last does not have an impact on costs.

✂ Technique No. 115. Manage Your Growth

This technique was also discussed in Chapter 3, but for a different reason. In Chapter 3, we were concerned about the impact of growth on the logistical and other systems needed to manage it. Here, we're concerned about the impact of growth on cash. The problem is that growth can eat up cash. To see this best, let's look at the situation in a nonprofit organization, where board members frequently insist upon a bottom line of zero, i.e., no profit (or "change in net assets," which is the current euphemism in the nonprofit world). Let's look at an organization that is growing at about 2 percent a month and that takes 2 months to collect its accounts receivable. The results, along with a few other assumptions, are shown in Table 5-1.

As Table 5-1 indicates, under these circumstances, there is a constant need for cash. As a result, if you use debt to finance your cash needs, you will not be able to repay the debt unless your growth rate slows or you take other measures (such as accelerating the collection of accounts receivable or delaying the payment of expenses) to lessen the need for cash. Clearly, under these circumstances, debt would be an undesirable alternative. Rather, a profit equivalent to the "Change in cash" line is needed to avoid the cash outflow.

The problem does not go away when we return to the for-profit world. It still is important to keep the five main factors in balance: growth rate, receivable collection period, inventory holding period (not shown here), payable period, and profit. Indeed, an article some years

Table 5-1   Cash Needs Associated with Growth

	MONTH					
	1	2	3	4	5	6
Operating statement:						
Revenue	100	102	104	106	108	110
Expenses	100	102	104	106	108	110
Net income	0	0	0	0	0	0
Cash flow:						
Cash collections[1]	96	98	100	102	104	106
Cash payments[2]	100	102	104	106	108	110
Change in cash	(4)	(4)	(4)	(4)	(4)	(4)
Cumulative change	(4)	(8)	(12)	(16)	(20)	(24)

[1]From revenue earned 2 months ago that went into accounts receivable.
[2]Same as expenses due to assumptions No. 3, No. 4, and No. 5. below.

Assumptions:

1. Growth in revenue and expenses of approximately 2 percent a month.
2. Accounts receivable collection lag of 2 months.
3. Accounts payable paid immediately.
4. Inventory, prepaid expenses, and other current assets grow at same rate as revenue.
5. Current liabilities (other than payables) grow at same rate as inventory, prepaid expenses, and other current assets.

ago in *Forbes* discussed how Manville was struggling to manage the cash flow implications of its growth. As the article put it, "There is more to Manville's financial troubles than those asbestos lawsuits." The article argued that the signs of Manville's cash flow problems could have been spotted as early as 2 years prior to the article, a year in which the company earned $115 million but in which its "excess cash flow—the amount it actually could spend on growth—had already begun to turn negative." The reasons given were declining earnings, compounded by rising interest expense and growing cash dividends. One year later, excess cash flow was a negative $137 million, and in the subsequent year, it was a negative $222 million.[14]

Make Sure You Avoid These YGBKs

YGBK No. 9. Seduction by the Immateriality Girl

Immateriality is that wonderful accounting technique that lets a company ignore generally accepted accounting principles (GAAP). The idea is that if some item will not affect the income statement or balance sheet in a "material way," it does not need to be given much attention. Used improperly, it becomes a neat way to avoid talking about ugly stuff. On the other hand, ignoring something on the grounds that it is not material can lead to problems. Rockwell International provides but one of what could be many examples. Rockwell did not reveal the amount of losses associated with a computer-leasing activity that allegedly involved some fraud. Rockwell claimed that the losses were "immaterial." The company's accounting firm reportedly said that losses totaling less than 10 percent of the company's $2.2 billion in shareholder equity were not material.

Although both Rockwell and its accounting firm insisted that the comment concerning materiality was taken out of context, it nevertheless highlighted the *possibility* that Rockwell did not need to disclose the reasons for any loss of $220 million or less.[15]

YGBK No. 10. Re-aging Accounts

What happens when a client misses a loan payment? Does the loan become delinquent? Does it become a bad debt? Can we wait a while to declare it as such? Or can we just roll it over to the end of the loan? What we do will influence what our expenses look like, but are we being honest? Consider the case of Household International, Inc. The major part of Household's business is its mortgage portfolio. Borrowers who are a couple of months overdue may receive an unsolicited call from a Household representative telling them that their late payments have been added to the end of their loans and that they are current again. While this practice does not make the company any money, it keeps delinquencies down. With its unsecured loan portfolio, the company waits some 18 months after a payment was last made to count the loan as a loss on its books. This is about twice the industry average.[16] These techniques make things look pretty good on paper, but what happens later on?

YGBK No. 11. Messing with Bad Debt Estimates
Bad debts are an estimate on an income statement. The matching principle of accounting requires organizations to include on their income statement any expenses that were associated with the revenues that they earned during the period. This means that if you earn $10 million in revenue in December from sales on account, you must *estimate* the amount of bad debts that you will incur on those sales. You can't wait until you find out what the actual amount is. The estimate results in a reserve (called, euphemistically, the "allowance for doubtful accounts"), from which the bad debts are subtracted when they are actually incurred.

Imagine the wiggle room this creates. Supposedly, an organization uses an estimating procedure that is consistent from one year to the next. But a firm's customers change from year to year, creating the possibility that the estimating procedure should be changed to reflect the new customer mix. Of course, this also creates the possibility of either hiding profits or increasing them. Barclays Bank appeared to do just that. Like most banks in the early 1990s, Barclays found that its profits were influenced significantly by bad debts. According to the *Economist,* in 1991, the bank had bad debts (an estimate, remember) of £1.55 billion, which cut its pretax profit to £533 million, giving it a return on equity of just 8 percent. Moreover, the *Economist* reported that analysts feared that Barclays' bad debt allowance was too small; it had set aside only 2.4 percent of its total loans to cover bad debts, compared to 3.0 percent for similar banks.[17]

But if you think this is bad, consider the situation in Japan, where the *official* estimate of bad loans is $135 billion. However, many analysts suspect that Japan's bad loans approach $1 trillion![18]

YGBK No. 12. Declaring Chapter 11

Okay, no one really *wants* to declare Chapter 11, but some people may be thinking of it as an easy way out. It's hardly easy, though. As an example, by one estimate, the final cost for Pacific Gas and Electric's Chapter 11 move was some $98 million. More generally, a company with $1 billion in assets can expect to pay about $60 million to advisers who help it strike deals with its creditors.

There may be better alternatives to Chapter 11. Recently, instances have been reported of a technique called a "distressed exchange," in which bondholders forgive a company's debt in return for cash, new bonds, and common stock. This sort of approach, while not yet common, has the potential to save both time and money.[19]

YGBK No. 13. Pushing the Envelope Too Far

Can you get it past the auditors? Is that the litmus test? Maybe, but it also may come back to haunt you if Wall Street gets wind of it. That certainly was the case with the Enron fiasco, but consider these examples as well (again, just a few of many possibilities). According to a *Business Week* article, Cisco Systems, Inc., subtracts payroll taxes on employee stock options when computing earnings per share. IBM and GE have increased their earnings by assuming that their pension plans were overfunded and therefore have cut the company's contributions to the plans. Motorola, Lucent, and Nortel have increased sales by lending money to customers to finance their purchases. While these may all be permissible under GAAP, they also can be misleading. For example, do Motorola, Lucent, and Nortel have appropriate bad debt estimates for those customers who may not be able to pay? If not, they have inflated their incomes artificially.[20]

6

NO TIME FOR LUDDITES
USING TECHNOLOGY FOR FUN AND PROFIT

Technological change has had an impact on almost every type of organization in the economy—service or manufacturing, for-profit or nonprofit, large or small. In some instances, technology's impact has been relatively minor, such as when a small organization decides to use accounting software to manage its checking account and prepare periodic financial statements. In others, it has been somewhat greater. For example, many organizations have discovered that the Internet can be used to promote—or even provide—new and expanded services. In still others, highly sophisticated technology has allowed an organization to undertake activities that its managers never would have thought possible only a few years ago. Database management, computer-aided design, shipment tracking, production scheduling, robotics, and a host of other activities that are now commonplace would have been considered the stuff of science fiction only a few decades ago.

Many of these technological improvements also offer the potential for cost savings. There's an enormous variety of possibilities. Let's look at a few.

✂ Technique No. 116. Use Technology to Increase Productivity

Usually, when a company reduces its labor force, its production has declined and it therefore needs fewer workers. But there's another way to either reduce labor or slow hiring: Increase productivity. The increases can be in both the "front room" and the "back office." In the back office, for example, Office Depot installed error-reducing scanners at 25 North American warehouses that serve online and catalog customers. The scanners helped reduce operating costs by 1 percent, and the company hopes to triple the amount over the next 3 years.[1] Similarly, by consolidating back-office software systems and eliminating duplications, Bank One was able to eliminate some 8000 jobs in about 18 months.[2] Amazon.com installed a system that would automatically route emails from customers to the appropriate service representative, thereby saving time and money.[3]

In the front room, consider the experience of some restaurants, where waiters have abandoned their pencils and pads for handheld devices on which they transmit an order directly to the bar or kitchen. The wait staff can also process credit card payments and print receipts at the table, and can signal to the parking valet to have the patron's car ready. This technology can be adapted to any service industry. One company is launching a system to help hospitals dispense medicine, for example.[4]

As yet another example of a situation where handheld devices can be useful, consider Honeywell. The company's heating, ventilation, and air-conditioning systems unit will soon start using handheld devices rather than handwritten invoices to transmit maintenance and repair requests to its 1500 field technicians. The company expects to save $4 million annually as a result.[5]

Similar things are also happening in health care. At a CareGroup Healthcare System clinic in Boston, for example, management spent $72,000 (about $6000 per physician) on wireless LAN equipment. It expected a return of about $1.1 million ($90,000 per physician) by reducing the average 20-minute patient visit by 2 minutes. The equipment lets the physician pull a patient's medical details from a central database. The 2-minute saving actually produces increased revenue, as it allows the physician to see more patients per day.[6] Of course, this technique is valuable only in an organization where demand remains high even during a slowdown in the economy.

And while were on the subject of health care, let's not forget the back office there. By installing cook-chill technology in his kitchen, the director of food and nutrition services for Baystate Health System was able to save about $150,000 a year in labor costs, giving him a payback period of about 2 years on the investment. A related investment in a cold preplate retherm system paid for itself in only 1 year. According to Bon Secours Cottage Health Services, the cook-chill system not only cut out labor costs but also eliminated mundane tasks like recording refrigerator temperatures. Best of all, according to Bon Secours's food manager, the system allowed her to view each unit in the hospital from her office and to troubleshoot potential problems before they adversely affected customer service.[7]

But handheld devices are not the only way to give key people the information they need. When Red Man Pipe and Supply Company in Oklahoma was unable to obtain information about customer orders quickly enough via telephone or fax, it developed a Web site where salespeople could look at the orders. Salespeople could determine what was in line to be shipped and what had already been shipped.[8]

Technique No. 117. Shift to Online Billing and Payment

We're not talking about bill-consolidation firms here—the folks who tried to convince consumers to pay $5 or $10 a month for the privilege of paying their bills online. Instead, the idea is to offer the service to your customers for free. That's what lots of credit card companies and others have done, not because they're being generous, but because it saves them money on processing costs. According to one study, 100 or so major billers have spent about $1.1 million each on their Web payment-processing systems. If just 20,000 customers can be convinced to pay their bills online, the entire investment will be paid for in just 1 year. Similarly, the IRS estimates that it saves about $1 for each return filed online, and it is now under a congressional mandate to see that 80 percent of returns are filed electronically by 2007.[9]

But the savings go beyond this into areas that are somewhat intangible and tricky to measure, but just as real. There seems to be some indication that online services raise buyers' switching costs. A study by Boston Consulting Group indicated that after customers have invested the time to understand a bank's online service and configure their accounts to send out regular monthly payments (such as for their automobiles), they are less inclined to switch banks.[10]

Technique No. 118. Use Technology to Assist Customers with Their Purchases

This sounds pretty basic, doesn't it? This certainly is what companies like Amazon.com, Dell, and other Internet vendors do. But how can you use technology to assist a customer with a purchase that will actually be made in a "bricks-and-mortar" setting? Crest Nissan, in Tewksbury, Massachusetts, has found a way. The dealership allows prospective buyers to cruise the new and used car inventory online, see photos, calculate monthly payments, and fill out loan applications. Crest and other dealers who do this say that it can cut 15 minutes from the 3 hours that customers typically spend at a dealership to buy a car. In fact, dealers report that "Customers come . . . at lunch with 45 minutes, . . . and they don't worry so much about how cheap something is if it's fast and easy to get."[11]

Technique No. 119. Use Technology to Shorten Your Supply Chain

Holding inventory is costly and carries the risk of obsolescence. In some industries, such as computer components, there is also a large opportunity cost, as unit prices decline on a weekly basis. To improve inventory management, some companies are beginning to examine their entire supply chain with the goal of making it shorter. Some are implementing supply-chain software, for example, and setting up Web supplier hubs. Everyone is seeking tighter collaborations with suppliers *and* timelier information from customers. These companies also are trying to make their supply chains shorter, more transparent, and as flexible as possible.[12]

Technique No. 120. Use Technology to Engage in Mass Customization

The oxymoronic technique now known as mass customization allows companies to use technology to more closely align costs and prices. When this is done properly, every customer feels as though the product and/or service has been customized to meet his or her needs, and yet, from the company's perspective, something approaching mass production is still at work. As a result, the most standardized product can be customized in some way—even a newspaper, as when customers provide a listing of their interests to the *Wall Street Journal* and then receive a daily online version of the paper that contains only the articles that match their interests.

Along the same lines, Hallmark offers a "reminder service" to its online customers, letting them know by email when it's time to send a greeting card and to whom. Dell Computer permits a customer to select the hardware configuration that suits his or her needs and then order that computer online. No dealers are involved, finished goods inventories are almost nonexistent, and customer payments are made directly, thereby reducing the company's accounts receivable to a negligible amount and keeping its inventory extremely low.[13] And each customer gets exactly the computer configuration that he or she wants.

Mass customization also can result in a complete rethinking of a company's pricing policies, as Delta Airlines demonstrated in the early 1980s. At that time, when deregulation had led to intense competition in the airline industry, Robert Cross, a marketing manager at Delta, concluded that if Delta unnecessarily discounted only one seat on each of its flights, it was losing $52 million a year in potential revenue.

Cross and his staff analyzed a vast amount of data to gain insight into Delta's customers' purchasing habits. They then trained Delta's "seat inventory control staff," who had been using their gut feeling to determine the number of discounted seats to offer on each flight, to think more systematically about discounting. They also used a computer model to flag flights that were filling up more slowly than expected, so that discounting could be used to sell the vacant seats. An investment of $2 million in this effort yielded an increase of $300 million in annual profits.[14]

Cross reported that Marriott Hotels, American Airlines, and other companies, some as small as a one-chair barber shop, were similarly successful with such efforts. In all instances, the approach is to customize the product for a segment of customers in such a way as to achieve the maximum possible amount of revenue per customer at the lowest possible cost, while at the same time leaving customers satisfied that they have received value.

To fully understand this, let's look at the spin that Marriott put on the mass customization idea, again using technology. Prior to Ben Ussery's arrival at Marriott's Desert Springs resort in Palm Desert, California, a planning coordinator called him to ask what he wanted to do. When everything was set, she faxed him a schedule. She had even ordered flowers for his wife. "Marriott made it a real smooth experience," says Ussery. "I'm ready to go back."

What makes such velvet-glove treatment possible is Marriott's use of customer management software. The software lets Marriott pull together information about its customers from different departments, so that its reps can anticipate and respond more quickly to their needs.[15] Similarly, many companies are beginning to develop customer tracking systems and interactive communication with customers. When combined, these sorts of activities allow an organization, if it wishes, to learn about and "manage" its customers more effectively than ever before, and to align its costs strategically with the places where they add the most value.

Engaging in this effort sometimes requires a nontraditional approach to market segmentation. In the banking industry, for example, small manufacturers generally do not like to pay fees for advisory services because they are used to being charged only for things that can be seen. Some banks have dealt with this issue by providing free advisory services to manufacturers but charging an interest-rate premium on their loans. By contrast, professional service firms are used to charging for their time and tend to accept fees for advisory services more readily. However, their egos frequently demand prime interest rates on loans. As a result, they are charged the prime rate for their loans but also are charged fees for advisory services.

In all these instances, the use of technology allows an organization to create customer satisfaction, perhaps at lower prices, but certainly with lower costs than would be possible if the same approach were attempted manually. Indeed, the ability of companies like Marriott to capture information on customer preferences and to use that information creatively to add value for their customers has become a key ingredient in maintaining a company's customer base. Since the cost of acquiring a new customer is many times the cost of retaining an existing customer, this approach can pay big dividends.

Technique No. 121. Use Technology to Study Complex Relationships

Just how complex is the set of activities that you must coordinate, and how do you do this? For many companies with complex relationships among their parts (varying product life cycles, whimsical style changes, seasonality, and inventory holding costs, to name just a few), using just a spreadsheet and gut feel may not be enough. There's nothing wrong with a little Zen on occasion, but maybe technology can help guide the decisions. Murray-Feiss, a lighting manufacturer whose product life cycles were very tricky to predict, used a $595 software package called ForecastX Wizard, with special functions for life cycles and new products, to replace procedures that had previously taken hours of time. The owner of Angove Proprietary Vineyard in Australia, using a $1000 package called CFO, discovered that producing even a little more wine than he could sell cost him a lot in terms of inventory holding costs. He was able to reduce his inventory by 10 percent and save over $50,000 a year. In effect, the software allowed him to manage several complex supply and demand variables affecting both his income statement and his balance sheet.[16]

Technique No. 122. Use Technology to Form an e-Marketplace

The Internet now allows companies to develop a variety of real-time arrangements to increase their purchasing power. Some do this by joining consortia that set up public e-marketplaces—Web sites where negotiations between potential purchasers and potential vendors take place. The concept can be very powerful. For example, Valeo, France's largest automobile component maker, planned to boost its procurement via the Internet from 8 percent to 20 percent of all transactions over a period of 12 to 15 months in an effort to lower costs.[17] General Electric Corporation, already a pretty powerful purchaser, made itself even more powerful by combining the purchasing functions of its 11 different businesses into a single private e-marketplace. It expected to save $600 million through this approach.[18]

Technique No. 123. Use Technology to Improve Logistics

Software is now available that can allow managers to see a wide variety of performance metrics and their associated costs, from hiring to sales closure rates. Using this kind of information, they can begin to think strategically about how they want to spend their time and resources. At Siebel Systems, for example, software lets the company know when meetings with the customer should take place, when contracts need to be drawn up, and how long it takes to get the customer to sign. The company also rewards its sales force for its ability to anticipate problems: Commissions are tied to a salesperson's *forecasts* as well as to the closing of the deal.[19]

Colgate-Palmolive has done much the same thing, but with a focus on inventory. C-P is on the other end of Wal-Mart's inventory control system (discussed in Chapter 4). It must respond to Wal-Mart's need for supplies, and it must do so quickly. How can it do that without building up too much inventory of its own? By improving its planning systems. Its agreement with Wal-Mart required it to link its information system to the retailer's cash registers, but C-P didn't stop there. It took the next step and began to monitor sales in such a way that it could adjust production to match consumer demand—on a real-time basis. C-P now can predict demand accurately 98 percent of the time and ships only as much product as the retailers can sell.[20] The technology helped C-P save $150 million by reducing inventories by 13 percent.

🪒 Technique No. 124. Use Technology to Improve Forecasting

This is a variation on using technology to improve logistics. Software is now available that can improve your ability to forecast the demand for your products by using external information, such as the weather and the economy. At Sioux Chief Manufacturing, for example, demand for many of the company's products was affected not only by the weather and the economy, but also by changes in building codes. By building a demand-forecasting model using relatively inexpensive software, the company was able to anticipate surges in demand and plan for them better, thereby saving on overtime and avoiding production disruptions. It also was able to improve its customer relations by avoiding the need to ask customers to take only partial delivery. And, finally, it was able to reduce its copper-tubing inventory by about 50 percent.

But improved forecasting can be useful in other industries as well. Internet companies can anticipate when they will get a lot of hits, allowing them to take steps to avoid server crashes; credit card companies can better anticipate which customers are likely to default; human resource departments can predict which employees are likely to quit; HMOs can predict hospitalizations.[21] The list is almost endless.

Technique No. 125. Use Technology to Limit Product Liability

Technology such as image scanning can be used for a variety of purposes, especially in the areas of quality control and product liability. Products that will be under tensile stress can be scanned for weak spots, products where a seal is important can be examined for flaws or misalignments, and so forth.

Clearly, there is a wide variety of industries where scanning of this sort can be helpful and can assist in lowering costs. But who would have thought that this technology would make its way into the meatpacking industry? Yet that's just what has happened, and not for the reasons you might expect. eMerge Interactive has licensed technology that is able to scan beef carcasses and detect the most minute traces of fecal matter, which may harbor harmful pathogens. An image of the meat slab is displayed on a monitor, with contaminated areas highlighted by a fluorescent glow. Meatpackers can then trim off the potentially harmful portions of the beef. The meat scans can then be archived and examined later if the safety of a batch of product is called into question.[22]

Technique No. 126. Use Technology to Shorten Design Cycles

Going from concept through engineering and product design to production specs can take a while for any company, especially one that outsources many of its components. Technology can now shorten that design cycle, leading to a shorter time from concept to market and perhaps reduced labor costs. Consider the case of Moen, Inc., a manufacturer of faucets. Moen found that suppliers of its components and other raw materials frequently could not meet the company's specs. A supplier would make or suggest changes and return the ideas to Moen on a CD. When Moen combined the suggested changes of some of its suppliers with those of others, it frequently found that there were incompatibilities, and the whole process would have to begin anew. The entire design effort sometimes took 16 weeks or longer. Given its need to remain competitive in its marketplace, Moen had to find a way to speed up the design of its new lines.

To solve the problem, Moen launched what it called "ProjectNet," an online site where it could share designs simultaneously with suppliers worldwide. The result was that the design cycle was shortened to just 3 days. More important, Moen's 50 engineers were able to work on three times as many projects as before.[23] Clearly, the use of technology had some significant cost savings in what have to be pretty expensive personnel.

Technique No. 127. Take Advantage of Technology to Lower Raw Material Costs

There is no limit on what the human imagination can do. Certainly technology such as the computer-aided design described in the Moen example can be helpful not only in testing various design options for their aesthetic qualities and gaining feedback from suppliers, but also in considering various raw material options and their costs. In this regard, Cargill Dow and the National Renewable Energy Laboratory have teamed up to break the mold. Working collaboratively, the two organizations have created a new corn-based (that's right, *corn*) biodegradable polymer called polyactic acid (PLA) that can be made into eco-friendly plastic (that's right, *plastic*). PLA can be used as a substitute for regular plastic in all sorts of products, including packaging, clothing, disposable cups, and carpeting. Not only can it reduce the demand for plastic (8 billion tons a year) and CO_2 emissions (10 million tons a year), but it can be cost-competitive to make.[24] Plastic from corn—everyone wins except OPEC.

✄ Technique No. 128. Use Technology to Help Consolidate Operations

Sometimes a geographically distributed set of data centers can be consolidated through the application of some new technology. Doing so not only can save some money but may provide some useful comparative information. Are there areas in your business where you might be able to use technology to help you group together several tasks or other activities so that you would be able to lower your operating costs overall? Colgate-Palmolive, for example, saved $430 million by installing software that helped it manage its financial accounts and planning worldwide. About $280 million of the savings came from consolidating 80 data centers scattered around the world into a single, highly efficient center in New Jersey.[25] That's not bad, but also consider the sorts of comparative analyses that now can be done with relative ease.

✄ Technique No. 129. Use Technology to Manage Your Vendors

When an order arrives, why should you spend time contacting your suppliers to get the raw materials you need? Why not just have the order go directly to them? Everyone can win. Indeed, based on a value-chain survey, *Industry Week* reported major benefits from improved value-chain management in the chemical, consumer durables, aerospace, automotive, pharmaceutical, printing and publishing, consumer packaged goods, industrial machinery and equipment, and high-tech industries. The significant benefits came from accelerated delivery times, improved quality, cost savings, and improved on-time delivery rates.[26] Cisco Systems is a case in point. According to Cisco's controller,

When an order comes in, our vendors can see it as if they were part of Cisco. Over the past several years, we figure this had allowed them to reduce inventories by about 45 percent. Also, we're able to do integrated testing of all our products over the Web before they ship, and still allow our partners to ship and build about 60 percent of our products without physically touching them ourselves.

In addition to saving its suppliers money, Cisco estimates that this and other Web-based initiatives, such as having 70 percent of the company's support calls handled over the Web, saved the company about $1 billion in 2000.[27]

Technique No. 130. Use Technology to Segregate Your Customers

This sounds, and is, a lot like redlining—the technique used by some companies in the mortgage lending and real estate industries to exclude certain ethnic groups from some communities. While using technology to segregate your customers may be legal, it's no more pleasant for the customers who are on the losing end than redlining is. Nevertheless, technology now allows a company to measure exactly what each customer-related service costs on an individual level, and to assess the associated returns. Management then can decide which services to deliver to whom, based on each customer's potential to produce a profit.

Some have called this the "dark side of technology." Companies that amass a large amount of data on their customers can now decide whom to pamper, whom to squeeze, and whom to toss away. The techniques include coding (grading customers on profitability), routing (sending important customers to a human being who will help solve the problem), targeting (giving reduced fees, waiving fees, or offering special promotions to a select few), and sharing (selling information about customers to other companies so that they, too, will know whether someone is a big spender or not).[28]

Many of us soon will be joining the Rodney Dangerfield club if we haven't already, and George Orwell no doubt is rolling over in his grave. Nevertheless, there are significant potential cost savings. At Fidelity Investments, for example, each phone call handled by a human costs about $13. The company not only created a Web site to handle customer questions, but also contacted about 25,000 high-cost callers—or "serials," in the company's jargon—and told them that they must use the Web or automated calls for simple account and price information. Each of these names was flagged, and, when they called, they were routed to a special representative who would direct them to automated services and tell them how to use the services.[29]

Continental Airlines has taken a similar approach. Continental has developed a customer information system that allows its 43,000 gate, reservation, and service agents to know immediately the history and value of each customer. The system can suggest remedies for problems, upgrades, and other perks in accordance with the customer's value. A Continental vice president was quoted as saying, "We even know if they put their eyeshades on and go to sleep." One result: According to the company, about 47 percent of Continental's customers now pay higher-cost unrestricted fares, up from 38 percent in 1995.[30]

Or take a look at All First Bank in Baltimore. At All First, only those customers who are considered "top" get the option of clicking on a Web icon that directs them to a live service agent for a phone conversation. The other customers never see the icon. First Union Bank codes its credit card customers for its service representatives. Green means that the person is a profitable customer and should be given "white glove" treatment. (Don't they mean "kid glove," or maybe "red carpet"?) Customers coded red are money losers and have almost no negotiating power. For those coded yellow, the service representatives are to use their discretion. According to a spokesperson, "The information helps our people make decisions on fees and rates."[31]

And these techniques aren't limited to service industries. Tech Data measured 150 costs, from average order size to freight charges, in order to calculate the gross expense and margin on every customer account. Unprofitable customers were abandoned or persuaded to order more efficiently (such as making one $1 million orders rather than ten $100,000 orders). As a result, Tech Data's expenses were reduced to 3.5 percent of sales, well below the 5 percent level of some of its competitors.[32]

Technique No. 131. Use Technology to Manage Your Customers

If technology can help you to segregate your customers, maybe it can also help you to manage them. It might even help you provide them with better service across the board, rather than selecting only a subset to receive better service. Trigon Healthcare, which was discussed in Chapter 2, does this when it hires caseworkers to help chronically ill patients better manage their conditions, thereby avoiding expensive emergency room visits, which not only are costly but are nowhere close to the high point of a patient's day.

But Trigon's cost-containment strategy doesn't stop there. The company does some pretty serious data mining using its claims archives. Lots of insurers do this, of course, but not all of them use the results as creatively as they might, and some don't even obtain the kinds of results that would allow them to think creatively. As an example, in one of its data-mining endeavors, Trigon discovered that doctors in Norfolk were prescribing proportionately more antibiotics than doctors in the rest of Virginia. Instead of penalizing those physicians for their use of antibiotics, which many HMOs would probably have done and which might have led physicians to curtail antibiotic use inappropriately, Trigon sent people to visit doctors' offices with educational posters and messages from the Centers for Disease Control. The messages explained the harm done by unnecessary use of antibiotics.[33] Since physicians operate according to a creed that begins, "First, do no harm," there's no better way to attract physicians' attention than to let them know that they might be doing some harm to their patients.

Technique No. 132. Use Technology to Better Inform Pricing Decisions

While this is not strictly a cost-reduction technique, it comes close. Many companies have customers who make initial, relatively large purchases from them, and then make multiple purchases following that. These downstream purchases may include supplies, parts, repairs, upgrades, and so forth. Others are purchases of replacement products. If that's the case in your business, keeping the initial purchase price low, perhaps close to or below your cost, may be a wise move. Polaroid did this for years with cameras, pricing them very low so that they would be in the hands of customers. Customers with cameras tend to be customers who buy film, which is where Polaroid made most of its money.

But technology can allow you to extend this idea much further. Consider the case of Crest Nissan, mentioned earlier in the chapter. Crest developed a database that allowed its salespeople to pull up a customer's entire record for as long as he or she had been purchasing from the dealership. The dealership's owner could see how much gross profit had been made from each customer on new car sales, sales of trade-ins, parts sales, and service. The dealership tends to give its best deals on new car purchases to customers whose purchasing history includes all the above items. The small markup over invoice is only the tip of the iceberg. As Crest's owner says, "I can see I'll have the ability to make another $1,800 or $2,000 on his trade-in, and I know he's going to service the new car, which will be another $1,000 over the next two years. So it's $3,500 in profit on the deal, not just $500." Parts, in particular, are high-margin items. According to the National Automobile Dealers Association, they make up about 12 percent of a dealer's sales but 47 percent of profits.[34]

Make Sure You Avoid These YGBKs

YGBK No. 14. Using Customer-Information Technology without Follow-up

Suppose you engage in a serious data-mining effort to identify some customers who fit into a particular category. You then have a choice: You may accept what you have learned and do nothing more, or you may make an effort to work with this customer segment in some way so as to maximize its profitability to you. What's risky is to do only half the job. Doing this comes about as close as you can get to telling your customers to buy from your competitors. As an example, First Dublin Bank (a disguised name) used some customer information technology to help it to contact many of its customers to alert them to the fact that their "Super Savings Accounts," which had been created with monthly sweeps of their regular savings accounts, were no longer good investments. The bank pointed out that with interest-rate declines and new tax regulations, the effective return on the Super Savings Accounts was only about 1 percent per annum. The bank said it would be contacting the customers shortly to advise them on how to invest the sum in a higher-return instrument.

But the bank didn't follow up with all of its customers, including some with accounts in the $75,000 to $100,000 range. Many of those customers, now alerted to the fact that they had a significant sum of money that was earning a low interest rate, took action on their own. Some moved their funds to a competitor's higher-interest-rate funds, and most ceased using the sweep function.[35]

YGBK No. 15. Offending (and Losing) Some Customers by Invading Their Privacy

Exactly how much data should you gather on your customers, and to what end? One of the concepts underlying the online gro-

(continued)

cery start-ups was that they would gather information on each customer's buying habits so that they could build up a database. Over time, a company would amass enough information about its customers' purchases to let any given customer know when he or she needed to restock a particular item. It's not clear that the online stores asked customers if they wanted those sorts of reminders, and we can all think of a few things that we'd rather not be reminded about.

And what about those banks, airlines, and other companies that begin to segregate customers? Is this the technology equivalent of first-class travel? In the world of travel, those who fly coach can see the first-class cabin in front of them. Should all of All First Bank's customers know about the existence of that little "first-class" icon that directs high-priority customers to a live service agent for a phone conversation? Should they know what kind of data are being gathered on their transactions with the bank and how those data are being massaged to determine if they're icon-worthy?

These are all pretty tricky "big brother"-like questions, and they basically have two parts: (1) Is it okay to do this? (2) If so, is it okay to do it without the customer's consent? The answer to the first question is probably yes, just as it's okay to have first-class air travel, private clubs with lounges, corporate boxes for valued customers, prime rates for big and frequent borrowers, and so forth. The answer to the second is a little less clear. Companies that move down this road need to consider carefully the ramifications of gathering data without their customers' approval, and the damage that exposure of this practice could cause to their business model. If the average customer, upon learning of the data being gathered on his or her activities, would respond with something like "You gotta be kidding!" this practice would appear to be a clear candidate for a YGBK.

7

IN THE LONG RUN . . .
INVESTING FOR PAYOFFS IN THE ALMOST HEREAFTER

Many of the techniques discussed so far are, in some sense, reactive. When revenues turn down, what do you do? More generally, if you must engage in layoffs (which, as Chapter 1 discussed, not all companies feel is wise), how do you do so in the most effective way possible? What other options are available to you in times of crisis?

But what if you're not in a crisis mode? This does not mean that you can ignore costs. Rather, it means that you have the opportunity to be proactive in managing your costs. Doing so requires the investment of time and effort to develop approaches that will allow a company to run "lean and mean" if it so chooses. We began to think that way in Chapter 6, but only with regard to the use of technology. It's possible to use some techniques other than technology to put into place cost-saving approaches that will have a long-term payoff. Those techniques are discussed in this chapter.

✂ Technique No. 133. Distinguish between Initiatives and Tactics

Most of the discussion so far has been devoted to tactics. Investing for long-term payoffs requires something more. Chapter 5 started to get us into that area, but its main focus was on investments in fixed assets. How about taking this idea one step further and considering investments in *initiatives*? During Jack Welch's 20 years as head of General Electric, for example, he began only four initiatives, yet each had a massive impact on the company's performance, and in particular its cost structure. Initiatives, in his view, "Live forever. They create fundamental change in a company. They build on one another. Everything in the GE operating system reinforces them."

Welch's four initiatives were six sigma, services, globalization, and e-business. The six sigma initiative is discussed later in this chapter. Services had more of an impact on the top line; it shifted the focus of the company away from manufacturing and allowed many divisions to create a constant stream of revenue from servicing an installed base. This was most apparent in the area of nuclear power plants, where the company ceased building plants in the United States but earned millions in revenue (and profits) from providing fuel and services to the existing plants.

Globalization and e-business, on the other hand, were cost savers. Globalization had two fundamental thrusts: sourcing from suppliers around the world, not just in the United States, and reducing the number of U.S. expatriates. Not only did these approaches save millions of dollars and put a "global face" on GE, but they put decisions in the hands of local nationals, who knew their country and its culture much better than expatriates did.

E-business, by contrast, allowed GE's managers and others to save considerably on international travel, again with savings extending into the millions of dollars. Moreover, the initiative had an impact on employees' work-life balance. As Welch put it, "Our people got fewer Frequent Flyer miles but stayed home and had better lives."[1]

✂ Technique No. 134. Use Work-Out Sessions

Pioneered at General Electric, these meetings, sometimes lasting several days, allow key line personnel to identify potential improvements in productivity, efficiency, and effectiveness. A central element of these meetings is the presentation of improvement ideas to managers, who then must react on the spot. For example, one manufacturer used a work-out session to reduce the number of signatures required for an authorization from 19 to 6, halving the time and cost of the authorization process.[2]

✂ Technique No. 135. Keep Customers Happy

By now, it's a pretty well established fact that for most organizations, the cost of acquiring a new customer is high. Incurring some costs to keep existing customers happy may be a wise investment, not only in future revenues but in avoided marketing costs.

The customer loyalty problem is particularly rampant in the markets for retail goods, where product differentiation is minimal and where upstarts such as Circuit City and Wal-Mart have been known to lure away the customers of such established firms as Federated and Kmart. Indeed, according to Frederick Reichheld, in his book *The Loyalty Effect*, the average U.S. corporation loses half its customer base every 5 years.[3] Clearly, reducing this by even a small amount not only would have some immediate effects, but would also be quite likely to have effects that extended far into the future.

Unfortunately, engaging in activities that increase customer satisfaction is sometimes seen as a last resort. Consider the case of Conning and Company, an insurance firm. Once it believed that it had squeezed out as much internal cost inefficiency as it could, Conning shifted its focus from improving operational efficiency to measuring and ensuring customer satisfaction. Conning is now focusing on improving client retention, reasoning that higher retention rates translate into higher profitability.[4] How come it took you so long, guys?

✂ Technique No. 136. Segment Your Market Creatively

How do you segment your market? One of the most difficult tasks in marketing is determining a set of market segments that clearly differentiates a company from its competitors. Clever and creative market segmentation can allow a company to set up a highly competitive marketing mix (sometimes called the "4Ps," product, price, place, and promotion). If it is successful, such an effort can lead customers to see the company as unique, and to view its products, which might be essentially the same as those of the competition, as desirable. Moreover, a nontraditional approach to market segmentation can sometimes yield targeted cost cutting, which, when aligned with targeted pricing, can produce substantial bottom-line results.

To illustrate how this might be done, consider the banking industry example from Chapter 6, in which manufacturers and professional service firms are charged different fees and interest rates. Southwest Airlines is an example of a company that is very explicit about its target market segment: people who do not want to (1) fly first class, (2) have meal service, (3) have their baggage transferred from one flight to the next, (4) receive seat assignments, or (5) use a travel agent and who are willing to fly to and from secondary airports in exchange for low fares and on-time flights. As will be discussed in a subsequent chapter, Southwest has directly targeted its 4Ps to this segment.

✂ Technique No. 137. Refocus Your Product Line

Note that in the banking example, the basic products that the banks offered—advisory services and loans—did not change. Instead, the pricing was reconfigured to more closely match each market segment's needs and desires. However, the product can also be changed. In some cases, this may mean reconfiguring an entire product line. For example, some retailers are finding that a broad product line requires too much inventory and doesn't allow customers to understand exactly what they sell. As a result, customers may go elsewhere to satisfy a need that the retailer could satisfy perfectly well. With this idea in mind, Sears remodeled its stores in late 2001 to focus on a narrower but "more potent" range of apparel lines, and to find a "unique position" between discounters and department stores. Toys 'R' Us took a similar approach, narrowing its product assortment and seeking more exclusive items in an attempt to be viewed as a "large-scale, multiple-outlet specialty retailer" rather than a "discounter."[5]

These approaches have a double whammy. On the one hand, they can lead to increased sales as a result of a better-defined focus on a particular market segment. But they also can lead to considerable cost reductions through a lowering of the amount of inventory that must be carried.

Technique No. 138. Redesign Your Production Process

Maybe looking at your products at the most basic level can yield significant payoffs, especially in an era in which teamwork and job satisfaction have become important ingredients in employee motivation. Have you considered whether your manufacturing processes are as effective and efficient as possible? Doing so may require thinking way outside the box, but with product life cycles dropping to only a few years—or a few months in some trendy industries—manufacturing flexibility has become imperative.

But manufacturing flexibility isn't the only benefit. Some changes can result in a lowering of defect rates, and maybe even in an improvement in cycle time. Levi Strauss is a case in point. The company shifted from using assembly lines for manufacturing clothing to a reliance on teams. Whereas a worker on the assembly line did only a small part of the total job, the teams completed entire garments on their own. The defect rate fell, and cycle time was reduced from 6 days to 7 hours (meaning that production can be switched more easily among products in response to customer demand).[6]

And it's not just in manufacturing that there can be payoffs. Cycle time is important in service industries, too. Healthsouth's CEO, Richard Scrushy, began teaching his case managers, nurses, administrators, and doctors (yes, doctors) to get patients in and out of the rehabilitation hospital faster. Rehabilitation hospitals deal with many chronic problems (such as spinal cord injuries, brain injuries, strokes, and the like) and usually have relatively long lengths of stay. But that didn't deter Scrushy. "I want all my doctors at work at 8 A.M.," he said. "We'll diagnose on Monday, operate on Tuesday, and start rehabbing on Wednesday." The result was that the average length of stay declined from 21.5 to 17.5 days over a 3-year period, and per-patient costs were reduced from $11,611 to $9600. Since Medicare pays an average of $11,200 per patient, the move turned Healthsouth from incurring a loss to significant profitability.[7]

✂ Technique No. 139. Use Activity-Based Costing to Understand How Costs Change

Activity-based costing, or ABC, has been around for about 20 years. It has proved very helpful to managers who wish to understand how manufacturing overhead costs are actually incurred. In effect, ABC attempts to identify the activities that lead to the existence of overhead costs, such as machine setups, and then establishes overhead pools that are driven by these activities.[8]

If ABC is useful in understanding overhead, it can also be useful (with perhaps some modification for the behavior of fixed and variable costs) for developing ways to measure the cost reductions resulting from the various techniques discussed in this book. As an example, a collaborative project between John Deere Horizon Works and one of its suppliers, Danfoss Fluid Power, led to a reduction in cycle time of more than 50 percent. How much was saved as a result? To determine the answer, the company looked at both the direct costs for the work on the product *and* the indirect costs related to support activities, giving John Deere a much better understanding of its full cost savings.[9]

Technique No. 140. Use ABC to Staff According to Need

Staffing according to need, while sounding simplistic, is a technique that has emerged in the wake of ABC. The idea is to determine how best to link direct personnel costs with value-adding activities. For example, Fireman's Fund supplemented routine expense information from its regular accounting systems with periodic sampling of costs. Since most of the company's costs were staff-driven, Fireman's focused these sampling efforts on getting a clear picture of how employees spent their time. This allowed the company to develop estimates of how much time was devoted to various products, activities, and tasks. Not only did this give Fireman's a more accurate picture of its internal costs so that managers could make more informed "make versus buy" decisions, but it helped the company to adjust the staffing of local offices based on their particular mix of business.[10]

In some quarters, this approach has become known as activity-based management. It represents a powerful way to manage costs.

Technique No. 141. Use Activity-Based Costing to Eliminate Unproductive and/or Redundant Activities

In addition to helping a company staff in accordance with its needs, ABC and/or ABM (activity-based management) can help a company dig into the black hole of overhead in a much more creative way than done previously. Of perhaps greatest importance is that these savings are not one-time in nature. If management is vigilant, once the unproductive or redundant activities have been eliminated, they can be gone forever. Chrysler, for instance, generated hundreds of millions of dollars in cost savings by simplifying product designs and eliminating unproductive, inefficient, or redundant activities. The savings were 10 to 20 times greater than the company's investment in ABC. At some sites, the savings were 50 to 100 times the implementation cost.[11]

✂ Technique No. 142. Use Target Costing

Target costing is a technique that begins with the price a customer is willing to pay and works backward to the maximum cost that can be incurred if the company is to earn a sufficient margin. It avoids a lot of the "if we build it, they will buy" wishful thinking. This sounds pretty logical, but how easy is it? Sometimes it's not too tough, but sometimes senior management may have to make some pretty tough decisions. Consider the case of H. J. Heinz Pet Products. Faced with declining prices in the cat food industry, and finding that going against the trend was resulting in an unacceptable drop in volume, Heinz turned to target costing. The company began by estimating the price that consumers would pay for cat food, and then developed cost targets. To reduce costs to the target level, the company needed to close some old plants and open some automated new ones.[12] There was no quick fix, but there certainly was the potential for a long-term payoff.

✂ Technique No. 143. Use Breakeven Time Measurement

Breakeven analysis is typically used in thinking about matters such as pricing, cost structure, and volume. It is described in Appendix B under the heading "Cost-Volume-Profit Analysis." But, breakeven analysis does not need to be restricted to costs, prices, and volume. At Hewlett-Packard, for example, it allowed management to establish some metrics that helped the company to control project development costs. In this instance, breakeven time was the number of months it took to repay an investment in product development. While long repayment periods were tolerated for some cutting-edge projects, the company sought to balance these with short time periods for modifications to existing products. In addition, the technique was used to measure the performance of product development managers.[13]

 But Beware! If too much emphasis is put on short breakeven periods, managers may be tempted to "game" the system by selecting only modification projects rather than projects with significant innovative qualities.

✂ Technique No. 144. Engage in a Systematic Review to Find Redundancy and Waste

In large organizations, especially those in the public sector, redundancy and waste sometimes creep in over time, and the only solution is a thorough spring cleaning. Usually, the folks who created the redundancy and/or waste are not the best ones to undertake the spring cleaning effort. In fact, sometimes the effort must wait for a change in management. This certainly was true in the federal government, where, in 1993, the National Performance Review led by newly elected Vice President Al Gore came up with 1250 cost-cutting recommendations.

But cost-cutting recommendations are just that: recommendations. The Gore Commission (as it was called) did not want to fall into the same trap as the 1984 Grace Commission, known more formally as the President's Private Sector Survey on Cost Control. The Grace Commission identified programs where it claimed intervention would reduce waste and improve management for total savings of $424.6 billion in 5 years.[14] But relatively few of its proposals were implemented.

Instead, the Gore Commission assigned responsibility for implementing its recommendations to specific agencies and offices, and each of these units was instructed to make annual reports to Congress. By 1995, 244,000 jobs had been eliminated, 2000 obsolete field offices had been closed, and 200 programs and agencies had been eliminated. The result was savings of $118 billion.[15] If only they could have eliminated the dangling chads!

✂ Technique No. 145. Reengineer and Benchmark

By now, this is pretty tried-and-true stuff. However, one spin that you may not have considered is the membership of the reengineering team, which should definitely include employees who are unhappy with the current processes.[16] Otherwise, you're likely to get something akin to pablum. Sometimes the team can include customers or others who are outside the normal boundaries of the process under consideration. When Matthew Thornton Health Care (an HMO) began a reengineering effort, for example, it assembled focus groups of physicians from around the state and asked them what they wanted from an HMO. It is likely that at least some of these physicians were not getting what they wanted from Matthew Thornton. The result was that Matthew Thornton changed its entire relationship with its affiliated physicians.[17]

Technique No. 146. Use Operational Auditing

This sounds like something you should turn over to the accountants, but they're the last people who should be doing this. Operational auditing is a technique that seeks to identify inefficiencies or uneconomical practices. People such as operations analysts, economists, and social psychologists are often the best ones to undertake such an effort.

Operational auditing frequently engages in process-flow analysis, in which it maps the flow of activities for a particular endeavor, identifies the key decision points, and analyzes the consequences of each. When this is done properly, there are no loose ends (i.e., decision-making paths that are left undefined), and so managers can view the decision-making process in its entirety and identify potential problem areas.

Process analysis has become an important activity for organizations implementing continuous quality improvement (CQI) and total quality management (TQM). It has also been an extremely important technique in many nonprofit organizations, where efficiency problems are not always readily apparent.[18]

A good example of the power of process analysis can be found in the case of Englehard, a specialty chemical and engineered materials company. At Englehard, process analysis resulted in the definition of six to twelve key processes in each of six business units. The teams undertaking the effort also identified leverage points for each process—places where a small improvement would produce a sig-

nificant performance improvement. In one instance, production scheduling was found to be a key leverage point, as a small improvement
in its accuracy led to a dramatic reduction in inventory levels.[19]

 But Beware! Operational auditors can sometimes get a little too full of themselves. For example, some years ago,
James Watkins, then head of the Department of Energy, created a special inspection force called "tiger teams" to enforce
compliance with federal rules on environmental purity, worker
safety, and public health. While some of the teams identified
serious problems, other focused on the trivial. In one reported
instance, a team member discovered a paintbrush left under
a fume hood in a laboratory. Someone in the lab had used it
to apply ordinary paint to a piece of equipment, then had set
it down to dry so that it could be disposed of safely in the trash
later. The tiger team threatened to cite the lab for a violation.
As a result, the lab staffer was forced to wrap the brush in two
layers of plastic and dispose of it as costly hazardous waste.[20]

Technique No. 147. Institute Six Sigma

This is the process for eliminating manufacturing defects that was
made famous by General Electric. In effect, six sigma defines the
quality goal as 3.4 defects per million operations in a manufacturing
or service process. To put this in perspective, many companies average 35,000 defects per million operations, and if you're down to 97
percent accuracy, you've achieved between three and four sigma. Jack
Welch put it in even more personal terms. In his words, three to four
Sigma means "5,000 incorrect surgical operations per week, 20,000
lost articles of mail per hour, and hundreds of thousands of wrong
drug prescriptions filled per year. Not much fun to think about."[21]

More specifically, prior to the introduction of six sigma at GE
Capital, mortgage customers had to use voice mail or call the company back 24 percent of the time because employees were busy or

unavailable. Under the leadership of a six sigma team, that percentage was reduced to 0.1 percent; i.e., customers had a 99.9 percent chance of getting a GE person on the first try. In the company's gas turbine power plants, rotors were cracking as a result of high vibration. Six sigma reduced vibrations by 300 percent. In the medical systems division, the time needed for a CT scanner to perform a chest scan was reduced from 3 minutes to 17 seconds. Overall, the company generated some $750 million in six sigma savings over and above its investment. Operating margins went from 14.8 percent in 1996 to 18.9 percent in 2000.

GE then took the idea to its customers. In 2000, the aircraft engine division had 1500 projects at over 50 airlines, leading to about $230 million in improved operating margins. The medical systems division had 1000 projects, creating over $100 million of incremental operating margin for its hospital customers.[22]

Former GE employees have taken the idea to other companies. At Allied Signal, Lawrence Bossidy believed that six sigma had helped generate 31 consecutive quarters of double-digit earnings growth.[23]

Technique No. 148. Use Surrogates to Monitor Cost Behavior

One of the great problems with trying to manage costs is that when the accountant's cost report arrives, it's too late to do anything—the costs have already been incurred. You might then think about what to do in the future, but the future is never quite the same as the past, and you are left fighting fires rather than engaging in fire prevention.

One technique that can help in this regard is finding surrogates for costs—elements that can be measured and evaluated on a day-by-day basis. This is a bit like the balanced scorecard idea (which will be discussed in detail in Chapter 8). If a surrogate gets out of line, this is an indication that costs are going to be out of line as well. This gives managers the opportunity to intervene and correct whatever problems are present before the situation worsens. Milliken & Co. is a case in point. Milliken adopted several surrogates, including (1) a reduction in lead, or throughput, time, (2) a reduction in change, or setup, time, and (3) a reduction in downtime. As a consequence of giving attention to these new areas, the company saw positive results in both process and cost control.[24]

These surrogates are sometimes called nonfinancial measures of performance. They no doubt have other names as well. Whatever they are called, they are powerful tools for cost management in that they allow a manager to focus his or her attention much more clearly on the *drivers* of costs than otherwise might be the case.

Technique No. 149. Focus on the Cost Drivers

The beauty of surrogates, as indicated above, is that they attempt to focus on the drivers of costs. In fact, when managers focus directly on the drivers rather than on surrogates, they can have a much more direct impact on costs. In a hospital, for example, the cost drivers are not nursing personnel or technician personnel but rather six quite distinct items.

- Type of case—each patient's diagnosis
- Volume—the number of patients of each case type
- The resources used per patient for a particular type of case
- The efficiency of resource delivery (e.g., the number of minutes needed to provide a particular resource)
- Factor prices (i.e., the cost per unit of each resource—nursing salaries, patient-related supplies, etc.)
- Programs—the readiness to serve clients or patients, including the hospital's administrative overhead[25]

Some hospitals have developed their budgeting and control systems in such a way that they can measure the impact of each of these drivers on their bottom line. What is important here is linking the driver with the individual or department that can control its use. For example, resources per case are controlled by physicians, but physicians have little control over the efficiency with which the resource is provided or the factor prices involved in its production.

✂ Technique No. 150. Align Activities with Goals

Sometimes an activity becomes an end in itself. When this is the case, a focus on improving the productivity of that activity might have some payoff, but questioning whether the activity is the best way to reach the actual goal may have a much larger payoff potential. At one time, for example, the U.S. Coast Guard measured its performance in terms of the number of inspections that its officers made. When it was pointed out that the goal was not inspections but reductions in marine fatalities, the Coast Guard examined the reasons for fatalities more closely. It discovered that most fatalities resulted from human rather than equipment error. Focusing on the boat towing industry, where there were above-average fatality rates, the Coast Guard became involved in restructuring the training for new workers. Not only did the fatality rate drop from 91 per 100,000 to 27 per 100,000, but the cost of training was well below the cost of inspections.[26]

✂ Technique No. 151. Ignore Sunk Costs

In February 1998, Steve Jobs eliminated Apple's Newton Division. Why? The Newton—the first personal digital assistant (PDA)—was struggling, and the eMate—a glitzy, low-power computer for kids that looked like a clamshell—was not gaining acceptance. Moreover, Apple had spent some $500 million over 6 years to develop the two products.[27] How could Jobs walk away from a $500 million investment?

Easily, some would say. The $500 million was a sunk cost. It was history. Nothing Jobs could do would change it. All he could affect were revenues and costs going forward, and he did not see these two products as making a positive difference. The conclusion: Get rid of them.

Ignoring sunk costs is something that is hard to accept emotionally, and one wonders whether Jobs would have been able to axe these two projects so easily if he had initiated them. Nevertheless, the only reason to look back is to think about lessons learned for the future. One should not pour good money after bad, as the expression goes. Nevertheless, how many people will refuse to sell a stock until its price returns to the level at which they bought it? It's the same problem. The purchase price is a sunk cost. But it's really hard to accept the idea.

Technique No. 152. Outsource a Manufacturing Activity

The purpose of outsourcing is to let others perform some activity that they can do better than you can, and perhaps, given their economies of scale, do it less expensively as well. Or, as Jack Welch once put it, everything we do in our back room is something that someone else does in their front room. Sometimes, a company has to be desperate before it considers what might have been a good decision much earlier on. For example, Hewlett-Packard was on the verge of shutting down its notebook division when it decided to try outsourcing to Quanta, a Taiwanese company. Now Quanta does just about everything for HP's notebook unit: assembling hardware, installing software, testing the final product, and shipping to the customer. It does so in fewer than 48 hours, which has allowed HP's division to return to profitability.[28]

IBM took a similar approach, announcing early in 2002 that it would outsource the manufacture of its desktop computers to Sanmina-SCI Corp. The company was seeking ways to reduce the $153 million in losses suffered by its personal computer division.[29]

🚫 **But Beware!** The cost analysis for outsourcing can be very tricky. Which costs actually go away and which ones stay can be quite difficult to analyze. Be sure you don't rely on a full-cost report, since many allocated costs will simply be reallocated. But some overhead costs may in fact be differential with respect to the outsourcing decision. The key is to find all the differential costs. See also in Appendix B.

Technique No. 153. Outsource Sales Returns

According to one source, if you're up to more than 1000 orders a week, outsourcing your sales returns may have cost advantages, and several new companies have sprung up to take some of the pain out of returns. According to one observer, outsourcing your returns can cut your losses in an unpleasant aspect of selling retail either over the Internet or by catalog. Some companies won't touch this idea with a 10-foot pole, however. Red Envelope, for example, staffs a central warehouse in Ohio with 20 to 30 of its own people. The company's CEO concedes that this is expensive, but he argues that since so many special arrangements and discounts are made, he doesn't want outsiders dealing with his customers.[30]

✄ Technique No. 154. Help Your Subcontractors Do Their Job Better

Okay, so you're already outsourcing. Can you reduce your costs anyway? Some companies have moved well beyond the "spot market" for outsourced purchases and have become more closely aligned with their suppliers. Clearly, the nature of the product will dictate how much of an alliance is needed. One can buy paper clips and stationery on the spot market, but components for a complicated subassembly no doubt would benefit from close collaboration between the two parties.

Close collaboration with suppliers may lead to some cost savings. General Motors is a case in point. Teams of GM employees—called PICOS teams—visited suppliers' plants to suggest ways to eliminate unnecessary activities. The teams were looking for overstocking, reworking, too many processing steps, idle equipment or space, and the inclusion of unneeded features. During their initial workshops with customers, the PICOS teams succeeded in increasing productivity by 65 percent. In addition, suppliers' inventories fell by 52 percent, and cycle times were reduced by 56 percent.[31] GM no doubt realized some of the resulting cost savings.

Doyle Wilson Homebuilder took a slightly different approach. Faced with the problem of spending a great deal of time rebuilding and repairing previously done work, Wilson started a program to improve customer satisfaction. Flying in the face of industry tradition, he eliminated the "builder bonus" policy. This policy had led some contractors to qualify for on-time completion bonuses by making side deals with customers to create "to-be-done-later" lists.[32]

Technique No. 155. Keep Subcontractors in Line

Outsourcing can be a great cost-saving idea for a company. Even the biggest companies are not fully vertically integrated. But how do you know if your subcontractor is in a position to hold you up by imposing unexpected price increases just at the time when you're most vulnerable, such as during your busy season? Even when it's not your busy season, how do you make sure that your subcontractor is charging you a fair price? Companies take a variety of approaches to dealing with this problem, but one of the most creative was taken by Pierre du Pont almost a century ago. As he was structuring the du Pont company, one of Pierre du Pont's main strategic thrusts was to engage in "just enough" vertical integration. He saw to it that the company was sufficiently backward-integrated to supply a large part, but not all, of its raw material requirements. In most cases, this forced suppliers to meet du Pont's own prices, yet it gave the company the ability to downsize without having its own capacity stand idle. During periods of slack production, the company used its own sources of supply, relying on subcontractors only when operating at peak production levels.[33]

Technique No. 156. Consider Both Volume and Unit Costs in the Outsourcing Decision

Outsourcing works best for those products and services that make up only a small part of your business but are a high-volume activity for the vendor. When that's the case, the vendor can attain economies of scale that are out of your reach, resulting in low unit costs and, one would hope, a price that is below your own unit cost. To illustrate, consider the case of a vibration chamber that is used to ensure that industrial equipment can take a good shaking. Such a chamber costs about $1 million, and its use is essential if a manufacturer is to meet its customers' expectations and avoid costly returns. But how much of the day would such a beast be used? If your company would use it for only a small fraction of the day, the investment doesn't make sense—the per-unit cost of each shake would be very high. Instead, the task can be outsourced to a company that does the shaking for many customers, thereby using the machine at close to its capacity and being able to charge a price that is below your unit cost.[34]

Make Sure You Avoid This YGBK

YGBK No. 16. Investing in Resources That Add Little Value for the Customer

A customer has little, if any, interest in the resources a company has to offer, however unique they may be. Instead, customers are interested in the benefits those resources provide. Nevertheless, many companies continue to invest in non-value-adding resources. Some years ago, for example, Xerox thought it had a competitive advantage in copiers because of its strong service network, but it failed to recognize that a customer's desired outcome (minimized copier downtime) could be achieved in other ways than through a service network (e.g., with improved machine performance or machines that lent themselves to easy repair by the customer). Xerox's loss of market share can be traced almost directly to this misperception of customer needs.[35]

Similarly, Lexus was able to take market share away from Mercedes by making a one-time investment in a manufacturing process that produced nearly defect-free cars, whereas Mercedes was expending considerable resources on an ongoing basis to catch mistakes. Since customers care little about a company's internal processes but care only about the end result—an absence of defects in this case—Lexus was able to meet customers' needs at a lower cost than Mercedes.[36]

Part III

BUILDING SYSTEMS AND NETWORKS FOR COST CONTROL

Warning! There's a rough road ahead. Proceed with caution. The next two chapters are substantially different from what you've read so far, and they are pretty heavy going. They're not for the faint of heart. They're for those managers who want to build systems and activities that make cost control a way of life rather than an ad hoc series of quick fixes during periods of intense panic, or even some investments in approaches that have a long-term impact.

Designing systems of the sort discussed in the next two chapters is hard. You may find that your accounting staff is reluctant to move in these directions—mainly out of fear that you will find out how much they don't know. This means that these moves will require your constant involvement. You will need to cajole, twist arms, and perhaps even yell and scream on occasion to make some of these changes happen. In effect, if you take some of the steps these chapters suggest, you will be building a new culture in your organization. And we're not talking about getting people to wear white shirts and striped ties and salute the company flag; we're talking about changing the fundamental assumptions that form the basis for line managers' decisions about the use of resources. These changes will not come easily.

Chapter 8, which covers the management control system, is concerned in part with the design of an appropriate responsibility-center structure. There are many available options. If you choose the correct one, managers will worry about exactly those things you want them to worry about. An incorrect choice is likely to result in a lack of either *fairness* (managers being held responsible for costs and/or revenues that they cannot control) or *goal congruence* (managers making decisions that are in their own best interest, but not in the best interest of the organization as a whole.

Chapter 8 also discusses the management control process, the regular cycle of programming, budgeting, measuring, and reporting. Designed appropriately, this process can result in managers proposing new programs that can improve the bottom line, building tight but attainable budgets, and using information effectively to make corrective decisions during the course of ongoing operations.

Chapter 9 puts the management control system into a larger context—the complete set of activities that a firm uses that, in effect, constitutes its strategy. Some organizations have been remarkably effective in designing a complementary, mutually reinforcing, essentially inimitable set of activities that create a highly sustainable competitive position in the marketplace. This chapter looks at some of those companies and examines how they do it.

8

BEYOND BEAN COUNTING
REEDUCATING (OR REPLACING)
THE ACCOUNTANTS[1]

Ironically, in many organizations, one of the greatest impediments to good cost control is the accounting staff. The accountants are trained as CPAs, and their skills are primarily in the areas of financial accounting, auditing, and taxation. Most of them—those who have neither an MBA nor a Certificate in Management Accounting (CMA)—have quite limited knowledge about the design of a good management control system. However, a good management control system is precisely what an organization needs if it is to push cost control down to the level of middle management—where it can take place most appropriately and most effectively.

The combination of the need for good management control and the inability of most members of the accounting staff to design the appropriate systems means that senior management must take the lead in this effort. It must make sure that members of the accounting staff facilitate rather than impede the design and installation of an effective management control system. Doing so will require both some reeducation of the accounting staff and, on occasion, some fairly heavy-handed encouragement on the part of senior management.

In its broadest sense, a management control system is concerned with *planning* and *controlling* the resources used in an organization. Like any system, it has both a structure and a process. When we discuss the human body, we consider both its structure (anatomy) and its process (physiology). The same is true when we discuss a management control system. Here, the *structure* consists of an organization's network of responsibility centers, and the *process* comprises programming, budgeting, operating and measuring, and reporting.

There is a wide variety of management control systems in organizations. Sometimes they function well, and sometimes they do not. Sometimes the management control system consists of highly formal procedures and regularly scheduled activities, and sometimes it is quite informal and sporadic. Sometimes the system requires a great deal of time on the part of senior management, and sometimes senior managers are only marginally involved. Sometimes a great deal of decision-making autonomy is delegated to divisional, departmental, or program managers, and sometimes line managers have almost no authority or responsibility in decisions concerning the use of resources. The principles in this chapter are designed to help you design the management control system that's right for your organization.

THE MANAGEMENT CONTROL STRUCTURE

A well-designed management control system focuses on the managers who are responsible for controlling the use of resources. This is the idea that underlies the notion of responsibility centers. More specifically, a responsibility center is an organizational unit headed by a manager who has been charged with achieving some agreed-upon results that help the organization accomplish one or more of its strategic objectives.

From the perspective of the management control system's structure, an organization can be thought of as a network of responsibility centers. Since everyone in an organization is responsible for something, and since most firms organize their employees into groups, each group can be thought of as a responsibility center. As a result, the important issue in designing the structure of the management control system is summed up in the question, "For what is the group responsible?" Senior management's objective is to design the organization's responsibility centers in such a way that individuals are responsible for those activities over which they exercise a reasonable amount of control. Unfortunately, this simple-sounding task becomes quite complex in practice.

Types of Responsibility Centers

Responsibility centers can take a wide variety of forms. In general, however, there are five main types: revenue centers, standard expense centers, discretionary expense centers, profit centers, and investment centers. The main factor determining senior management's selection of one type over another for a given operation is the kind of resources controlled by the responsibility-center manager. These different types of responsibility centers are listed in Table 8-1.

As Table 8-1 indicates, if a manager has a great deal of control over revenue, as is ordinarily the case in a sales office, for example, his or her department would generally be considered a revenue center. This is true even though the responsibility center incurs some expenses. That is, the manager's performance is evaluated in terms of the amount of revenue generated by the department. On the other hand, if a manager has a great deal of control over the department's expenses but has no ability to generate revenue, the department would ordinarily be an expense center.

The distinction between standard and discretionary expense centers is quite important. The use of a standard expense center is appropriate when a manager can control the expense per unit of output but not the number of units of output. The laundry department of a hotel, for example, might be designated as a standard expense center. That is, the manager would be responsible for the expense per pound but not for the total expenses of the department. This is because total

Table 8-1   Types of Responsibility Centers and Associated Responsibilities

Type	Responsible for	Examples
Revenue center	Revenue earned by the center	A divisional sales office. The development office in a large university.
Standard expense center	Expenses per unit of output, with a flexible budget used to compute total allowable expenses for each period	Many manufacturing plants. The laundry in a hotel.
Discretionary expense center	Total expenses incurred by the center, regardless of the volume of output	An accounting department. A corporate staff department.
Profit center	Total revenues minus total expenses of the center, i.e., the center's profit	A product line in a large company.
Investment center	Total revenues minus total expenses of the center, computed as a percentage of the assets used by the center, i.e., the center's return on assets (ROA)	A division in a multidivisional conglomerate.

expenses depend on the number of pounds of laundry sent for washing, which is not under the manager's control.

A discretionary expense center, by contrast, is an organizational unit in which there is no easily measurable unit of activity (such as a pound of laundry). This is the case in, say, a personnel or accounting department. Under these circumstances, the department would ordinarily receive a fixed budget, negotiated with senior management, that is not tied to any units of activity. The department's manager would be expected to adhere to this budget during the budgetary period.

If the manager has control of both revenue and expenses, the center is a profit center. Over the past several years, many large, and even some small, organizations have instituted profit centers as a way to give their managers incentives to both control expenses and worry about the generation of additional revenues.

Finally, it is possible that a manager also exerts some control over the acquisition and use of certain assets, such as machines, production equipment, accounts receivable, or inventory. If this is the case, then the manager could reasonably be expected to have control over the productivity of those assets in addition to the center's revenue and expenses. This would imply that the unit should be an investment center. In this case, the manager is responsible for the profit earned in his or her center as a percent of the center's assets, i.e., the center's return on assets (ROA).

Design Principles

In considering the design of an organization's responsibility centers, senior management should begin with the fundamental premise that the organization itself is an investment center. That is, all organizations must obtain a sufficiently high return on assets to (1) help finance the acquisition and replacement of assets, (2) provide the cash needed to support growth and perhaps weather bad times, and (3) satisfy investors. Even nonprofit organizations need a return on assets to satisfy the first two needs. This means that the fundamental design question for a management control system is how to decentralize investment responsibility among the various organizational units—divisions, sales offices, plants, and so forth.

The Concept of Fairness A key factor driving the determination of the most appropriate responsibility-center structure is the fairness criterion. In effect, the structure must be designed in such a way that managers have reasonable (even if not total) control over those items for which they are being held responsible.[2]

✂ Technique No. 157. Make Sure That Fairness Is Present Whenever Possible in the Design of Responsibility Centers

While complaints in this area may sound like whining, violations of the fairness criterion can cause some considerable difficulties. Violations frequently occur when cost accounting gets mixed up with management control. Sometimes this can work, but usually it does not. At Crown Cork and Seal in the 1980s, for instance, each plant was designated as a profit center, and plant managers were compensated on the basis of their bottom-line performance. However, corporate overhead was allocated to the plants using standard cost accounting allocation bases. Fortunately, Crown's CEO at the time (John Connelly) ran a very lean operation: SG&A as a percent of sales was kept very low, and even decreased throughout his tenure, so the plants had little to complain about.[3] Nevertheless, allocating overhead removed the plant manager's ability to control all the elements involved in profit. More generally, while overhead allocation may be useful for computing the "full cost" of operating a plant, and hence is an appropriate cost accounting technique, it also means that a portion of a plant's profitability is not under the control of the profit-center (plant) manager. This leads to a violation of the fairness criterion.

✂ Technique No. 158. Instead of Allocating Actual Overhead to Responsibility Centers, Assign an Agreed-Upon Amount Each Month

In general, all responsibility centers benefit from membership in the corporation, and therefore they should bear their "fair share" of corporate overhead. The real question is how to both determine each responsibility center's fair share and ensure that the fairness criterion is being met. While a responsibility center's fair share no doubt will always be subject to question, the issue can be discussed openly and frankly at budget formulation time, and an amount for the year can be agreed upon. One-twelfth of this amount can then be assigned to the responsibility center each month. Not only does this approach abide by the fairness criterion, but it allows the management control system to identify the variance between assigned and actual overhead. Assuming that all *budgeted* corporate overhead was assigned to responsibility centers, this variance then serves as a measure of the ability of the corporate office to control its costs.

The Management Control Structure and Motivation

As you might imagine from the preceding discussion, a firm's management control structure can provide a powerful motivating force for middle- and lower-level managers. It is therefore extremely important that senior management consider the incentives the structure provides to the affected managers. In particular, senior management needs to pay attention to the concept of goal congruence, since a lack of goal congruence is a problem that frequently plagues an organization's management control system.

Technique No. 159. Make Sure That Goal Congruence Is Present Whenever Possible

Goal congruence, a term borrowed from social psychology, is the idea of aligning the goals of the managers of individual responsibility centers with the goals of the organization as a whole. A lack of goal congruence ordinarily takes the form of dysfunctional behavior—i.e., behavior by responsibility center managers that is not in the best interests of the organization as a whole. Its presence ordinarily means that some changes in the nature of the organization's responsibility centers are needed. As an illustration, consider the example of Rural Health Associates (RHA), a small physician group practice located in Franklin, Maine. RHA had designated each of its physicians as a revenue center. Physicians were encouraged to see as many patients as possible, and a sizable portion of their annual compensation was based on the amount of revenue they generated. Senior managers at RHA were puzzled when one physician insisted—upon threat of leaving the group practice—that he be given a full-time nurse practitioner to assist him. Unfortunately, his increased productivity as a result of the NP would not generate enough revenue to cover the person's salary.[4]

This lack of goal congruence arose because the physician was motivated to increase his revenue in any way he could—regardless of the associated costs. He thus had no incentive to consider the tricky economics associated with hiring a nurse practitioner. Yet for the group practice overall, those economics were very important.

Similarly, at General Electric one year, a division had a great fourth-quarter revenue line, but no income to speak of. When asked what happened, the division general manager responded that the division had had a fourth-quarter sales contest and "everyone did a good job." When queried about the margin on those sales, the manager responded, "We didn't ask for margin." In Jack Welch's words, "That's the simplest example of a universal problem: What you measure is what you get—what you reward is what you get."[5]

In sum, at a revenue center at RHA, physicians were motivated to increase the amount of revenue they billed in any way they could, regardless of the cost. At General Electric, salespeople were probably motivated to offer deep discounts or to push products with very small margins in an effort to increase revenue. In both instances, there was a lack of goal congruence: People were pursuing activities that were in their own personal best interest but not in the best interest of the organization overall. Changing physicians to a profit center and making them responsible for their direct expenses (such as their nurse practitioners), as well as for some portion of the group's overhead, would probably have altered their behavior considerably. Changing the sales contest to emphasize margins rather than sales revenue would likely have had the same effect at GE.

Technique No. 160. When Feasible, Set Up Profit Centers

The use of profit centers is a well-established technique that many companies employ to encourage managers to think about both revenues and expenses. But profit centers can also work in nonprofit organizations. At Harvard University, for example, each school is a profit center. Similarly, many hospitals designate their clinical departments (such as surgery and pediatrics) as profit centers. Even the tiny Kelmscott Rare Breeds Foundation in Lincolnville, Maine, has set up profit centers. The managers of the farm, the gift shop, and the educational program are all expected to manage both their revenues and their costs, even though some are budgeted to operate at a loss.[6]

Profit centers can even work in the public sector, where the center has no ability to earn revenue. This counterintuitive notion was illustrated a few years ago in New York City when the manager of the repair garage of the New York City Sanitation Department created a "profit-center mentality" among the department's employees, even though the department was a public-sector agency with no earned revenue. To do this, he used market prices in outside, private garages to create a pseudo revenue figure, and then compared it to the expenses of each operating unit. By making a game of beating the private-sector garages, he was able to achieve a dramatic increase in the department's productivity.[7]

Many nonprofit managers consider profit centers to be anathema to the nonprofit mission. However, for other managers, they reinforce the oft-stated nonprofit maxim: no margin, no mission.

Transfer Prices A lack of goal congruence can appear in a number of other situations, but one of the most common is with transfer prices—the internal prices that are used for transactions when several divisions in a multidivisional organization buy and sell products and services from one another.[8]

✂ Technique No. 161. When Feasible, Set Transfer Prices at Market Rates

Careers in accounting have been made on the back of transfer prices. Tenure has been awarded, and learned papers have been written. Indeed, the classic paper on transfer pricing was written by an economist, suggesting that the idea has a multidisciplinary focus as well. (Don't ask!)

In general, however, despite all the hubbub, the basic notion of setting transfer prices at market rates remains a strong guiding principle. Although doing so is not always feasible, when it is, goal congruence can be achieved. To understand why, consider the following hypothetical but fairly typical problem.

A company has several profit centers that engage in buying and selling transactions among themselves. One profit center is the Automated Component Division (ACD); another is the Laboratory Testing Division (LTD). The ACD charges outside customers $11 for a component that is used in the manufacture of a camera. The component's full cost includes all direct materials and labor (both of which are minimal), purchased services, and a fair share of overhead. To this full-cost amount, the ACD adds a small profit margin to arrive at the $11 price.

A sophisticated test is needed to analyze the component and ensure that it works properly before it is shipped. This test is currently "purchased" by the ACD from the LTD. The LTD charges all of the company's divisions $6 for this test and others like it. The price is based on variable costs of $2 per test (mainly supplies and labor), plus $3 of fixed costs and $1 of profit.

The ACD's manager has discovered that tests of comparable quality and with equivalent turnaround time can be obtained for $4.50 from a freestanding laboratory located nearby. By purchasing these tests, the ACD's manager could increase the ACD's contribution to overhead by $1.50 (from $5 to $6.50), as shown in Table 8-2.

Table 8-2   Comparative ACD Performance Using Tests from the LTD versus Tests from a Freestanding Laboratory

	Automated Components Division	*Laboratory Testing Division*	*Company Overall*
Buy From			
Laboratory Testing Division			
Revenue	$11.00	$6.00	$11.00
Variable cost	6.00	2.00	2.00
Contribution to fixed costs and overhead	$ 5.00	$4.00	$ 9.00
Freestanding Laboratory			
Revenue	$11.00	$0.00	$11.00
Variable cost	4.50	0.00	4.50
Contribution	$ 6.50	$0.00	$ 6.50

Note: Figures are for one component only.

While the ACD could improve its financial performance by having tests conducted by the freestanding laboratory, the company's overall profits would decline if it were to do so. That is, the company pays $2.00 "out-of-pocket" for every test done by the LTD. All other costs are fixed. Therefore, each test done by the LTD reduces the contribution to the company's profits by $2.00. If, on the other hand, the ACD buys tests from the freestanding testing laboratory, the company incurs an out-of-pocket cost of $4.50 instead of $2.00. As a result, the contribution to profits falls from $9.00 to $6.50 per component.

Clearly, the company would prefer to have the ACD purchase tests from the LTD rather than from the freestanding testing laboratory, whereas the ACD would prefer to purchase tests from the freestanding laboratory. If the ACD is forced to buy from the LTD in order to maximize the company's overall profit, the ACD's profits will fall, as will the ACD's manager's bonus. As a result, the ACD's goals are not congruent with those of the company as a whole.

If the market price were used as the transfer price in this example, the problem could be solved quite easily. Senior management might have to establish a shadow price for the LTD so that the manager's bonus would not be affected. However, the larger question that senior management now can ask is why the internal price is so much higher than the outside price.

The market-price approach is not always possible because of the unavailability of information for some internally provided goods and services. Nevertheless, the key question remains: Do an organization's transfer pricing policies motivate managers to take actions that are in the best interest of *both* their individual responsibility centers *and* the organization as a whole? If so, the policies would seem to be appropriate. If not, they most likely need to be modified.

Design Complications

Determining the appropriate responsibility centers for a company's product lines would be relatively easy if each line (1) sold its own products or services, (2) were staffed by personnel who worked for no other product line, and (3) were the responsibility of a manager who had reasonable control over hiring and other personnel decisions, as well as over decisions on program supply purchases. Then, each product line would likely be designated as an investment center or profit center.

However, most organizations are not set up in a way that permits such a tidy and well-defined formal structure. Many companies operate over large geographic areas and must consider this fact when designing their structures. For example, does a multidivisional corporation have one manager of home appliances with broad geographic responsibilities, or does it have several area managers, each with responsibility for all products in his or her area, including home appliances?

In general, a separate formal structure is needed when responsibility for a product line's success depends on more than one supporting functional unit. For example, the director of a master's degree program in a large university draws on faculty from several different departments (e.g., accounting, marketing, organizational behavior) who work in the program. Moreover, while faculty may teach in a particular program, they generally do not report only to the director of one program within the organization. A similar blurring of product and functional lines takes place in companies like Boeing and McKinsey, where project managers may require personnel from several functional units to carry out their projects successfully.

Technique No. 162. Consider the Use of a Matrix Structure

Although the product line structure need not match the organizational structure, there typically is a manager who has identifiable responsibility for each product line. The need for a fit between the organizational and product line structures often results in a matrix organization. The matrix consists of product line managers along one dimension and managers of functionally organized responsibility centers along the other. It is illustrated in Figure 8-1.

In this sort of arrangement, each product line manager is accountable for his or her line's profitability. Functional unit managers, by contrast, are held accountable for the skill mix and quality in their units. In this example, most employees would have a home base in a functional unit, but they also would be "purchased" at a transfer price by one or more product lines.

Since product line managers call on the functional units for work that is done on their products, responsibility is divided between the functional units and the product lines. The product line managers, whose units are probably designated as profit centers, are responsible for the profitability of their lines. The functional units may be standard expense centers, with their managers responsible for recruiting the needed skill mix and undertaking the requisite training to meet the needs of the product lines. In some instances, a functional unit specialist might be needed for a relatively short period of time, such as on a consulting project. In others, such as in the construction of an aircraft, the functional specialist might spend 1 or more years working for a given product line.

One particularly interesting example of a matrix organization comes out of the federal government. In the Department of Defense

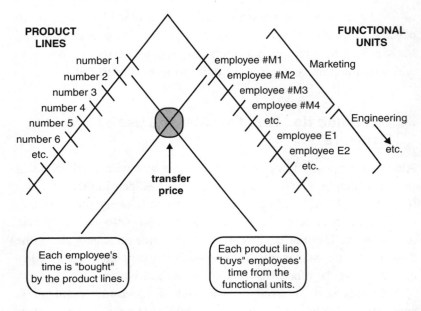

Figure 8-1   A typical matrix structure.

(DoD) in the 1960s, the lines of organizational responsibility ran to the secretary of the Army, the secretary of the Navy, and the secretary of the Air Force, whereas defense programs cut across these lines. For example, the DoD had a strategic mission that was related to a possible nuclear exchange with the Soviets. Different parts of this program were the responsibility of the Army (antiballistic missiles), the Navy (Polaris submarines), and the Air Force (strategic missiles and bombers). The DoD needed a mechanism that facilitated decision making for the program as a whole.[9] A matrix organization was the result.

✂ Technique No. 163. Consider Using ETOB

When an organization has investment or profit centers, senior management must decide whether there will be cross-subsidization among them. Investment or profit centers that are independent—i.e., that do not cross-subsidize one another and that have managerial rewards linked to bottom-line performance—constitute a powerful motivating device in an organization. In effect, they create a series of small business units, sometimes referred to as "every tub on its own bottom," or ETOB.

At General Electric, for example, each business is an investment center, and each is expected to earn a reasonable return on its invested assets. At Harvard University, where the ETOB idea originated, each school is expected to operate at a surplus, even if small. As you might imagine, the business school, the law school, and the medical school think the ETOB idea is just fine, whereas the divinity school, the educational school, and a few other "poor sisters" are not so happy with it.

One of the problems with an ETOB structure is that it can create a fortresslike mentality among the affected responsibility-center managers, leading to a quite different culture from that in an organization with cross-subsidization among its responsibility centers. On the other hand, a strategy of cross-subsidization inevitably raises the question of how large a subsidy should be and for how long it should exist. As a result, managers who are concerned about cost cutting must make sure that subsidies are not leading to slack or other inefficiencies in the units that are being subsidized. In hospitals where the clinical departments are profit centers and where there is cross-subsidization among them, for example, the departments of pediatrics, psychiatry, and a few others are constantly attempting to justify their deficits as being appropriate. At the same time, the very profitable surgical departments constantly complain about having to subsidize "those lazy pediatricians."

THE MANAGEMENT CONTROL PROCESS

Much of the management control process is informal. Meetings, hallway and lunchtime conversations, ad hoc memoranda, and the like can all influence how managers make decisions about the use of resources. Nevertheless, in most organizations, there is also a more formal process. This formal process usually consists of a set of regularly scheduled activities through which decisions are made about the kinds and quantities of products and services the organization expects to produce during an upcoming period of time and the resources needed to generate that output. During each fiscal year, records of actual results (revenues and expenses) are usually kept, and most organizations prepare regular reports on these results that senior and middle managers can use as a basis for determining whether corrective action of some sort is needed.

In most organizations, these activities are considered to be part of the formal management control process. They can be classified into four separate phases:[10]

1. Programming
2. Budget formulation
3. Operation and measurement
4. Reporting

As indicated in Figure 8-2, these phases recur in a regular cycle and build upon one another. Thus, by describing each phase, we can gain an appreciation for the nature of the formal aspects of the management control process.

Programming

In the programming phase of the process, senior management makes a variety of decisions of a long-term nature concerning the product lines the company will produce, the programs it will undertake, and the approximate amount of resources it will devote to each. As Figure 8-2 indicates, these decisions are made within the context of the organization's overall strategy, coupled with whatever information is available concerning new opportunities, increased competition, new or pending legislation that might affect the organization's efforts, and other similar considerations.

Frequently, each division in an organization prepares its own strategic plan, in which it defines such things as the elements of its

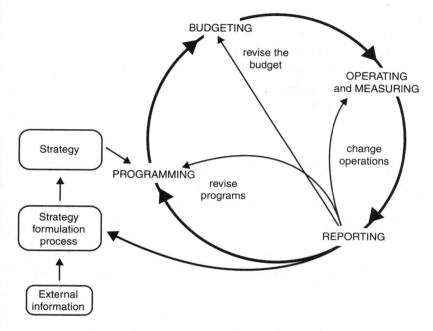

Figure 8-2   Phases of the management control process. (*Adapted from Robert N. Anthony and David W. Young, Management Control in Nonprofit Organizations, 7th ed., Burr Ridge, Ill.: McGraw-Hill/Irwin, 2003*)

business, its competitors, and its competitive advantages and disadvantages. In effect, this plan establishes the framework for the organization's programming activities.[11]

Because programming decisions are generally long range in nature, the programming phase of the management control process frequently looks ahead by as much as 5 or 10 years. In some large organizations, there is a lengthy program planning document that describes each program proposal in detail, estimates the resources needed to accomplish it, and calculates the expected returns.

Programming can also be an inherently creative activity, bordering on strategic change. Gary Hamel, a leading strategic thinker, demonstrates this when he contrasts programming at Nabisco (stuffing "twice as much white gunk between two chocolate cookies as you used to" to get Double Stuf Oreos) and at The Gap (which "went from selling Levi jeans and a motley assortment of teen clothing in an undistinguished mall format, to owning a portfolio of couldn't-be-cooler brands sold in some of the freshest retail digs around").[12]

Budgeting

In contrast to programming, which looks ahead several years, budgeting generally is for a single year. Ordinarily, it looks at both existing programs and the new programs that emerged from the programming phase, and attempts to determine the revenues, expenses, and other activities that will be associated with each.

In some organizations, programs fall neatly into responsibility centers, so that each responsibility-center manager prepares a budget for each of his or her programs. Alternatively, each program may be a separate responsibility center, most likely a profit or investment center. When neither of these arrangements is possible, a more complex, matrixlike structure may be needed.

It is important that the budgeting phase fit with the programming phase of the management control process. Moreover, by having line managers budget for nonfinancial as well as financial goals and objectives, senior management can relate each program to the organization's overall strategic direction. This is not a new idea. Ford Motor Company included nonfinancial items in its budgets some 35 years ago. The approach was refined about 25 years ago by Texas Instruments. Today, it is used in many companies in many different forms.

Despite these changes, and despite the importance of budgeting to an organization's success, the budgeting phase of the management control process is anathema to many senior managers. They see it as taking up a lot of valuable time and as being something that is to be finessed rather than taken seriously. As a result, many line managers devote considerable energy to game playing in the budgetary process rather than using this process as a tool to help them improve their performance. When this happens, the budget plays a far less valuable role than it otherwise could.

Operating and Measuring

Once a budget has been agreed upon, an organization commences operating. This is an oversimplification, of course, since all organizations except newly established ones operate continuously. However, if new programs have been approved, or if additional funds have been made available for existing programs, it is quite likely that a variety of new or different types of operation will also commence at the beginning of a new budget year.

From a somewhat more general perspective, senior management must focus on the kinds of information needed by responsibility-center and program managers. The primary goal of the measurement phase—to collect information that meets managers' needs—is complicated by three factors: (1) New programs frequently require new kinds of information, (2) different managers in an organization make different kinds of decisions, and (3) any given manager will make a variety of decisions at various times, depending on the particular circumstances that he or she faces at those times.

These factors mean that the measurement phase of the management control process, must both collect a wide variety of information and be flexible and dynamic. In any growing or evolving organization, the information needed by senior and line managers not only will differ from one responsibility center or program to the next, but will be changing constantly.

Many organizations collect a variety of nonfinancial as well as financial information. The types of nonfinancial information collected will vary within and among organizations, based on such considerations as each manager's responsibilities, the nature of customers and their needs, and the kinds of action that senior management expects line managers to take in response to a problem. In many instances, senior management may need to work closely with the accounting department to develop the appropriate nonfinancial measures, since dealing with this sort of information is not the most comfortable activity for people with a strong financial orientation.

Reporting

The final phase of the management control process is the preparation of reports for program and responsibility-center managers. The information collected in the measuring phase of the process is thus classified, analyzed, sorted, merged, totaled, and finally reported to senior management and line managers. The resulting reports usually compare planned outputs and inputs with actual ones, and thereby allow managers to evaluate their performance. This information, along with whatever other information (e.g., from conversations, informal sources, industry analyses, etc.) is available, generally leads to one of three possible courses of action, as indicated in Figure 8-2.

1. *Change the operation.* If a manager is not satisfied with the results shown on the reports, he or she may need to take corrective action. This can include such activities as investigating sources of supply to attempt to obtain lower prices, asking about the use of overtime, speaking with salespeople about customer satisfaction or dissatisfaction with products, and so forth. The action taken can also include praise for a job well done, constructive criticism, reassignment, or, in extreme cases, termination.

2. *Revise the budget.* In some instances, certain key aspects of the activities in a responsibility center are not under the control of the manager of the center. For example, if a factory's production volume is determined exclusively by the sales force and the orders it submits, the factory manager has little ability to control that volume. If supply prices are the responsibility of the purchasing department, or if wage rates are determined by senior management in its negotiations with unions, managers of the affected responsibility centers generally will have little control over the associated variances

from the budget. Moreover, the effect of a strike or a natural disaster may mean that it is all but impossible for a responsibility-center manager to meet his or her budgeted targets. In these instances, some organizations will revise the budget.

3. *Revise programs.* The reports can also be used as a basis for program evaluation and revision. For any of a number of reasons, a programming decision may not be optimal. The anticipated demand for the product may not materialize, competition may be stronger than the organization thought it would be, technological improvements may have made the product obsolete, or the organization may not be able to recruit or develop people with the skills necessary to implement the program successfully. In extreme situations, the reports may indicate a need not only to revise or discontinue one or more of the organization's programs, but also to change the organization's overall strategy. Thus, as indicated in Figure 8-2, the reports can also feed into the strategy formulation process.

Role of the Accounting System If the measurement aspect of this phase of the management control process is to be effective, the organization must have a well-developed accounting system. From a management control system perspective, we are concerned with the kinds of information that flow to responsibility-center and program managers, and its role in facilitating decision making. The goal of the measurement phase of the management control system, then, is to determine the appropriate information to gather to meet the needs of these managers.

In addition, the financial reporting process must be designed in such a way that managers can "drill down" to understand the elements of different variances from budget (e.g., volume, price, mix, wage, efficiency, productivity, and the like). Without an ability to understand which of these elements caused how much of a variance, a line manager is likely to have difficulty determining which product lines need to be the focus of quality-improvement and/or cost-reduction efforts.

In addition to reporting on financial performance, a good management control process reports on nonfinancial (or programmatic) performance. Nonfinancial objectives tend to fall into two general categories: (1) those that will have an impact on the organization's long-term performance, such as gaining market share or ensuring product quality, and (2) those that are oriented toward social responsibility, such as providing a safer, more fulfilling workplace.

Central to measuring and reporting programmatic performance is the task of selecting the relevant measures. The challenge here is to develop some clear-cut indicators of performance so that nonfinancial objectives can be established during the budgeting phase of the management control process, and then measured and reported at regular intervals during the budget year.

Clearly, the specific characteristics of nonfinancial reporting in a given organization will depend on the nature of the relationship among customers, programs, and resources. In general, however, nonfinancial reports provide information on such items as minutes spent per activity, the number and kind of customers served, the nature of the services delivered, the results of those services, customer satisfaction, and progress toward overall organizational goals. Table 8-3 shows some examples.

The classic work in the area of nonfinancial performance measures is John Rockart's article "Chief Executives Define Their Own Data Needs," which was published in the *Sloan Management Review* more than 20 years ago.[13] The most popular book on the topic at the moment is Robert Kaplan and David Norton's *The Balanced Scorecard.*[14] This book has generated a great deal of thinking on the part of senior management about the kinds of nonfinancial measures that are useful and how they interrelate. Kaplan and Norton break the nonfinancial measures into three categories, each of which is related to a different area of importance to an organization, and each of which has a causal, usually lagged, relationship to financial performance: customer satisfaction, employee skill development, and internal processes.

Table 8-3 Measures of Programmatic Performance

Area	Positive Measures	Negative Measures
Manufacturing quality	First-pass yields	Percentage defects
Vendor quality	Percentage of on-time performance	Percentage returns
Customer quality	On-time delivery	Percentage returns Percentage complaints

✂ Technique No. 164. Develop and Measure a Variety of Leading Nonfinancial Indicators of Performance

These indicators will vary considerably from one organization to the next, and they may undergo constant evolution in any given organization until a workable set of indicators emerges. Milliken & Co., for example, developed several nonfinancial measures of performance related to its operations: (1) a reduction in throughput time, (2) a reduction in setup time, and (3) a reduction in downtime. As a consequence of these new areas of attention, Milliken saw positive results in both process control and cost control.[15] As another example, Pioneer Petroleum tied only 60 percent of its executives' bonuses to financial performance (which consisted of a weighted average of five components: operating margins, return on capital, cost reduction versus plan, and growth in both existing and new markets). The remaining 40 percent was based on the Balanced Scorecard's indicators concerning customer satisfaction, internal process improvements, and employees' learning and growth perspectives.[16]

Presenting the Information The presentation format for nonfinancial information is important. Given the wide variety of feasible measures in each of several areas of concern to senior management, it is possible for the information to become overwhelming. In response, some companies have begun to use a "spidergram," like that shown in Figure 8-3. This technique allows senior management to see several different measures in several different categories at a glance. In a spidergram, the inner circle is the minimum acceptable level of performance, the outer circle is the goal, and the jagged line is actual performance for the period in question. This spidergram, which is for a large integrated health-care delivery system, shows several areas where the jagged line is inside the minimum acceptable line. Senior management can use this information to focus its conversations with line managers and others who have responsibility for the different measures.

Technique No. 165. Make Sure You Can Revise Your Management Control System Quickly in Response to Changing Managerial Needs

Some organizations are finding that the measurement and reporting phases of the management control process must be in constant revision. This is especially true in a growing or evolving organization, where the information needed by senior and middle managers not only will differ from one responsibility center or program to the next, but will be changing constantly. In addition, the whole management control system must be attuned to managers' needs if the organization is to make cost-reducing improvements on a constant basis. To illustrate, consider the case of Toyota. Toyota defines the ideal plant as one "where a Toyota customer could drive up to a shipping dock, ask for a customized product or service, and get it immediately at the lowest possible price and with no defects." If a plant does not achieve this ideal, the shortcoming "is a source of creative tension for further improvement efforts."

To help achieve this goal, Toyota has developed the Toyota Production System (TPS). This system requires workers and managers to use the scientific method to experiment constantly with improvements in the company's production process. The system relies on four basic rules: (1) All work shall be highly specific as to

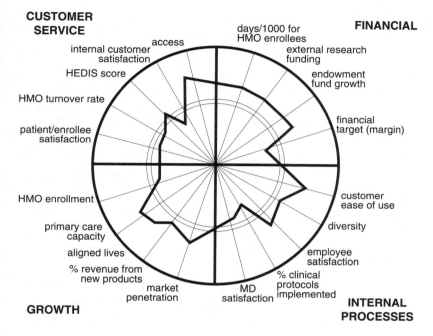

Figure 8-3 Example of a spidergram. (*From Robert N. Anthony and David W. Young, Management Control in Nonprofit Organizations, 7th ed., Burr Ridge, Ill.: McGraw-Hill/Irwin, 2003*)

content, sequence, timing, and outcome; (2) all requests and responses between customers and suppliers must be unambiguous; (3) the pathway for every good and service must be simple and direct; and (4) improvements are made under the guidance of a teacher at the lowest possible level in the organization.

In the TPS environment, anyone can challenge the established production process. A worker who encounters a problem is expected to ask for assistance at once. The problem is a signal that some sort of learning is needed, either by the person on the assembly line or by his or her superiors in the form of a process improvement. If two or more line workers are involved in the problem, they are expected to collaborate in seeking a solution, using a superior as coach if need be.

Changes, when made, are accompanied by goals (e.g., the number of minutes needed for a changeover on a production line), and data are collected to measure performance against those goals. Considerable responsibility is thus delegated to line workers, and yet there is almost no chaos. The rules and norms of expected behavior are all quite clear and are adhered to throughout the organization.[17]

The success of the TPS is due, in no small measure, to Toyota's management control process. Toyota is prepared to accept new programmatic efforts based on changes initiated at the floor level. Budgets are developed with a recognition that time will be spent on process improvements, conflict management, and data collection as well as on actual production activities. New measures are constantly developed to address the experiments that are taking place. And the resulting reports, prepared for both line managers and senior management, are always in flux.

Many companies in a variety of industries have tried, unsuccessfully, to imitate the TPS. In part, their failure can be traced to a poor management control process. In fact, despite its importance for cost control and improved bottom-line performance, the management control process is generally neglected in both the popular business literature and management education. Its neglect is partially a result of the fact that in most organizations the design of the management control process is the responsibility of the accounting department, but accounting studies in most schools and universities give the topic only cursory treatment. The goal of most undergraduate accounting programs is to prepare students to become CPAs and to enter public accounting, and there are almost no questions on the CPA exam concerning management accounting or the management control process. Since many CFOs began their careers in public accounting, the unfortunate conclusion is that they have had little formal education in management control principles. What they know about the process they have learned on the job, and, as a result, their knowledge is frequently incomplete and sometimes ill informed. For this reason, senior management involvement with the management control system is crucial.

9

STRATEGIC POSITIONING IS NOT AN 'R'-RATED MOVIE
MAKING COST CONTROL A WAY OF LIFE

When Steve Jobs returned to Apple Computer in 1997, his turn-around efforts were not directed solely toward new products, such as the iMac. Indeed, because of his flair for marketing, and especially for product promotion, Jobs frequently is seen as more flashy than substantive. However, he also demonstrated an ability to look at what goes out the back door as well as what comes in the front door. He took some of the tried and true steps toward cost cutting that have been discussed in earlier chapters, such as instituting layoffs, requiring most employees to travel coach, ending Apple's sabbatical plan, and centralizing a number of functions, thereby eliminating duplication and permitting some job reductions.

But Jobs also cut costs in some unusual ways. For example, by consolidating the number of product lines from fifteen to three, he was able to close some facilities and reduce the advertising and other promotional costs associated with having so many different product lines. And by changing Apple's distribution system, he was able to focus on national chains and eliminate thousands of relatively small retail outlets, each of which required company resources to support it. Similarly, he reduced Apple's cash conversion cycle from 55 to 25 days between 1997 and 1998, mainly by almost doubling the company's inventory turnover in the space of a single year and tripling it from its 1995 level. Although Apple did not reach Gateway's 2 days or Dell's *negative* 6 days,[1] the shortened cycle nevertheless led to some significant cost savings.

Whether Apple will rise, Phoenix-like, from the ashes of Jobs's predecessors is still an open question. However, his attempt to rescue the company relied on a technique that goes well beyond cost cutting per se, namely, the idea of strategic repositioning. There are a number of positioning options, but in all instances, as the discussion below highlights, there is a need for tradeoffs.

Technique No. 166. Focus Your Strategy in an Area Where You Can Have a Cost Advantage

Strategic positioning is one of the most important concepts in all of corporate strategy, but it's difficult to pull off. The difficulty arises because, among other things, focusing requires making trade-offs and thus requires you to decide not only what you are going to be as a company, but also what kind of company you are *not* going to be. One of the most dramatic examples of the trade-off idea comes from the banking industry, where Lan and Spar, a small Danish bank, adopted a strategy focusing on white-collar workers. But the next step must not have come about without some heated and gut-wrenching discussions. The bank actually sent letters to its corporate customers—who now were not a part of the strategy—asking them to move their accounts to another bank. In part because of this highly focused strategy, and in part because of the ability it now had to focus its costs in those areas where there was a clear relationship between a cost item and some associated revenue, the bank is now the most profitable in Denmark.[2]

Apple was not so fortunate. Even after Jobs had focused it more precisely, the company was still in trouble. In large part, the company's continuing problems were the result of some of its products not producing the revenue stream that Jobs and others had anticipated. But in addition Jobs had made some questionable business decisions, such as acquiring retail outlets. These problems do not minimize the importance of the cost-reduction efforts, however, many of which were made possible by the strategic focus that Jobs gave the company, and most of which were in line with the longer-term ideas discussed in Chapter 7.

Jobs's need to take immediate action to cut costs arose in large part because Apple had not been designed as a cost-conscious organization. Other organizations have been designed in this way, however. In fact, many companies that seem poised not only to survive but to thrive in the twenty-first century are well known for being highly cost-conscious and cost-efficient.

This chapter examines the stories of several of these organizations: Southwest Airlines, Airborne Express, Wal-Mart, Dell, and General Electric. The chapter's main point is that building a cost-conscious organization does not happen by accident. Nor is it something that can be accomplished overnight. Nevertheless, if it is dedicated to the task, senior management can build an enterprise in which a focus on cost control is a way of life. The chapter concludes with a set of general principles for doing just that—making cost control a way of life.

SOUTHWEST AIRLINES

Let's start with Southwest Airlines. So much has been written about this airline's success story that little more need be said. The analysis of what makes Southwest so lean and mean was presented by strategy guru Michael Porter.[3] In his analysis, Porter emphasized that the key to Southwest's success was its activity system—a collection of strategic choices and accompanying operating policies that made Southwest not only cost-efficient but also almost impossible to imitate. Table 9-1 shows some of Southwest's strategic choices and the associated operating policies.

Some cost-reducing policies appear in more than one place, which is by design. Southwest's activities are all interconnected—like love and marriage in the popular song of the 1950s, you can't have one without the other. For example, highly motivated ground crews help to speed gate-turnaround time, but that's not enough. The fact that the fleet is standardized means that everything is always in the same place on each aircraft. Since there are no meals and no baggage transfers, there are no delays in getting items on and off the planes. Since there are no seat assignments, people don't have to search for their seat; it's first come, first served. The use of secondary airports means lower landing fees and less congestion. And on and on.

What does all this mean? Well, among other things, when you tease out the consequences of a 15-minute gate-turnaround time

Table 9-1   Southwest Airlines Strategic Choices and Associated Operating Policies

Strategic Choice	Associated Operating Policies
Offer limited passenger service	No meals, no seat assignments, limited use of travel agents, no baggage transfers, no connections with other airlines, automatic ticketing machines
Offer frequent, reliable departures	Short gate-turnaround times, use of secondary airports, short-haul flights, standardized fleet of 737 aircraft
Use lean, highly productive ground and gate crews	High compensation of employees, flexible union contracts, high level of employee stock ownership, standardized fleet of 737 aircraft
Charge very low ticket prices	Limited use of travel agents plus high aircraft utilization coming from short gate-turnaround times and a standardized fleet of 737 aircraft

compared to the industry average, you find that Southwest needs far fewer aircraft than other airlines to serve the same number of passengers. Return on assets can be increased either by raising profits or by reducing assets, and Southwest has done both. As a result, it has been, and remains, the only really profitable airline (measured by return on assets) in the United States. It even earned substantial returns in 2001 despite the economic slowdown and the falloff in business that resulted from the September 11 terrorist attacks.

AIRBORNE EXPRESS

How do you break into an industry that is dominated by one or two very big players? In the overnight delivery industry, Federal Express and United Parcel Service pretty much had the market to themselves. By making some strategic choices just as Southwest did, and then developing an activity set to reinforce them, Airborne Express was able to enter the industry. Airborne's choices and policies are shown in Table 9-2.

A more complete depiction of Airborne's activity system, showing the various interconnected elements, is contained in Figure 9-1.

Airborne had some difficulties in 2000 and beyond, largely because of strategic moves by its competitors, such as FedEx's alignment with the U.S. Postal Service, which reduced its need for home-based pickups and deliveries, and zone-based pricing by FedEx and UPS, which took away some of Airborne's price advantages. Nevertheless, Airborne remains an excellent example of how to make cost control a way of life.

WAL-MART STORES

How do you go from being a small, little-known, Bentonville, Arkansas-based discount store to being the largest discount retailing chain in the world? Wal-Mart did it, again with an activity system that focused on squeezing out all unnecessary costs while simultaneously investing in those assets and incurring those expenses that allowed the

Table 9-2   Airborne Express Strategic Choices and Associated
                 Operating Policies

Strategic Choice	Associated Operating Policies
Offer two-day service	Limited pickup and delivery sites, no retail service centers, balance between air and land transport
Be selective about customers	Focus on corporate customers with large shipping needs who are price-sensitive, no catalog customers, no residential customers, and no infrequent shippers
Obtain higher capacity utilization	More pickups and deliveries per stop, wait until aircraft is close to fully utilized before taking off, own the hub so as to eliminate constraints on takeoffs and landings
Maintain low unit costs	Purchase secondhand aircraft, use company-owned vans selectively for deliveries, use less sophisticated technology than competitors, pay lower taxes via the community reinvestment act (CRA) zone, do not have mass media advertising

company to establish and maintain its competitive position as the low-cost provider to a mass market. Table 9-3 shows Wal-Mart's strategic choices and operating policies, and how they reinforce one another.[4]

Let's look at some hard measures of what this activity system creates. Wal-Mart's prices reflect the latitude the company has given its managers. According to one study, when a store was adjacent to a Kmart, so that customers could go back and forth easily, Wal-Mart's prices, using a base of 100, were 100, whereas Kmart's were 101.3. When a Wal-Mart store was close to a Kmart (4 to 6 miles), so that customers were likely to make a decision to drive to one store or the other for all their shopping needs, the comparison was Wal-Mart 99.9, Kmart 110.3. When a Wal-Mart store was remotely situated, with no Kmart nearby, Wal-Mart's prices were 106.[5]

Wal-Mart's inbound logistics amounted to 2.8 percent of revenue, compared to 4.8 percent for the industry overall. Its shrinkage

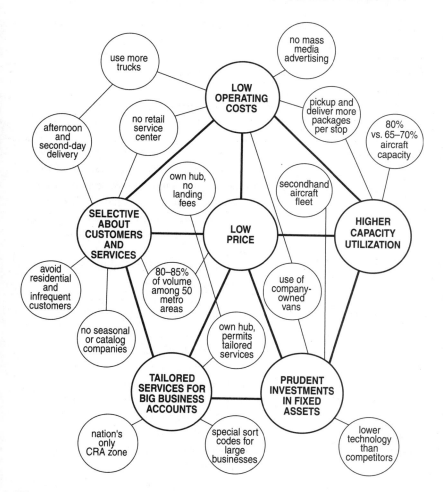

Figure 9-1 Airborne Express activity system. (*Courtesy of Yingyan Guan, MBA student, Boston University School of Management, 2001*)

was 1 percent of revenue, compared to 1.6 percent for the industry. Its advertising was 0.5 percent, compared to 1.2 percent for the industry. Rental was 0.8 percent, compared to an industry figure of 1.8 percent. Payroll was 10 percent, compared to the industry average of 10.4 percent. And administrative expenses (a reflection of the com-

Table 9-3 Wal-Mart Strategic Choices and Associated Operating Policies

Strategic Choice	Associated Operating Policies
Satisfy customers	Have a people-greeter at each store, provide a satisfaction-guaranteed return policy, be open long hours, tailor merchandise to individual markets
Operate at a low cost	Rent expandable space, devote only 10 percent of square footage to back-of-house inventory storage, offer few promotions, keep trucks 60 percent full on back hauls, emphasize self-service and cash and carry, institute a shrinkage incentive plan, share hotel rooms when traveling, walk instead of taking taxis
Build employee loyalty	Give responsibility and recognition, have profit sharing, open accounting books to all employees, develop various incentive plans
Use a sophisticated distribution system	Adopt e-scanning, use bar codes to link inventory information with vendors for seamless supply chain, build warehouses strategically as stores expand, use cross-docking to minimize merchandise time in warehouse, have highly automated warehouses, deliver to stores within 24 hours to minimize stock-outs
Manage vendors carefully	Educate vendors to use IT for automatic shipments when inventory reaches reorder point, use only socially responsible vendors, invite vendors to managers' meetings, eliminate manufacturers' representatives, negotiate prices in spartan surroundings
Give store managers significant responsibility	Make each store a profit center; give managers latitude to adjust prices based on nearby competition; base managers' bonuses and stock options on store profits; use IT system to show inventory movements, thereby allowing store managers to adjust inventory as needed

pany's culture of intense frugality) were 15.8 percent compared to a whopping 21.2 percent for the industry. Overall, because its low pricing results in a higher cost of goods sold percentage, Wal-Mart has about a 0.6 percent advantage in net income.[6]

How significant are these numbers? With $40 billion in sales and $8 billion in assets, each $1/10$ percent cost advantage translates into a $40 million profit advantage, or an incremental return on assets of $1/2$ percent. Overall, Wal-Mart's 0.6 percent advantage would mean an additional $240 million in net income and a 13 percent increase in its return on assets.

In short, Wal-Mart did not become a legend by accident. It managed its growth carefully by expanding across America, much like the blob's infamous creep, and backfilling with warehouses as needed. Wal-Mart made some mistakes, to be sure, notably its entry into the German retail industry when it did not fully understand the German culture, competitive landscape, or regulatory system.[7] And it has received some criticism for its treatment of women.[8] In general, however, the company is considered a paradigm of success, and it is one of a handful of companies that *Fortune* magazine cited as prepared to thrive during a recession.[9]

Southwest Airlines was another of those companies, as was Dell Computer. Let's look at how Dell does it.

DELL COMPUTER CORPORATION

It all started in a college dorm room.[10] The 18-year-old Michael Dell began configuring hard drives, modems, disk drives, and the like to make PC clones, and selling the resulting computers for 40 percent less than a comparably configured IBM machine. All the while, he was hiding his inventory in his bathtub when his parents came to visit so they wouldn't see what he was spending his time doing instead of studying. As business began to boom, however, Dell dropped out of college, formed his company, and began to pursue the business full time.

Dell's decision no doubt was noticed by his parents, but it took a while before his company was noticed by the big players. In 1989 his share of the PC market in the United States was less than 1 percent, compared to 17 percent for IBM, about 11 percent for Apple, and 62 percent for the white boxes (i.e., PC clones with no brand identification). Other than the white boxes, IBM saw its major threats as being Compaq and Packard Bell.

Not until the mid-1990s did Dell become more than a blip on the industry's radar screen. In 1995, Compaq had almost 11 percent of the market, Apple was hanging in at just under 11 percent, Packard Bell had just over 14 percent, and IBM and the white boxes had fallen to 8 and 40 percent, respectively. Dell had 4.9 percent of the market.

Imagine the reaction of a PC manufacturer in 1995. Who is this upstart with almost 5 percent of "our" market? He can't possibly survive. He doesn't have any retail outlets to sell his computers. He won't be able to move his products through the channels. Sure, some people might buy a computer sight unseen, but not many. People like to see, touch, and play with the computer before they buy it. That's how our industry works. Besides, he builds to order, and what you really need in this industry is a big inventory of products out there in the retail stores so that people can come in, look, touch, talk, buy, and walk away with the computer.

But Dell was not interested in the traditional channels. Nor was he interested in playing by the established rules of the game. Instead, he developed an activity system that was focused on one of the most profitable niches in the industry: company purchasing managers who bought in large volume and had no need to see, touch, or play with a computer before purchasing it. Indeed, the purchasing manager was rewarded for obtaining acceptable quality and service at the lowest possible price. And that's exactly what Dell Computer Corporation was providing. Table 9-4 shows Dell's strategic choices and operating policies, and how they reinforce one another.[11]

What does all this mean? Well, for one thing, when you're in an industry where component prices are declining by about 1 percent a *week*, delaying your purchase of raw materials for a few weeks can result in some substantial savings. In addition, Dell has no working capital cost

Table 9-4 Dell Computer Corporation Strategic Choices and Associated Operating Policies

Strategic Choice	Associated Operating Policies
Satisfy knowledgeable customers	Focus on corporate and institutional customers who purchase over $1 million per year in PCs, who know exactly what features they want, and who seek low prices; provide service to minimize support costs (which averaged some $8000 to $12,000 per year per computer)
Operate at low cost	Locate close to supplier to facilitate just-in-time production; build to order, with the result that Dell can purchase raw materials later than competitors; coordinate with some suppliers (such as Sony) to have a component (such as a monitor) delivered directly to the customer rather than passing through Dell's plant
Produce to order for direct sale to customer	No advertising to resellers, no channel markup, no price protection needed, no buybacks
Sell over the Internet	Customers pay in advance, giving Dell working capital and avoiding financing costs; a handful of online staffers can do the work of hundreds of telephone salespeople
Manage suppliers carefully	Suppliers are required to use sophisticated software that wires them straight into Dell's factory floor; Dell's plants order supplies over the Internet many times a day, replenishing only what is needed when it is needed

for carrying inventory—of either raw materials or finished goods. Dell's warehouse stock was 4 days, compared to 24 days for Compaq.

When you put all these strategic choices together, the result was that in 1996, Dell's cost per computer was some $400 below its competitors'. Its computers were priced at about $2300 at the time, compared to about $2900 for the competition. For a corporation with a $1 million PC budget, this $600 difference translated into about 90 additional computers that could be bought by using Dell instead of one of its competitors. Purchasing managers who used Dell no doubt earned some serious bonuses at year-end.

But this was only the beginning of the story. Just as Continental failed miserably in its attempt to match Southwest Airlines, IBM, Compaq, and the rest failed in their attempts to match Dell. It was just too hard for them to abandon the retail stores, and their half-hearted attempt to do so—by, say, directing some customers to the Web and encouraging them to purchase directly—only angered the retail outlets, who then emphasized some other company's computers.

Caught between that rock and its complementary hard place, IBM announced in 1999 that it would halt retail sales of desktop PCs. Meanwhile, not content to rest on a quite reasonable market share, Dell began to push its prices even lower. In March 2001, as the recession was becoming a serious factor in everyone's thinking, Dell announced that it would include free delivery, a free printer, and free Internet access to customers who bought a PC through its Web site.[12] The result was that through the second quarter of 2001, Dell had earned $361 million in profits, while the rest of the industry had incurred losses of $1.1 billion. In September 2001, hit hard by these losses, Compaq announced that it would be acquired by Hewlett-Packard.[13]

Is this luck? Hardly. It's all in the activity system, which Dell is constantly working to improve. And it's not just one thing in the activity system. Rather, it's the entire collection of mutually reinforcing and interdependent activities that not only give Dell its cost advantage but also make the company very difficult (maybe even impossible) to imitate.

GENERAL ELECTRIC CORPORATION

So far, we've been looking at the business-unit level—companies that operate in a single market and must create a model of sustainability against the forces that would disrupt their ability to be profitable. What about at the corporate level? That's the question that companies like General Electric, General Motors, Textron, Emerson Electric, Cooper Industries, Disney, and a host of others face.

In his autobiography, *Jack: Straight from the Gut,* Jack Welch discusses the idea of an activity system at a conceptual level that is somewhat higher than the more operationally oriented discussions of the preceding four companies.[14] Welch was not so much concerned with individual business units per se (except when he did what he called "deep dives") as with creating an infrastructure that promoted both excellence *within* any given business unit and a high level of coordination *among* the business units. In effect, Welch was dealing directly with the question that the CEO of any multidivisional corporation must address: What does the corporate office do to add value to the business units so that each business unit is more successful as a member of *this* corporation than it would be either alone or in any other corporate setting? His activities fell into the three broad categories shown schematically in Figure 9-2: expansion of the business units, discipline within individual units, and coordination among the units.

Expansion (and Contraction) Activities

Expansion takes place for many reasons. In Welch's case, it was frequently a cashflow hedge against competitive forces. The purchase of RCA was undertaken in an attempt to get into a business where the Japanese could not compete as well. But Welch also addressed the question of divesting unprofitable businesses with weak potential. His mantra was, "No. 1 or No. 2 (in the industry), and, if not, fix, sell, or close it." This theme drove home the point that if the discipline he was imposing did not work, it was time for GE to get out of the business. Shortly after he arrived, he identified the corporation's three main areas of business: the core, high technology, and services. Several existing businesses that fell outside those three areas were targeted for closing, exemplifying an important cost-control technique for almost any corporation made up of a set of unrelated businesses.

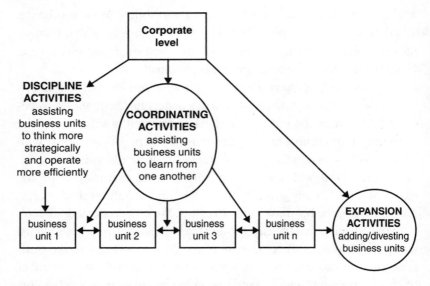

Figure 9-2   Three Categories of Corporate Activities

✂ Technique No. 167. If a Business Can't Make a Reasonable Profit, Sell It or Close It without Emotion

Welch did this with air conditioners. GE's air conditioners had a very small market share in comparison with other GE appliances, and they were contributing very little to the bottom line. Part of the problem was a lack of control over costs. In Welch's words,

> You sold the GE-branded product to a local distributor like "Ace Plumbing." They installed it with their hammers and screwdrivers and drove away, leaving the GE-branded air conditioners behind. How Ace installed our products and how it serviced its customers reflected directly back on GE. We were getting customer complaints that had nothing to do with us. We were being tarred by something we had no control over.

Welch used the gains obtained by selling the air-conditioning business to improve the company's overall competitiveness. In his words, "In 20 years we never permitted ourselves or any of our businesses to use one-time restructuring charges as an excuse for missing an earnings commitment."

That, of course, doesn't explain what was done to ensure that the businesses *did* meet their earnings commitments, which leads to another important cost-control technique.

Technique No. 168. Institute Reality Checks

As Welch describes it, many of GE's business units were a little (perhaps a lot) sloppy in their strategic thinking, and also lacked emphasis on cost control. Welch imposed what he called "reality checks," sometimes with remarkable success. As he put it, reality checks sound simple but are not. He recalled his mother's words when he was a youth: "Don't kid yourself. It is the way it is." One example he cites is that of GE's Nuclear Power Division. Early in his tenure as CEO, Welch conducted a 2-day review with the division's leadership team. The team was proposing a business plan based on the receipt of three or four new orders for nuclear plants every year. Welch, pointing out the potential (and real, as it turned out) impact of the Three Mile Island disaster, forced the team to assume zero(!) new orders, and to redirect its emphasis toward providing fuel for and servicing the installed base instead.

Not only was he right in his analysis (in the next 20 years, only four orders were received, all from outside the United States), but he managed to shift the cost structure of the division away from large manufacturing plants with a high level of fixed costs toward fuel and nuclear service sales, activities with mainly variable or semivariable costs. Moreover, the new strategy also brought dollars in the front door: The division's net earnings grew from $14 million in 1981 to $116 million in 1983.

Reality checks can come in a variety of ways. At Disney, Michael Eisner uses large (100-person) "Synergy Group" meetings, in which key managers question and test one another on various aspects of what Disney calls its "profit multiplier" model. All managers and other key people need to consider how cross-promotion will work from their point of view, and anyone can challenge anyone else's assessment.[15]

✂ Technique No. 169. Hire a SWAT Team

Cooper Industries has taken the idea of a reality check to the extreme. Cooper uses something that it calls the Manufacturing Services Group, a corporate-level SWAT team that includes experts in facilities, automation, environmental engineering, materials management, quality control, and management information systems, to promote manufacturing improvements, administer the capital budget, improve quality control, and run a manufacturing training program. The group spends about 60 percent of its time on new acquisitions and 40 percent on existing Cooper divisions. There is no charge for the group's services, and the group never enters an old division unless it is invited.[16] However, it's hard to imagine divisional CEOs not using these services if they felt their divisions were in some trouble. What's the downside?

✂ Technique No. 170. Reward Behavior That Is in Line with Corporate Strategy

A divisional CEO at Cooper Industries will be more inclined to seek help from the Manufacturing Services Group if his or her performance is rewarded not on the basis of the problems that gave rise to a need for the group, but rather on the results his or her division attained, presumably either profits or meeting ROA expectations. To make this happen, however, the corporation must reward the right kinds of things, with rewards including both compensation and promotion. At GE, for example, Jack Welch instituted a personnel ranking system called the "vitality curve," in which each division general manager was required to rank no more than 20 percent of his or her managers as being in the top 20 percent and no fewer than 10 percent as being in the bottom 10 percent. The ranking was based on GE's four Es and one P: energy, energize, edge, execute, and passion. A manager needed energy, the ability to energize his or her team, a lot of edge and passion, and the ability to execute a plan. Those managers who ranked in the lower 10 percent were assisted to leave the organization, those in the top 20 percent were given substantial rewards, and those in the middle 70 percent were mentored and otherwise helped to move into the top 20 percent.[17]

Although GE is somewhat unusual in its method of seeking out and retaining the best performers, it is not alone. Microsoft also rewards employees solely on the basis of performance. However, management understands that people spend 50 percent of their time doing something that is destined to fail, and, as a result, Microsoft expects failures from everybody. At the same time, nobody can rest on his or her past successes; people are rewarded only for their most recent performance. Because of the company's rapid growth, there are always opportunities for promotion. However, the open positions are filled not by the people with the most seniority, but by the best person available. One result is that managers always have a powerful incentive to do a good job. Moreover, as they move up the hierarchy, the competition increases dramatically. Only the best survive.[18]

Technique No. 171. Develop Ways for Business Units to Learn from One Another

A good cost-saving idea in one organizational unit may be applicable in other units. The key is to find ways for the various units to learn from one another. There are many ways to do this. Disney's profit multiplier model depends on every Disney business unit cooperating with every other unit, so that a given theme (such as the Lion King) is carried throughout the entire range of Disney's profit centers: movies, videos, television, theme parks, retail stores, and so forth. At GE, the cross-divisional learning problem was somewhat different, as there was no single theme that needed to be built upon by each division. Rather, Welch's concern was how to foster the transfer of technology and other ways of thinking from one division to another. To do so, he introduced the concept of "boundaryless." His idea was that a boundaryless culture would open GE up to the best ideas and practices, not only from other divisions within GE, but from customers and suppliers as well.

To foster boundaryless behavior, Welch engaged in several activities: (1) He made sure that the concept was emphasized at Crotonville, GE's in-house training facility for managers; (2) the concept was raised at every meeting, and people were chastised for not sharing ideas; (3) rewards were given to people who recognized and developed a good idea, not just to the person who came up with the idea; (4) the personnel evaluation system (the one that used the vitality curve) rated people on the basis of their boundaryless behavior; (5) terminations were instituted when, in Welch's words, managers "didn't practice our [boundaryless] values"; (6) the balance between individual bonuses and stock option grants was shifted heavily toward stock option grants, meaning that managers' rewards were tied more closely to overall company performance than to the performance of their individual businesses; and (7) the number of managers and others who were eligible for stock options was increased from about 500 people in 1989 to 15,000 people in 2000.

Worthy of note is the fact that boundaryless behavior came about not just because Welch said he wanted it, but because several different organizational processes were linked to the initiative. In effect, Welch was changing the organization's culture, an effort that has frequently failed in other companies because the desired new culture was not reinforced with the various tools at a manager's command.[19]

SOME GENERAL PRINCIPLES

Although these company examples could be considered simply anecdotal, they can also be viewed as a series of "ideal types," as an economist might call them, illustrating some important techniques for keeping costs low. More generally, they suggest the importance of an activity system that, while focused on a variety of strategic matters, includes cost control as a key element.

How does a senior manager create such an activity set, or perhaps analyze the organization's existing activity set to see where it may need modification? Clearly, such an analysis is highly dependent on the organization's strategy: how it is attempting to position itself in the marketplace, what sorts of competition it faces, and a variety of other matters that make each organization unique. Nevertheless, there are four principles that managers may wish to consider as they undertake this crucial endeavor.

Principle 1. Seek to Understand and Act on the Real Environment

A manager never knows what the organization's real environment consists of. He or she may know some of the business or other opportunities it presents, know something about the competitive threats it poses, and have a sense of the constraints that it may impose on operations in the future. However, it is impossible to forecast all these matters with 100 percent precision. Yet getting as close as possible to the real environment is crucial to success. How might this be done?

There are many examples of failures by the highest-performing companies to understand the real environment. Jack Welch's misreading of the European Commission's view of GE's proposed acquisition of Honeywell is a case in point. Similarly, in *The Innovator's Dilemma*,[20] Clayton Christensen describes the evolution of the computer disk from a 14-inch device for mainframes to the 3.5-inch floppies currently used by most personal computers. The manufacturers of the 14-inch drives were listening to their customers—the perceived environment—who told them that they wanted 14-inch drives with more capacity and a lower cost per megabyte. Meanwhile, the *real* environment was moving to 8-inch drives for use on minicomputers, then to 5.25-inch drives for early PCs, and finally to 3.5-inch drives.

While customers were asking for improvements on the current drives, the market was moving to the next-generation disk drive.

In part, as Figure 9-3 illustrates, senior managers can have difficulty understanding the real environment because the opportunities and threats that it is presenting pass through a filter of managers, professionals, and others before they reach senior management.

The effectiveness of this filter in preventing the entry of important information tends to be inversely related to the number of middle managers, professionals, and other members of the organization who are involved in the strategy formulation process, the opportunities given to them to express their views, and their rewards for providing good information. In general, the more managers and others who are involved in the process, the greater the opportunity for senior

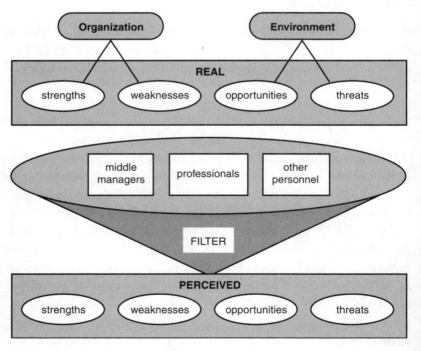

Figure 9-3   Real versus perceived environment.

management to see the *real* environmental opportunities and threats, as well as the organization's *real* strengths and weaknesses. However, as more people become involved in this so-called SWOT (for strengths, weaknesses, opportunities, and threats) analysis, the process becomes more complex, time-consuming, and costly. How senior management makes this trade-off, how it decides whom to involve, and how it determines the nature and timing of these other people's involvement are all extremely important decisions.

✂ Technique No. 172. Transfer Knowledge Whenever and Wherever Possible

This is a bit like Welch's reality checks, but it can be somewhat more formal. Using regular meetings and other activities to seek out information (which may include potential bad news), using formal rewards for people who bring important environmental information to senior management's attention, and other such techniques are all ways to reduce the density of the filter. Indeed, misreading the European Commission was one of the few times in Welch's tenure as CEO that he missed an environmental signal. His term for eliminating the filter was "maximizing the organization's intellect." As he put it,

> Getting everyone's mind into the game is a huge part of what the CEO job is all about . . . The first step is being open to the best of what everyone, everywhere, has to offer. The second is transferring that learning across the organization . . . Searching for a better way and eagerly sharing new knowledge has today become second nature at GE.[21]

Although GE is unusual in its quest for knowledge of the real environment, it is not alone. In part this sort of knowledge is what Michael Eisner is seeking at Disney with his Synergy Group. Also, Cooper Industries' Manufacturing Services Group is attempting to bring some of the real environment into a division general manager's thinking when it engages in its internal consulting activities.

Contrast this sort of information-seeking behavior with the behavior at Yahoo!, where it seems clear that the senior management team effectively insulated itself from the real environment—the one in which advertisers (Yahoo!'s principal source of revenue) were becoming increasingly frustrated with the company's arrogance. Not only did senior management not seek input from below, but it had what some have characterized as an insular board of directors, with only one true outsider out of seven members. Having failed to spot some fundamental changes in the Internet advertising market, when the recession hit, Yahoo! was unable to convince its already somewhat estranged customers that there was a revenue payoff from placing their banners on Yahoo!'s Web page. As a result, the company's revenue plummeted. Similarly, this isolation from the environment kept the "Three Amigos" (as Yahoo!'s senior management team was called) from purchasing an old media company to diversify away from its exclusive Internet focus. As a *Business Week* article put it, Yahoo!'s senior managers' approaches and styles "kept them from anticipating vital adjustments, and this left the company vulnerable when Yahoo's world began to spin out of control."[22] Indeed, in the ultimate display of its failure to understand its environment, and in a desperate attempt to recover advertising revenue, Yahoo! connected an "adult and erotica" store to its main shopping channel. The online store offered thousands of hard-core DVDs and videos. The move was later abandoned, but not before Yahoo! had perhaps just slightly sullied its mom-and-apple-pie image.

✂ Technique No. 173. Use Training and Other Educational Activities for All Employees

One way to reduce the density of the filter and to encourage "out of the box" thinking is to make sure your employees *get* outside the box. At Chaparral Steel, for example, 85 percent of the company's personnel are involved in a training course at any given time. Moreover, all Chaparral personnel are *required* to take an annual educational sabbatical, which might include any of a variety of activities, including visiting a customer's plant or taking a course at a local university.[23]

Principle 2. Create a Culture That Embodies a Focus on Cost Control

A strong and well-understood culture—a set of ideas and attitudes that embodies the notions of good and bad—identifies what is desirable or undesirable in an organization. Having such a culture is important in that it constitutes one of two approaches to encourage managers and other employees to do what is necessary for the organization's success. If employees understand and believe in the organization's culture at its most fundamental level, they will make decisions consistent with, and supportive of, the organization's overall strategic directions, including its cost-control strategies. When this is the case, senior management needs to intervene very little in employees' decision-making activities. But when employees do not share the organization's basic assumptions, senior management must intervene to ensure that employees' decisions are consistent with the organization's strategy.

Indeed, in a 1945 book that contributed to his receipt of the Nobel Prize in Economics, Herbert Simon observed that most organizations engage in four activities to maintain their cultures: hiring, training, severance, and internal communication.[24] Organizations with homogeneous cultures use these activities to help influence the way middle managers, professionals, and others go about making decisions.

Technique No. 174. Hire and Promote Only the Best, but Be Sure They All Embody the Company's Culture

As any senior manager knows, hiring and promoting are among the most difficult processes that a company undertakes. An especially good discussion of the issues involved in obtaining the needed skills is contained in the book *Topgrading,* which argues that companies should hire only "A players," i.e., those who are in the top 10 percent of talent at their salary level.[25] The best companies, the author argues, hire A players and remove their C players as quickly as possible. This policy is an attempt to avoid "mis-hires," which, over time, can cost the company millions of dollars.

Unfortunately, *Topgrading* and several other books like it do not address the importance of a cultural fit, which many would argue is as important as a candidate's intelligence and/or skills. At Disney, for example, a candidate may be superior in every measurable category, but, since Disney values dreaming and risk taking, a cultural mismatch is likely to occur if he or she is not a dreamer or is risk-adverse. Similarly, Microsoft's policy is to hire only very smart, highly analytical people regardless of their computer expertise, reasoning that it can train them to do the job. To do so, it uses a rigorous series of job interviews—mainly with the team with which the candidate will work if hired—to ensure that there is a fit with the company's intense, market-driven, high-technology culture.

✂ Technique No. 175. Be Sure That Training Includes an Emphasis on the Company's Culture

Training that imparts an organization's culture as well as the requisite skills is not uncommon. In particular, to create a set of consistent cultural values and basic assumptions, senior management may need to develop an *ongoing* training process. Such an ongoing program not only helps to develop needed skills, as training usually does, but also, if it is designed properly, communicates and instills a set of cultural values and basic assumptions about the organization. At Disney, for instance, the overriding value is "to provide the finest in family entertainment." This is supported by 10 principles, including such basic assumptions as "dream, take risks to make innovative ideas work, pay close attention to detail, and support, empower and reward employees." To infuse this culture into its employees, Disney uses a formal training institute, known as "Disney University." Part of the training is skill-related, but a big part of it is cultural, instilling such values as "treat customers like guests in your home." Thus, in addition to being trained to do their jobs, employees learn why their jobs are important to the company and are made to feel that their efforts make a difference. In essence, just as Disney treats its customers as guests, it treats its employees with dignity and respect. As a result, it is almost impossible to find a discourteous employee at any of the Disney theme parks.[26]

Starbucks has a similar policy. At Starbucks, training includes not only techniques for brewing "the perfect cup of coffee," but also classes on customer service and retail skills. In addition, the training immerses new employees in a culture that embodies respect and dignity for both customers *and* one another.[27] Anyone who has been in a Starbucks store can feel the mutual respect that exists among the employees.

In some companies, training goes beyond the formal classroom experience and extends into an employee's day-to-day activities. Even this training can be culture-maintaining (or culture-building) as well as skill-based, however. At Disney, each employee receives constant on-the-job reinforcement from his or her "coach," who praises the employee's success and gradually instills the company's basic cultural assumptions into his or her behavior. Indeed, the idea that a manager is a *coach* reflects a significantly different basic cultural assumption from the idea that a manager is a *supervisor.*

Technique No. 176. When Necessary, Use Severance to Maintain the Culture

The severance activity is not just about ensuring that a company has employees with the requisite skills and knowledge. The policies of companies like Microsoft and 3M (where failure is expected, since without it, employees would not be stretching themselves enough) say a great deal about the company's culture. In particular, these companies' basic assumptions begin to define the correct way for employees to perceive, think, and feel in relation to problems. But what happens when these basic assumptions are violated? How many chances does someone get? Sometimes none. Consider the experience of Arthur Andersen following the Enron debacle, for instance.

Or how about another large public accounting firm? On February 28, 2000, *Business Week* carried a story entitled "This Scandal Changes Everything." The story discussed breaches of auditor independence at PriceWaterhouseCoopers (PWC). The article contained the following paragraph:

> Half of PWC's 2,700 U.S. partners owned stock in companies the firm audits, according to the report by law firm Lankler Siffert & Wohl, done at the behest of the [Securities and Exchange Commission]. The report also revealed that 1,885 people at the firm—1 in every 20 employees—committed violations, prompting Lankler Siffert to conclude that PWC has serious structural and cultural problems.

As a result, "five partners were forced to resign, a sixth [was] on the way out, and five other managers and staffers were dismissed."

Clearly, as a result of highly intense public scrutiny, the *severance* activity was being used as part of an attempt to develop a culture of auditor independence.[28]

Similarly, during the late 1990s, some of the high-performing employees at GE Capital decided that they should have a piece of the action in the companies in which they invested GE's money. Jack Welch's response was a clear indication of the need to preserve the company's culture: "We told them to take a hike. In our shop, there's only one currency: GE stock with GE values."[29]

Technique No. 177. Reinforce the Culture with Internal Communication

Internal communication is a little more slippery than the other activities. It can include hallway conversations, company newsletters, formal reports, performance reviews, and employee-of-the-month plaques, among other things. It can even include such subtle signals as body language during a meeting. Sometimes it can be a little brutal. Under Jack Welch's leadership, for example, no General Electric division general manager was allowed to keep a good idea to himself or herself. When Welch visited a manager, if he learned of a particularly innovative idea or solution to a production problem, one of his first questions was always, "With whom have you shared this?" It was unacceptable to say, "No one." As a result, GE became a true learning organization, with ideas that solved problems in, say, the aircraft engine division frequently finding applicability in other divisions, such as home appliances.[30]

Principle 3. Embrace and Manage Conflict

It is a well-known fact of organizational life that salespeople think differently from manufacturing people. Similarly, doctors think differently from nurses, R&D engineers think differently from product line managers, professors think differently from deans, and basic researchers think differently from applied researchers. In part, these differences are personality-driven, but in those instances where organizational (as distinct from interpersonal) conflict emerges, the participants are usually from different occupational groups. These groups have differing time horizons for measuring their performance, differing degrees of tolerance for ambiguity in their jobs, and, more generally, highly contrasting demands put upon them by their work environments. As a result, they approach organizational decision making from vastly different perspectives.

For example, a sales manager's work environment may be driven by such factors as quarterly revenue quotas, shifting customer preferences, established customers who want preferential treatment, and potential new customers who may be testing the organization's capabilities by, say, asking for a small order on a tight time schedule. Salespeople may also have to deal with customers who are moving toward or have established just-in-time manufacturing or product availability strategies, and who therefore demand rapid delivery schedules. In short, sales managers and their staffs face an uncertain and frequently turbulent environment.

By contrast, the typical plant manager's environment is one of tight production schedules, machine performance concerns, externally imposed work standards, and a wide variety of cost and quality considerations. Plant managers tend to dislike turbulence, preferring instead predictability and order.

When these worlds collide, as they do when, say, sales has a small rush order for a potentially valuable customer that will disrupt the plant's schedule, there is certain to be friction. There also is friction when a physician wants the time to do a thorough diagnostic workup on a patient, while the nurse must respond to the family's request for information on the patient's condition. And there is friction when marketing wants to get a product to market quickly, while R&D wants more time to perfect its features. The Microsoft mantra, "Can we ship it yet?" in reference to a new software product[31] is reflective of this tension.

This is not interpersonal conflict, although it can become so at times. The sales and manufacturing managers may socialize after work, and they and their families may get together on weekends. They may be great friends. Inside the organization, however, their head-butting, and similar conflicts among many other managers and professionals, is rooted in their occupational positions in the organization, their work environments, and the ensuing cognitive and emotional orientations that they bring to the decision-making table. *Organizational,* as opposed to interpersonal, conflict is the inevitable result.

Perhaps surprisingly, this kind of conflict is desirable, as it can bring out the best in everyone. Managed properly, it can be a source of enormous strength. It can help an organization to achieve previously unimagined levels of performance, whether they be in the form of a blockbuster movie, such as *The Lion King,* at Disney, higher passenger loads at Virgin Air as a result of the novel idea of in-flight massages, or collaboration between two highly disparate entities, such as the aircraft engine and home appliance divisions at General Electric (which results from regular meetings to explore, discuss, and decide upon what GE calls cross-business synergies). Left unmanaged or poorly managed, however, conflict can wreak organizational havoc.

Perhaps most important, conflict can be highly beneficial to an organization. The tension that exists between line managers and the controller's staff during budget formulation is an example of potentially beneficial conflict that exists in almost all organizations. Each party brings an important, but usually conflicting, perspective to the table, the resolution of which can lead to improved organizational performance. For a good decision to emerge, however, the conflict must be well managed. In this case, well-managed conflict might lead to a tight but attainable budget that directly supports an organization's strategy, helps to ensure that customers receive high-quality products, and motivates line managers to stretch themselves to attain the agreed-upon goals.

Types and Modes of Conflict Management   Managing conflict requires a focus on two related elements: *type* and *mode*. The five basic types of conflict management are shown in Table 9-5, along with an example of where each might be appropriate. As the table indicates, the types of conflict management can range from information flows (such as the exchange of interoffice memos or emails) to the creation of permanent committees. A manager might use the former to schedule a meeting (where there is usually a relatively low level of one-time conflict) and the latter to make capital investment decisions (where there tends to be a relatively high level of continuing conflict).

As Table 9-5 suggests, the particular conflict management process chosen must correspond with the nature and degree of the conflict. For example, using email to make capital investment decisions would be just as inappropriate and ineffective as the formation of a permanent committee to schedule a one-time meeting. In each instance, senior management must consider the degree of conflict that exists, whether it is one-time or ongoing, what perspectives are involved, who holds those perspectives, and what approach might be most effective to address the differences and reach an acceptable resolution.

Table 9-5   Types of Conflict Management

Type of Conflict	Example	Conflict Management Mechanism
Low-level, one-time, with multiple perspectives	Scheduling a meeting	Information flows (paper, email, telephone)
Moderate, one-time, with two perspectives	Determining who will attend a conference	Hierarchy
Moderate, one-time, with multiple perspectives	Designing and launching a new product	Ad hoc cross-disciplinary teams
High, continuing, with two perspectives	Resolving differences between engineering and manufacturing	Integrator or integrating department
High, continuing, with multiple perspectives	Capital investment decisions; production scheduling for several product managers	Permanent cross-disciplinary teams

Conflict management modes tend to fall into six categories, which are shown in Table 9-6. The mode chosen depends, in part, on the issue at hand. As Table 9-6 indicates, there is no one mode that is best for all circumstances. Although avoiding and smoothing tend to be somewhat dysfunctional in most organizations, the other modes can to be used effectively at different times and under different circumstances. Sometimes the situation calls for a unilateral approach, for example, or for bargaining. And sometimes it calls for a confronting mode.

In general, a successful mode of conflict management must fit with an organization's authority structure as well as with the type of conflict being addressed. To attempt to use a *unilateral* or *forcing* mode in an organization with a collegial culture would be difficult and perhaps counterproductive, as would the use of a *confronting* mode in an organization where the decision ultimately will be made by the supervisor of the conflicting parties. Indeed, in this latter

Table 9-6 Modes of Conflict Management

Mode	Characteristics	Uses
Avoiding	Substantive issues are not brought out into the open.	Useful if interpersonal friction is so severe that improved understanding of the issue will not lead to resolution; however, may lead to many decisions being left open and worsening organizational performance.
Smoothing	The issues are raised, but are not discussed to the point of making a decision. Differences among the participants frequently are ascribed to personalities.	Like avoiding, indicates that there are differences that are not being discussed.
Unilateral	A manager makes a decision independently, depending on how he or she sees fit. Sometimes the manager seeks to fully understand the issue, and sometimes he or she does not.	Usually better than avoiding or smoothing in that a decision gets made and usually gets made quickly. However, the decision may have adverse effects on those organizational units that were not consulted.
Forcing	Issues are raised and discussed, but one party uses power to attain the approach that he or she feels is best.	If the decision maker has the most relevant perspective, this mode may result in the best decision with the lease amount of effort. However, the approach may mean that some decisions get made without all relevant information in hand or with a bias toward the interests of the decision maker.

(continued)

Table 9-6 Modes of Conflict Management (*continued*)

Mode	Characteristics	Uses
Confronting	Issues are raised, and the parties mutually explore them and seek the most favorable solution, using all relevant information.	Has a high potential for reaching a quality decision, especially if organizational goals are used to frame the discussion. Can be time-consuming and emotionally draining, however.
Bargaining	Similar to confronting, but the parties each give up something in an attempt to reach a compromise that is acceptable to all.	May be useful for resource allocation decisions where a zero-sum game is at work, but tends to limit information sharing and openness in a discussion.

Source: Martin Charns, personal communication.

instance, the confronting mode would be quite likely to be a questionable use of time for the involved parties.

A *confronting* mode tends to be most appropriate in situations where two professionals or managers of equal status need to make a decision or reach an agreement. Examples include researchers from chemistry and physics laboratories seeking an appropriate study design, engineering and marketing departments agreeing on a product development schedule, primary-care physicians and specialists finding a suitable test or procedure for a patient, manufacturing and sales departments developing a policy for rush orders, and so on.

Technique No. 178. Create as Many Opportunities for Conflict as You Can Manage Successfully

Although this idea may sound somewhat far-fetched or academic, it in fact describes exactly what some senior managers have done. For example, consider the comments by Michael Eisner in an interview published in the *Harvard Business Review*. When he was asked, "How do you create the environment for supportive conflict?" his response included the following:

> We're entertaining people, so we should have an energized culture . . . That kind of culture doesn't just happen—you have to make it happen. That's one of the reasons we started doing our own internal "gong show" back in the 1970s. It started as a concept where, once a week, we'd invite everybody to come to a conference room, and anyone could offer up an idea or two and, right on the spot, people would react. We loved the idea of big, unruly, disruptive meetings . . . *The Little Mermaid* came out of a gong show, and so did *Pocahontas*. Lots of ideas came out of those meetings.
>
> Another way we get creative juices going and ideas flowing is with "charettes." These are meetings with our architects and

theme park designers. I love them because they are so brutally honest. Because everybody has a different opinion about color and style and size and look and landscaping and all the rest, these meetings take on an event stature. Eventually resolution arrives, but not before every possible idea is put on the table . . .

There is no pecking order. All of a sudden it gets really creative. You may have a ten-hour meeting, but it's during the last half hour that the best ideas come out. Everybody starts driving each other crazy with ideas, and then somebody says something and it all comes together.[32]

Clearly, Eisner is not waiting for conflict to happen and then designing a conflict management mechanism to deal with it. Rather, he is investing considerable company resources (such as a 10-hour meeting involving many high-level people) in an activity that is designed to generate conflict and then manage it.

A similar approach was used some years ago at the Palo Alto Research Center (PARC) when the senior manager, Robert Taylor, set up a series of weekly meetings run like academic conferences, in which the scientists were expected to challenge the work of their peers. In addition to improving communication and helping to create a learning culture, the meetings also helped with the generation—and resolution—of considerable conflict.[33]

Eisner and Taylor are not alone. In his book *Wide Angle Vision,*[34] Wayne Burkan makes the point that companies that fail to generate conflict often miss strategic opportunities. His "ideal team" is one that helps a company question its own rules and assumptions. He cites examples of companies such as Smith Corona (which was battling Brother Industries, its biggest rival in typewriters, but the wrong competitor given where the market was heading), Schwinn Bicycle Company (a dominant player in its industry that failed to see the trend toward mountain bikes), and Hewlett-Packard (which rejected a "lowly" technician's idea of a personal computer; that technician, Steve Wozniak, then went on to co-found Apple Computer).

Principle 4. *Align Reward and Recognition with the Desired Behavior*

What motivates people to perform well in organizations, how senior management designs appropriate *motivation* (as distinct from *compensation*) packages, and what role monetary compensation plays in this effort are all quite controversial. Indeed, Stanford's Jeffrey Pfeffer, who has studied the impact of compensation on performance, concludes in *The Human Equation* that a firm's compensation system is a relatively *unimportant* factor in its success. While he does not disagree with the importance of compensation per se, he cites employee surveys showing that a pleasant, challenging, and empowered workplace often has a greater impact on employee behavior than monetary incentives.[35]

Harvard's Dorothy Leonard and Tufts's Walter Swap make a parallel argument in their book *When Sparks Fly.* They emphasize the importance of employees' passion for work, which leads them to lose the distinction between work and play, and they give the examples of 3M, where R&D employees are allowed to use 15 percent of their time to pursue any individual project they want, and Hewlett-Packard, where R&D employees may set aside 10 percent of their time to work on potential projects. As a result, they argue, both 3M and Hewlett-Packard are among the most innovative companies in the world.[36]

Although these authors and others consider financial rewards to be of secondary importance, most observers tend to agree that financial rewards work best when they take the form of incentive—or contingent—compensation. These incentives can range from piece rates to stock options. For example, Starbucks's CEO, Howard Schultz, emphasizes the importance of the company's "Bean Stock" plan, which makes all employees (including part-timers who work at least 20 hours a week) eligible for stock options after only 6 months of work. In Schultz's view, this plan goes a long way toward explaining employees' dedication to the company and their constant quest for innovative ways to cut costs. Similarly, stock options have been shown to be effective in companies like Wal-Mart, Pitney Bowes,

Home Depot, and Southwest Airlines.[37] The overwhelming conclusion seems to be that when employees receive a share of profits (whether through bonuses, stock options, or some other means), they work to keep costs low and seek ways to increase revenues.[38]

✂ Technique No. 179. Link Rewards to Organizational Strategy

Many organizations, especially those in the nonprofit sector, have difficulty finding a link between organizational strategy and rewards.[39] Some nonprofit organizations seek to develop this link by encouraging entrepreneurial behavior and providing supplemental resources to successful managers. Others, and some for-profit professional service firms as well, provide nonfinancial bonuses, such as sabbaticals.

Some companies are tougher than others in establishing this link between rewards and strategy. The City of Phoenix, Arizona, for example, makes life pretty easy. Phoenix has a suggestion program that encourages employees to submit ideas that promote cost savings or measurable improvements in productivity, product quality, employee morale, or safety, and it pays cash awards of up to $2500. The Phoenix system has received several national awards.[40]

In contrast, at Intel, the company's commitment to its employees includes a willingness to assist them in making intelligent career choices, but there is no guarantee of continued employment. Intel employees are expected to review the company's quarterly business updates to determine which areas of the company are growing and which are shrinking, and to use that knowledge to focus their career decisions and training activities.[41]

Sometimes there needs to be a major realignment of the organizational structure as well as a change in the way rewards are determined. 3M Company is a case in point. Traditionally, each of 3M's 57 departments (producing a total of 60,000 products) had approached customers separately. The company realized that it was sending multiple sales representatives to the same customer, creating excessive costs and customer confusion. In response to this problem, 3M introduced a Customer Focused Marketing initiative that was designed to encourage cross-selling among divisions. Under this initiative, sales representatives got their commission even if some other department sold the product. The company also rewarded representatives for selling other divisions' products. The initiative led to a doubling of the sales force's productivity.[42]

Technique No. 180. Link Rewards to Cultural Values

As Stanford's Pfeffer says, incentive compensation systems "can be used to shape how people think about the organization and how they approach their work." He believes that pay is important symbolically, in that it sends signals about how the firm values its employees.[43] There are lots of examples that substantiate this point. At General Electric, anyone who cannot operate as a team player, who is not prepared to work up, down, and across the organization, and who is unwilling to work with both customers and suppliers should, as the euphemism goes, "plan to seek a job elsewhere."[44] At Starbucks, in addition to receiving health benefits and stock options after only a few months on the job, employees also receive training in the importance of treating customers and one another with respect and dignity. The result is a commitment to the company's culture, and an employee turnover rate that is about half the industry average.[45]

Similarly, in his successful effort to restore the Toro Company to profitability, Ken Melrose created a culture that would help Toro reach its goals. He asked managers to trust their subordinates and to allow them to do things themselves without constantly asking their superiors' advice or approval. As part of a program called *Pride in Excellence,* Melrose wrote a corporate philosophy statement which said that management was going to fully support individual employees of the company, helping them to achieve their highest potential. To reinforce that philosophy, Melrose based a significant part of his managers' annual incentive awards on the way they followed the philosophy.[46]

✂ Technique No. 181. Link Rewards to Nonfinancial as Well as Financial Performance

Organizational excellence can be defined in many ways, and some nonfinancial measures are predictors of future financial performance. In most instances, compensation and other rewards can be linked to nonfinancial measures as well as financial ones. For example, IBM surveys its customers once a quarter and uses the data to calculate a "net satisfaction index," which it then uses to rate each department and each employee on the basis of customer perception. A significant amount of employees' compensation and bonuses depends on that rating.

Similarly, in one large oil company, employees were asked to define their own performance objectives and the steps needed to achieve them. They were then compensated not only on the basis of their progress toward those objectives, but also on their understanding of corporate goals.[47]

The idea of linking compensation and other rewards to corporate goals brings us full circle. The first technique discussed in this chapter was to focus your strategy in an area where you can have a cost advantage. If you are to do this successfully, you must be sure that you understand your environment as fully as possible so that you can be certain that you can establish and maintain a cost advantage. Then you must link your strategic focus to a variety of other activities that encompass culture, conflict, and motivation. To illustrate how this might be done, this chapter has both examined the experience of several organizations that have made cost control a way of life and introduced some techniques that senior management can use to build an enterprise with a focus on cost control as well as broader strategic objectives.

APPENDIX A

A Primer on Capital Investment Analysis

A typical capital investment proposal involves an outlay of money at the present time in order to realize a stream of benefits at some time in the future. For example, a proposal might be to install storm windows at a cost of $10,000, with an estimated savings in heating bills of $3000 per year. In evaluating this proposal, one must ask: Is it worth spending $10,000 now to obtain benefits of $3000 per year in the future? There are several approaches to answering this question.

PAYBACK PERIOD ANALYSIS

In this approach, we determine the number of years that the benefits will have to be obtained in order to recover the investment. The payback period for the storm window can be calculated as follows:

$$\text{Payback period} = \frac{\text{initial investment}}{\text{annual benefits}} = \frac{\$10,000}{\$3000} = 3.3 \text{ years}$$

If the storm windows are expected to last fewer than 3.3 years, the investment is not worthwhile. After 3.3 years, however, the storm windows will have "paid for themselves," and any future benefits will contribute to the organization's surplus.

PRESENT-VALUE ANALYSIS

Payback period analysis assumes that savings in the second and third years are as valuable as savings in the first year, but this is not realistic. No rational person would give up the right to receive $3000 now in return for a promise to receive $3000 two years from now. That is, if a person loans $3000 to someone now, he or she expects to get back more than $3000 at some time in the future. The promise of an amount to be received in the future therefore has a lower *present value* than the same amount received today.

The concept of present value rests on the basic principle that money has a *time value*—that is, that $1 received 1 year from today is worth less than $1 received today. To illustrate the concept, consider the following situations:

Question: A colleague offers to pay you $1000 one year from today. How much would you lend her today?

Presumably, unless you were a good friend or somewhat altruistic, you would not lend her $1000 today. You could invest your $1000, earn something on it over the course of the year, and have more than $1000 a year from now. If, for example, you could earn 10 percent on your money, you could invest your $1000 and have $1100 in a year. Alternatively, if you had $909 and you invested it at 10 percent, you would have $1000 a year from today.

Thus, if your colleague offers to pay you $1000 a year from today, and you are an investor expecting a 10 percent return, you would most likely lend her only $909 today. With a 10 percent interest rate, $909 is the *present value* of $1000 received 1 year hence.

Question: Under the same circumstances as the previous question, how much would you lend your colleague if she offered to pay you $1000 two years from today?

Here we must incorporate the concept of compound interest—that is, the fact that interest is earned on the interest itself. For example, at a 10 percent rate, $826 invested today would accumulate to roughly $1000 in 2 years, as shown by the following:

Year 1: $826 × 0.10   = $ 82.60
Year 2: ($826 + $82.60) × 0.10   = $ 90.86
Total at end of Year 2 = $826 + $82.60 + $90.86 = $999.46

Thus, you would be willing to lend her $826.

Question: The previous question consisted of a promise to pay a given amount 2 years from today, with no intermediate payments. Another possibility to consider is the situation in which your colleague offers to pay you $1000 a year from today and another $1000 two years from today. How much would you lend her in this situation?

The answer requires combining the analyses in the previous two examples. Specifically, for the $1000 received 2 years from now, you would lend her $826, and for the $1000 received 1 year from now, you would lend her $909. Thus, the total you would lend her would be $1735.

Our ability to make these determinations is simplified by present-value tables. Two such tables are given here. Table A-1, "Present Value of $1," is the table we would use to determine the present value of a single payment received at some specified time in the future. For instance, in the first example we gave, we could find the answer to the problem by looking in the column for 10 percent and the row for 1 year; this gives us 0.909. Multiplying 0.909 by $1000 gives us the $909 that we would lend our colleague. Similarly, if we look in the row for 2 years and multiply the entry of 0.826 by $1000, we arrive at the answer to the second example: $826.

Table A-1 Present Value of $1

Years Hence	1%	2%	4%	6%	8%	10%	12%	14%	15%	16%	18%	20%	22%	24%	25%	26%	28%	30%
1	0.990	0.980	0.962	0.943	0.926	0.909	0.893	0.877	0.870	0.862	0.847	0.833	0.820	0.806	0.800	0.794	0.781	0.769
2	0.980	0.961	0.925	0.890	0.857	0.826	0.797	0.769	0.756	0.743	0.718	0.694	0.672	0.650	0.640	0.630	0.610	0.592
3	0.971	0.942	0.889	0.840	0.794	0.751	0.712	0.675	0.658	0.641	0.609	0.579	0.551	0.524	0.512	0.500	0.477	0.455
4	0.961	0.924	0.855	0.792	0.735	0.683	0.636	0.592	0.572	0.552	0.516	0.482	0.451	0.423	0.410	0.397	0.373	0.350
5	0.951	0.906	0.822	0.747	0.681	0.621	0.567	0.519	0.497	0.476	0.437	0.402	0.370	0.341	0.328	0.315	0.291	0.269
6	0.942	0.888	0.790	0.705	0.630	0.564	0.507	0.456	0.432	0.410	0.370	0.335	0.303	0.275	0.262	0.250	0.227	0.207
7	0.933	0.871	0.760	0.665	0.583	0.513	0.452	0.400	0.376	0.354	0.314	0.279	0.249	0.222	0.210	0.198	0.178	0.159
8	0.923	0.853	0.731	0.627	0.540	0.467	0.404	0.351	0.327	0.305	0.266	0.233	0.204	0.179	0.168	0.157	0.139	0.123
9	0.914	0.837	0.703	0.592	0.500	0.424	0.361	0.308	0.284	0.263	0.225	0.194	0.167	0.144	0.134	0.125	0.108	0.094
10	0.905	0.820	0.676	0.558	0.463	0.386	0.322	0.270	0.247	0.227	0.191	0.162	0.137	0.116	0.107	0.099	0.085	0.073
11	0.896	0.804	0.650	0.527	0.429	0.350	0.287	0.237	0.215	0.195	0.162	0.135	0.112	0.094	0.086	0.079	0.066	0.056
12	0.887	0.788	0.625	0.497	0.397	0.319	0.257	0.208	0.187	0.168	0.137	0.112	0.092	0.076	0.069	0.062	0.052	0.043
13	0.879	0.773	0.601	0.469	0.368	0.290	0.229	0.182	0.163	0.145	0.116	0.093	0.075	0.061	0.055	0.050	0.040	0.033
14	0.870	0.758	0.577	0.442	0.340	0.263	0.205	0.160	0.141	0.125	0.099	0.078	0.062	0.049	0.044	0.039	0.032	0.025
15	0.861	0.743	0.555	0.417	0.315	0.239	0.183	0.140	0.123	0.108	0.084	0.065	0.051	0.040	0.035	0.031	0.025	0.020

Notes:
1. Tables A-1 and A-2 are truncated versions of most present-value tables, which typically have factors for up to 50 percent and up to 50 years.
2. Tables A-1 and A-2 use 4 decimal places only; calculators and spreadsheet packages with present-value functions use many more decimal places and thus will give slightly different results.

Table A-2, "Present Value of $1 Received Annually for *N* Years," is used for even payments received over a given period. Looking at Table A-2, we can see that the present value of $1.735 (for a payment of $1 received each year for 2 years at 10 percent) multiplied by $1000 is $1735. This is the amount we calculated in the third example. We also can see that 1.735 is the sum of the two amounts shown in Table A-1 (0.909 for 1 year hence, and 0.826 for 2 years hence). Thus, Table A-2 simply sums the various elements in Table A-1 to facilitate calculations.

The present-value technique is important in the capital budgeting process. By incorporating the time value of money into the analysis, the technique recognizes that money received in the future does not have as much value as money received today.

NET-PRESENT-VALUE ANALYSIS

The present-value (or *discounting*) technique is used in what is called the *net-present-value approach* to capital budgeting analysis. Net present value is the difference between the present value of a project's estimated benefits and the amount to be invested in the project. The benefits are often called the project's "cash flows." The approach involves the following steps:

1. Determine the estimated annual cash flows (CF) associated with the project. These may be either increased revenues (net of increased costs) or decreased costs to the organization, but they must result exclusively from the project itself and not from any activities that would have taken place without the project.
2. Determine the estimated economic life of the investment. This is not necessarily the physical life of the investment. Rather, it is the time period over which the cash flows will be received. The economic life may be shorter than the physical life because of obsolescence, change in demand, or other reasons.

Table A-2 Present Value of $1 Received Annually for N Years

Years N	1%	2%	4%	6%	8%	10%	12%	14%	15%	16%	18%	20%	22%	24%	25%	26%	28%	30%
1	0.990	0.980	0.962	0.943	0.926	0.909	0.893	0.877	0.870	0.862	0.847	0.833	0.820	0.806	0.800	0.794	0.781	0.769
2	1.970	1.941	1.887	1.833	1.783	1.735	1.690	1.646	1.626	1.605	1.565	1.527	1.492	1.456	1.440	1.424	1.391	1.361
3	2.941	2.883	2.776	2.673	2.577	2.486	2.402	2.321	2.284	2.246	2.174	2.106	2.043	1.980	1.952	1.924	1.868	1.816
4	3.902	3.807	3.631	3.465	3.312	3.169	3.038	2.913	2.856	2.798	2.690	2.588	2.494	2.403	2.362	2.321	2.241	2.166
5	4.853	4.713	4.453	4.212	3.993	3.790	3.605	3.432	3.353	3.274	3.127	2.990	2.864	2.744	2.690	2.636	2.532	2.435
6	5.795	5.601	5.243	4.917	4.623	4.354	4.112	3.888	3.785	3.684	3.497	3.325	3.167	3.019	2.952	2.886	2.759	2.642
7	6.728	6.472	6.003	5.582	5.206	4.867	4.564	4.288	4.161	4.038	3.811	3.604	3.416	3.241	3.162	3.084	2.937	2.801
8	7.651	7.325	6.734	6.209	5.746	5.334	4.968	4.639	4.488	4.343	4.077	3.837	3.620	3.420	3.330	3.241	3.076	2.924
9	8.565	8.162	7.437	6.801	6.246	5.758	5.329	4.947	4.772	4.606	4.302	4.031	3.787	3.564	3.464	3.366	3.184	3.018
10	9.470	8.982	8.113	7.359	6.709	6.144	5.651	5.217	5.019	4.833	4.493	4.193	3.924	3.680	3.571	3.465	3.269	3.091
11	10.366	9.786	8.763	7.886	7.138	6.494	5.938	5.454	5.234	5.028	4.655	4.328	4.036	3.774	3.657	3.544	3.335	3.147
12	11.253	10.574	9.388	8.383	7.535	6.813	6.195	5.662	5.421	5.196	4.792	4.440	4.128	3.850	3.726	3.606	3.387	3.190
13	12.132	11.347	9.989	8.852	7.903	7.103	6.424	5.844	5.584	5.341	4.908	4.533	4.203	3.911	3.781	3.656	3.427	3.223
14	13.002	12.105	10.566	9.294	8.243	7.366	6.629	6.004	5.725	5.466	5.007	4.611	4.265	3.960	3.825	3.695	3.459	3.248
15	13.863	12.848	11.121	9.711	8.558	7.605	6.812	6.144	5.848	5.574	5.091	4.676	4.316	4.000	3.860	3.726	3.484	3.268

3. Determine the net amount of the investment (I). This is the actual purchase price of the new asset, plus any installation costs, plus any disposal costs for the asset it is replacing, and less the salvage value received for the asset being replaced.

4. Determine the required discount rate, or rate of return (discussed in greater detail later), and combine it with the economic life to get the present-value factor (pvf).

5. Compute the proposed project's net present value (NPV) according to the formula

$$NPV = (CF \times pvf) - I$$

6. If the NPV is greater than zero, the investment is financially feasible. That is, once we have determined a desired rate of return, a project that yields a NPV of zero or greater is earning the desired rate and therefore is acceptable from a purely financial perspective.

As discussed previously, when the cash flow is the same every year, the present-value factor can be obtained from Table A-2 by looking at the intersection of the year row and the percent column selected in steps 2 and 4. Present-value factors for one-time cash flows can be found in Table A-1. The ($CF \times pvf$) portion of this equation is known as *gross present value*; it becomes *net present value* when the investment amount is deducted from it.

Example. Assume that we estimate that the storm windows in the example given at the beginning of the appendix will last 5 years, and that our required rate of return is 8 percent. The analysis would be performed as follows:

Step 1.   Annual cash flow = $3000
Step 2.   Economic life = 5 years
Step 3.   Net investment amount = $10,000
Step 4.   Rate of return = 8 percent

Step 5.   NPV $= (\text{CF} \times pvf) - I$
$$= (\$3000 \times 3.993) - \$10,000$$
$$= \$11,979 - \$10,000$$
$$= \$1979$$

Step 6.   The investment has a NPV that is greater than zero, and therefore it is financially feasible.

Points to Consider

There are several important points that should be made about an analysis of net present value. First, the example assumed identical cash flows in each of the years, which permits us to use Table A-2. If the cash flows were not the same in each year, we would need to calculate the term (CF $\times$ pvf) for each year separately, using Table A-1, and add the results together.

Second, although an analysis of this sort appears to be quite precise, we should recognize that its significant elements are estimates or guesses, and therefore may be quite imprecise. Specifically, cash flows projected beyond a period of 2 to 3 years ordinarily are not precise, nor are estimates of the economic life of most investments. Thus, we should be careful about attaching too much credibility to the precision that the formula seems to give us. Because of this, many managers look for the NPV to be a *comfortable margin* above zero. Of course, what is comfortable for one manager may not be so for another.

Third, inflation is a factor. It is quite likely, for instance, that potential increases in wage rates will cause labor savings from an investment to be greater 5 years from now than they are today. However, if we are to adjust our cash flow factor for the effects of inflation, we also need to adjust the required rate of return to reflect our need for a return that is somewhat greater than the rate of inflation. By excluding an inflation effect from both the cash flow calculations and the required rate of return, we neutralize the effect of inflation. We thus do not need to undertake the rather complex calculations that otherwise might be necessary.

Finally, the financial analysis is only one aspect of the decision-making process. Clearly, there are many more considerations, including political analyses. Managers must be careful not to let the financial analysis dominate a decision that has political or strategic consequences that cannot be quantified. In these instances, a manager's judgment and "feel" for the situation may be as important as the quantitative factors. Indeed, if a project is *required* for nonquantitative reasons (e.g., to meet life-safety codes), its net present value is irrelevant. In short, in almost all capital budgeting proposals, there is a wide variety of nonquantitative considerations that will influence the final decision. The use of present value or any related technique serves mainly to formalize the quantitative part of the analysis.

BENEFIT/COST RATIO

Since most organizations do not have sufficient capital investment funds to engage in all financially feasible projects, managers must devise some method for ranking projects in order of their financial desirability. One such method is to calculate their *benefit/cost ratio,* as follows:

$$\text{Benefit/cost ratio} = \frac{\text{gross present value}}{\text{investment}}$$

To illustrate this approach, suppose we have two proposals, one requiring an investment of $2000 that yields a cash inflow of $2400 1 year from now, and the other requiring an investment of $3000 that yields a cash inflow of $900 a year for 5 years. If the required rate of return is 10 percent, the benefit/cost ratio indicates that the second proposal is preferable, as indicated in Table A-3.

In this instance, Proposal B is more valuable on a benefit/cost basis than Proposal A.

INTERNAL RATE OF RETURN

Another way of ranking projects is by their *internal rate of return (IRR).* The IRR method is similar to the net-present-value method,

Table A-3

Proposal	Investment	Cash Inflow	Present Value Factors at 10 Percent	Gross Present Value	Benefit/ Cost Ratio
A	$2000	$2400, year 1	0.909	$2182	1.09
B	$3000	$900, years 1–5	3.791	$3412	1.14

but instead of determining a required rate of return in advance, we set the net present value equal to zero and calculate the *effective rate of return* on the investment. Proposed projects can then be ranked in terms of their rates of return.

To use this method, we usually assume identical cash flows in each year of a project's life. Given this assumption, the IRR method begins with the net-present-value formula

$$NPV = (CF \times pvf) - I$$

but sets NPV equal to zero, so that

$$CF \times pvf = I$$

or

$$pvf = I \div CF$$

Once we have determined the present-value factor, we can use it in conjunction with the project's economic life to compute the effective—or *internal*—rate of return. We do this with Table A-2. For instance, in our storm window example, if we divide the $10,000 investment amount by the $3000 annual cash flows, we get 3.33. We now look for the figure 3.33 in the row for 5 years in Table A-2, and we can see that it lies somewhere between 15 and 16 percent. This is the internal rate of return for the storm window project.

CHOICE OF A DISCOUNT RATE

In any capital investment analysis, the choice of a discount rate is an important consideration. The approach used by many organizations, both for-profit and nonprofit, is to calculate an entity's weighted cost of capital, which is then adjusted as necessary to account for the riskiness of the proposal under consideration.

Weighted Cost of Capital

An organization's assets are financed by a combination of liabilities and equity. Some liabilities, such as accounts payable, are usually interest-free, but the organization must pay interest on short- and long-term debt. Equity generally comes in two forms: (1) contributed capital (or contributions and grants in nonprofit organizations) and (2) retained earnings (which are usually called unrestricted net assets in nonprofit organizations).

In choosing a discount rate, we begin with the cost of each of these sources of capital and weight them by their relative amounts. For example, assume that the right side of an organization's balance sheet appears as shown in Table A-4, with interest rates as shown.

Table A-4

Item	Amount	Interest Rate
Accounts payable	$ 3,000	0.0%
Accrued salaries	2,000	0.0
Short-term note payable	10,000	12.0
Total current liabilities	15,000	
Long-term note payable	75,000	10.0
Mortgage payable	150,000	8.0
Total liabilities	240,000	
Contributed capital	150,000	12.0
Retained earnings	50,000	12.0
Total liabilities and equity	$440,000	

In calculating a weighted cost of capital, we (1) determine the percentage of the total liabilities and equity that each source represents, (2) multiply this by the appropriate interest rate, and (3) add the resulting totals together. The calculations for the situation in Table A-4 are shown in Table A-5.

Cost of Equity The weighted cost of capital in this example used an interest rate of 12 percent for equity. There is an ongoing debate in many organizations concerning the appropriate interest rate for equity. In general, however, most people agree that this should be the rate of return that investors expect. Sometimes this is adjusted for the riskiness of the industry in which the organization operates. In addition, the weighted cost of capital will differ from one organization to the next, depending on the organization's capital structure and interest rates.

Table A-5

Item	Amount	Percent of Total	Interest Rate	Weighted Rate
Accounts payable	$ 3,000	0.6	0.0%	0.00%
Accrued salaries	2,000	0.5	0.0	0.00
Short-term note payable	10,000	2.3	12.0	0.28
Total current liabilities	15,000			
Long-term note payable	75,000	17.0	10.0	1.70
Mortgage payable	150,000	34.1	8.0	2.73
Total liabilities	240,000			
Contributed capital	150,000	34.1	12.0	4.09
Retained earnings	50,000	11.4	12.0	1.37
Total liabilities and equity	$440,000	100.0		10.17%

INCORPORATING RISK INTO THE ANALYSIS

Capital investment proposals are not risk-free. Since all capital investment projects involve future cash flows, there is always the possibility that the future will not be as anticipated. This element of risk should be incorporated into the analysis. If risk is not considered explicitly, then a very risky proposal might be evaluated in the same way as a proposal that has a high probability of success.

There are a number of ways to incorporate risk into an analysis. With all of them, an increase in risk reduces the net present value of a proposal. Many organizations adjust their weighted cost of capital either upward or downward to account for perceived risk. The problem with this approach is that there is no easy way to establish a meaningful risk scale or otherwise make adjustments to the required rate of return. Statistical techniques for incorporating the relative risk of a project are available, but they require analysts to estimate the probabilities of possible outcomes. This is quite difficult to do.

Another approach, which is taken by many organizations, is to heavily discount any projected cash flows beyond some predetermined time period, such as 5 or 10 years. Organizations taking this approach use the weighted cost of capital as the discount rate for all cash flows in, say, the first 5 years of an investment. They then use a much higher rate for cash flows in all subsequent years. Some even exclude all cash flows beyond a certain number of years. The reasoning behind this is that the future is highly uncertain and that the further out the projections, the greater the uncertainty. While this approach tends to bias decisions in favor of projects with short payback periods, many organizations in industries that are experiencing rapid technological change believe that demanding short payback periods is justified.

Finally, in considering risk, some organizations give greater weight to projections of cost savings than to projections of additional revenues. When a particular technological improvement, say a new piece of equipment, has demonstrated its ability to produce certain cost savings in other organizations, managers reason that projections of cost savings are quite reliable. In contrast, a projection that a certain investment will result in new business and hence additional revenue is far more uncertain. Factors such as customers' willingness to use the new product or service, competition, and so forth will also affect a new investment's return. Some organizations incorporate this risk into the analysis by using lower discount rates for projects with cost savings and higher ones for projects that are expected to yield additional revenues.

In summary, when we consider the formula

$$\text{NPV} = (\text{CF} \times pvf) - I$$

the only element that is reasonably certain is the amount of the investment. Estimates of both cash flows and economic lives can be highly speculative. Organizations can adjust for this uncertainty either by shortening the estimated economic life or by raising the required rate of return. Either approach requires managers and analysts to exercise considerable judgment.

SUMMARY

Managers of most organizations frequently must choose between two or more competing proposals. When this is the case, some attempt to quantify both benefits and costs can usually assist in the decision-making effort.

When two or more proposals have roughly the same benefits, the comparison is relatively easy, since only costs need to be calculated. Similarly, when competing proposals have the same costs but one clearly produces more benefits than the other, the decision is usually quite easy. The decision becomes complicated, however, when benefits and costs extend over several years (as is the case with almost all proposals), and when competing proposals have both different benefits and different costs.

When both benefits and costs can be expressed easily in monetary terms, calculating either present values or internal rates of return can facilitate a decision. When these types of analyses are being used, the choice of a discount rate is a key decision.

Frequently, benefits and costs cannot be expressed easily in monetary terms. This happens, for example, when managers attempt to incorporate risk into the analysis, because risk is inherently difficult to measure. In addition, there is a variety of nonquantitative considerations that are part of almost every proposed project. In all these instances, although some quantitative analysis can usually be carried out, managers must be careful not to allow the quantitative factors to dominate the decision. In most capital investment decisions, managers will need to exercise their judgment, which occasionally will override the results of the quantitative analysis.

APPENDIX B

A Primer on Cost Behavior

One of the most significant aspects of cost accounting is the notion that *different costs are used for different purposes.* In general, full-cost accounting reports are not appropriate for several types of decisions that managers frequently must make. These decisions, called *alternative choice decisions,* include (1) keeping versus discontinuing a product line or service, (2) making versus buying (e.g., making a subassembly yourself or contracting with another company to have it made for you), (3) accepting versus rejecting a special request (e.g., selling a product below full cost in order to use a certain amount of otherwise unused capacity), or (4) selling obsolete supplies or equipment. For alternative choice decisions, the appropriate information is differential costs.

The key question asked in the context of an alternative choice decision is, "How will costs (and revenues) change under the alternative arrangements?" If a product line or service is discontinued, for example, some costs will be eliminated, but so, usually, will some revenues. In a make versus buy decision, by contrast, certain costs will be eliminated, but other costs will be incurred. In the special request and obsolete asset situations, certain revenues will be received, but the change in costs will not be consistent with the indications of a full-cost analysis.

As this appendix discusses, the use of full-cost information as a basis for deciding which costs will change or how costs will change under alternative arrangements can lead managers to make decisions that are financially detrimental to the organization.

THE NATURE OF COSTS

Fundamental to any discussion of differential cost analysis is the question of cost behavior. Differential cost analysis divides costs into fixed and variable categories, since doing so lets a manager see more clearly how a change in the volume of activity of a given cost center will affect cost behavior. The distinction also needs to include the refinements of semivariable and step-function costs. The four types of costs are shown in Figure B-1. A discussion of each follows.

Fixed Costs

Fixed costs are costs that are independent of the number of units produced. While no costs are fixed if the time period is long enough, the *relevant range* for fixed costs (i.e., the span of units over which they remain unchanged) and the time period within which they are considered generally are quite large, so they can be viewed graphically as shown in quadrant *a* of Figure B-1.

A good example of a fixed cost in most organizations is rent. Regardless of the number of units produced or other volume of activity, the amount of rent the company pays will remain the same.

Step-Function Costs

Step-function costs are similar to fixed costs in nature, but they have a much narrower relevant range. Therefore, they do not change in a smooth fashion, but are added in lumps, or "steps." The result is that,

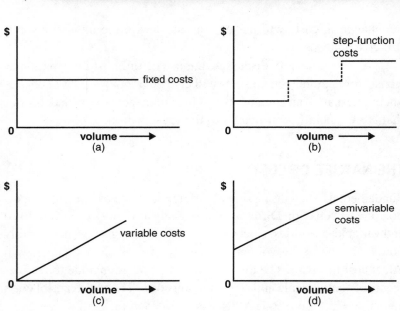

Figure B-1 Types of cost behavior.

graphically, they take the form shown in quadrant *b*, where the dotted lines represent discontinuous jumps.

A good example of a step-function cost in most organizations is supervision. As the number of workers increases, supervisory personnel must be added. Since it is difficult for most organizations to add part-time supervisory help, supervisory costs will tend to behave in a step-function fashion.

Variable Costs

Variable costs are those costs that increase or decrease in a roughly linear fashion along with changes in volume. That is, as volume increases, total variable costs will increase in some constant proportion. The result is a straight line, the slope of which is determined by the amount of variable costs associated with each unit of output, as shown in quadrant *c*.

An example of variable costs in many manufacturing organizations is raw materials, which will increase in almost direct proportion to increases in the number of units of product manufactured. Some organizations will have relatively high variable costs per unit, resulting in a line that slopes upward quite steeply; other organizations will have variable costs that are relatively low for each unit of output, so that the variable-cost line slopes upward more gently.

Semivariable Costs

Semivariable costs (sometimes called *mixed* or *semifixed* costs) have features of both fixed and variable costs. There is a minimum level of costs that is fixed, but the cost line then increases with increases in volume. The result is a line that begins at some level above zero and then slopes upward in a linear fashion, as shown in quadrant *d*.

A good example of a semivariable cost is electricity. Typically, there is some base cost each month for electricity service that an organization must incur even if it uses no electricity at all. Costs then increase in a linear fashion in accordance with the number of kilowatt-hours used. Similar cost patterns exist for other utilities as well, such as telephone, gas, and water.

Estimating Cost-Volume Relationships

In working with cost information, it sometimes is difficult to separate fixed from variable costs. This is especially true when a cost is semivariable in nature. To make the separation, one needs at least two historical or projected data points, and preferably more. There are a variety of techniques that then can be used to draw the cost lines. Those techniques are beyond the scope of this appendix.

Relation of Cost Behavior to Full-Cost Accounting

The analysis of differential costs would be simplified if, as is occasionally assumed, all service-center costs were fixed and all production-center costs were variable. Unfortunately, this is almost never the case. Some production-center costs are relatively fixed, such as equipment depreciation, and some service-center costs, such as housekeeping supplies, are relatively variable.

Cost Behavior in Organizations

Generally, an organization can classify its costs as fixed, step-function, variable, or semivariable. Doing so requires analyzing the actual or expected behavior of each cost item and attempting to determine how that cost item will change with changes in the volume of activity.

COST-VOLUME-PROFIT ANALYSIS

An important technique used in differential-cost situations is cost-volume-profit (CVP) analysis. The purpose of cost-volume-profit analysis is to determine (1) the volume of activity that is required if an organization is to achieve its profit goal, (2) the price that an organization needs to charge in order to achieve its profit goal, or (3) the cost limits (fixed and/or variable) that an organization needs to adhere to in order to achieve its profit goal.

CVP analyses are usually done for a particular activity within an organization, such as a product line or program. A CVP analysis thus begins with the fundamental equation

$$\text{Profit} = \text{total revenue (TR)} - \text{total costs (TC)}$$

For many activities, total revenue is quite easy to calculate. If we assume that an organization's price is represented by the letter p and its volume by the letter x, then total revenue is price times volume, or

$$\text{TR} = px$$

Total costs are somewhat more complicated. CVP analysis requires a recognition of the different types of cost behavior in an organization: fixed, step-function, variable, and semivariable. Let us begin with the simplest of cases, in which there are no step-function or semi-variable costs. In this instance, the formula would be quite simple:

$$\text{Total costs} = \text{fixed costs} + \text{variable costs}$$

Fixed costs are generally represented by the letter a and variable costs per unit by the letter b. Thus, total variable costs can be represented by the term bx, where, as before, x represents volume. The resulting cost equation looks like this:

$$TC = a + bx$$

This means that the fundamental profit equation can be shown as

$$\text{Profit} = px - (a + bx)$$

Graphically, we can represent the formula as shown in Figure B-2.

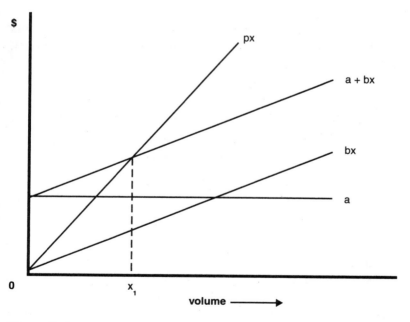

Figure B-2

Point x_1, where $px = a + bx$, is the *breakeven volume*, or the point at which total revenue px equals total costs $a + bx$. At a volume above x_1, the organization earns a profit; below x_1, it incurs a loss.

To illustrate how this formula can be used, let's assume that an organization wishes to determine its breakeven volume, i.e., the volume at which profit is zero. If we know the price, fixed costs, and variable costs per unit, we can solve the formula algebraically for x, which would be our breakeven volume. Similarly, if we know any three of the four items in the equation, we can solve for the fourth. Let's look at this in terms of a simple problem.

Problem: Littleton News, Inc., publishes a monthly magazine for the town of Littleton. The company has fixed costs of $100,000 a month and variable costs per magazine of $0.80, and it charges $1.80 per magazine. What is its breakeven volume (number of magazines sold per month)?

To answer this, we begin with the cost-volume-profit formula and substitute the known elements. We then solve for the unknown, which, in this case, is volume, or x.

$$\text{Profit} = px - (a + bx)$$

At breakeven, profit $= 0$, and therefore

$$px = a + bx$$
$$1.80x = 100{,}000 + 0.80x$$
$$1.00x = 100{,}000$$
$$x = 100{,}000$$

Breakeven is 100,000 magazines. To confirm:

Revenue: $1.80 (100,000) =		$180,000
Less costs:		
Variable: $0.80 (100,000) =	$ 80,000	
Fixed	100,000	
Total		180,000
Profit		$ 0

Unit Contribution Margin

An important aspect of CVP analysis is the idea of unit contribution margin. This is the contribution to fixed costs that comes about as a result of the sale of each additional unit. In effect, the unit contribution margin is the difference between price and unit variable cost, or $p - b$. By rearranging the terms of the CVP formula, we can arrive at the conclusion that breakeven volume is simply fixed costs divided by unit contribution margin, as follows:

$$px = a + bx$$
$$px - bx = a$$
$$x(p - b) = a$$
$$x = a \div (p - b)$$

In effect, price minus unit variable cost tells us how much each unit sold contributes to the recovery of fixed costs. When we divide this amount into fixed costs, we arrive at the volume (number of units of activity) needed to recover all our fixed costs. This is our breakeven volume.

To illustrate, Littleton News has a unit contribution margin of $1.00 ($1.80 − $0.80). When we divide this amount into its fixed costs of $100,000, we arrive at its breakeven volume of 100,000 magazines.

Incorporating Other Variables into a CVP Analysis

Thus far, we have been using CVP analysis to solve only for the breakeven volume. Clearly, if we knew how many units of our product we were likely to sell, our fixed costs, and our unit variable costs, we could then determine the price we would need to charge in order to break even. Similarly, if we were in an environment where price was market-driven and we knew about how many units we could sell at that price, we could set up either fixed costs or unit variable costs as the unknown and solve for either one.

Profit Considerations We also can incorporate a need for profit into CVP analysis. The easiest way to do this is to add the amount of desired profit to our fixed costs, and then calculate a breakeven point with that new level of "fixed costs." Similarly, if we were planning to pay dividends or if we needed a margin of safety, we could incorporate these amounts into our so-called fixed-cost figure.

Special Considerations in Cost-Volume-Profit Analysis

There are a number of special considerations that can complicate a CVP analysis. Two of the more important are the presence of semivariable costs and the presence of step-function costs. Let's look at each of these.

CVP Analysis with Semivariable Costs Incorporating semivariable costs into a cost-volume-profit analysis is relatively easy. Since semivariable costs have a fixed component and a variable component, we simply need to add the fixed component to the fixed-cost total and add the unit variable cost figure to the existing unit cost figure. For example, assume that, in addition to its other costs, Littleton News has electricity costs that are $2000 a month regardless of usage, plus an additional amount per kilowatt-hour of use. Electricity usage is tied directly to the number of magazines produced. The company's accountants have determined that the rate is about $0.04 per magazine.

Littleton's monthly breakeven volume (number of magazines) can now be computed as follows:

$$px = a + bx$$
$$1.80x = (100{,}000 + 2000) + (0.80x + 0.04x)$$
$$0.96x = 102{,}000$$
$$x = 106{,}250$$

Breakeven is 106,250 magazines.

CVP Analysis with Step-Function Costs The introduction of step-function costs is somewhat more difficult than might at first be imagined. Ideally, we would like to be able to assume that, for any given relevant range, we could simply add together the step-function costs and the fixed costs to give us the total applicable fixed costs. We then could use the formula as described previously. Unfortunately, the process is not quite that simple, as the following example illustrates.

Problem: Return to the first problem for Littleton News (i.e., ignore the electricity costs). In addition to the $100,000 in fixed costs stipulated in the first problem, Littleton also has supervisory costs. These costs behave as follows:

Volume	Costs
0–50,000	$10,000
50,001–100,000	20,000
100,001–150,000	30,000
150,001–200,000	40,000

If we attempt to solve the breakeven formula at the first level of fixed costs, we have the following equation:

$$1.80x = (100,000 + 10,000) + 0.80x$$
$$1.00x = 110,000$$
$$x = 110,000$$

The problem with this solution is that, while the breakeven volume is 110,000 magazines, the relevant range for the step-function costs was only 0–50,000 magazines. Thus, a breakeven of greater than 50,000 magazines is invalid, and we must move to the next step on the step function, which gives us the following equation:

$$1.80x = (100,000 + 20,000) + 0.80x$$
$$1.00x = 120,000$$
$$x = 120,000$$

This solution is also invalid. Only when we get to the third level do we encounter a valid solution, as follows:

$$1.80x = (100,000 + 30,000) + 0.80x$$
$$1.00x = 130,000$$
$$x = 130,000$$

The conclusion we must draw is that the incorporation of step-function costs in the cost-volume-profit formula requires a trial-and-error process to reach the breakeven volume.

THE DIFFERENTIAL-COST CONCEPT

In addition to using an understanding of the fixed, step-function, variable, or semivariable nature of cost behavior for CVP analysis, we can use it to undertake a differential-cost analysis. Effectively, differential-cost analysis attempts to identify the behavior of an organization's costs under one or more different scenarios. These scenarios are related to the type of alternative choice decision we are making. Consider the following problem.

Problem: Clearwater Taxi Service operates two taxis. It charges 50 cents a mile for each passenger-mile driven. Last year, Taxi 1 drove 60,000 passenger-miles, and Taxi 2 drove 30,000 passenger-miles. The variable cost per mile (gasoline, tires, wear, and tear) for each taxi was 20 cents. Each driver was paid a salary of $5000 per year (the remainder of each driver's income was earned in tips). Rent and administration are fixed costs totaling $15,000; they are allocated to each taxi on the basis of the number of miles driven. As a result, total revenues and expenses for the year are as shown in Table B-1.

Would the profitability of Clearwater Taxi Service have been improved if Taxi 2, which lost money, had been discontinued at the beginning of the year? By how much would the company's profits have improved or worsened?

An answer to this question must be structured in terms of differential costs. The question is not whether Taxi 2 lost money on a *full-cost* basis (as it did), but rather the nature of its differential costs and revenues; that is, how would Clearwater's revenues and costs have changed if Taxi 2 had been discontinued?

Although the data are not as good as we might like, we nevertheless can see that discontinuing Taxi 2 would have eliminated its

Table B-1

Item	Taxi 1	Taxi 2	Total
Revenue	0.50 × 60,000 = $30,000	0.50 × 30,000 = $15,000	$45,000
Expenses:			
Variable costs	0.20 × 60,000 = 12,000	0.20 × 30,000 = 6,000	18,000
Drivers	5,000	5,000	10,000
Overhead costs (rent and administration)	10,000	5,000	15,000
Total expenses	$27,000	$16,000	$43,000
Profit (loss)	$3,000	$(1,000)	$ 2,000

revenue and its variable costs as well as the fixed cost of the driver. From all indications, however, the overhead costs (rent and administration) would have continued (i.e., they were not differential). The result would therefore have been a shift from a profit of $2000 to a loss of $2000, as Table B-2 indicates.

This situation illustrates several important principles.

Table B-2

Item	Taxi 1
Revenue	0.50 × 60,000 = $30,000
Expenses:	
Variable costs	0.20 × 60,000 = 12,000
Driver	5,000
Overhead costs (rent and administration)	15,000
Total expenses	$32,000
Profit (loss)	$(2,000)

Principle #1. Full-Cost Information Can Be Misleading

The kind of information that is available from most full-cost accounting systems can produce highly misleading results if it is used for alternative choice decisions—in this instance a keep versus discontinue decision. In the Clearwater case, the full-cost data would seem to indicate that we could increase profits by dropping Taxi 2, but this clearly is not the case.

Principle #2. Differential Costs Can Include Both Fixed and Variable Costs

Although this is perhaps counterintuitive, you should note that differential costs can include *both* fixed and variable costs. In the Clearwater example, the driver was a fixed cost of Taxi 2, and yet the elimination of Taxi 2 eliminated this fixed cost. The key point is that as long as we operate Taxi 2, we have the fixed cost of the driver's salary; it does not fluctuate in accordance with the number of miles driven (within the relevant range). But when we eliminate the taxi, we also eliminate this cost in its entirety; thus, it is differential in terms of the alternative choice decision we are making. In effect, we have moved outside the relevant range when we reduce the number of miles to zero; at that point the fixed cost falls to zero also.

Principle #3. Assumptions Are Needed

Differential-cost analysis invariably requires assumptions. Although the analysis of the Clearwater situation focused on what would have happened in the prior year, the real intent of the analysis is to assist management in a decision that it must make concerning the future. The assumption that underlay our analysis, therefore, was that next year's prices, costs, volume, etc., would be the same as last year's.

Of course, it is not true that next year will be just like last year. Inflation will affect our costs, and it may be possible for us to raise our prices. The general state of the economy, along with a wide variety of other factors, will affect our volume next year so that it is quite likely to be different from last year's. This raises some important concerns about the reliability of our analysis.

Despite these concerns, since we do not have perfect knowledge of the future, we must speculate about how costs will behave. In the Clearwater example, we made two important assumptions that went beyond the general ones just mentioned: (1) The number of miles driven by Taxi 1 will not increase with the elimination of Taxi 2, and (2) we will not be able to reduce or eliminate any rent or administrative costs with the elimination of Taxi 2. Changes in either of these assumptions clearly would have an impact on the new profit (or loss) figure and might, in fact, actually make it financially beneficial to eliminate Taxi 2.

The Need for Causality   A key aspect of differential analysis is causality. Specifically, for an item to be included in a differential analysis, the change must be *caused* by the alternative under consideration. For example, if we are to assume here that there will be an increase in the number of miles driven by Taxi 1, that increase would need to be *caused* by the elimination of Taxi 2. If Taxi 1 would have driven more miles anyway, then the increased mileage is irrelevant for the differential analysis. If, however, we assume that the elimination of Taxi 2 means that some passengers who would have used Taxi 2 now will use Taxi 1 instead, then the increased mileage is relevant for the differential analysis. We would need to include that additional mileage in computing Taxi 1's revenue and variable expenses under the alternative scenario.

The same issue must be considered for cost items such as rent and administrative costs. If we were planning to decrease our administrative costs with or without Taxi 2, then the change is irrelevant for the differential analysis. If, on the other hand, the elimination of Taxi 2 will *cause* a decrease in administrative costs (such as the elimination of a portion of the dispatcher wage expense), then we would need to include this decrease in the differential analysis.

The Use of Sensitivity Analysis   Because assumptions play such a crucial role in a differential analysis, it is important to identify them and document them as completely as possible. Furthermore, it is important to explore how changes in the assumptions would affect the conclusions of the analysis. This latter activity is called *sensitivity analysis*. If we were doing a sensitivity analysis for the Clearwater Taxi situation, we might try to determine how many more miles Taxi 1 would need to be driven in order for the organization to maintain its $2000 profit. Or, if we thought we might be able to reduce our rent and administrative costs with the elimination of Taxi 2, we might ask by how much they would need to fall in order to maintain the $2000 profit.

A sensitivity analysis could be followed by an assessment of whether managerial action could be taken that would allow the assumptions to become reality.

Principle #4. Information Must Be Structured Appropriately

The Clearwater Taxi example illustrates the importance of structuring information for decision-making purposes. For example, one way to structure the information is the approach shown in Table B-2.

THE CONCEPT OF CONTRIBUTION

Another way of structuring differential-cost information is in terms of *contribution*. As the Clearwater example indicates, an important question in differential-cost analysis is the behavior of overhead (or service center) costs. A key assumption was that overhead costs (rent and administration) for the taxi service would not be reduced by eliminating the second taxi. As indicated previously and as is discussed in greater detail later, an assumption of this sort is not necessarily valid. Nevertheless, in most instances, an analysis of differential costs is most easily performed when the direct fixed and variable costs of the particular activity are analyzed separately from the overhead costs of the organization.

An analysis that separates costs in this way is usually structured in terms of the contribution of the particular program, product, or service to the organization's overhead costs. The term *contribution* means the amount that each product or service has left after its product- or service-specific costs have been deducted from its revenue. Product- or service-specific costs include variable, semivariable, fixed, and step-function costs. The amount left after deducting these costs *contributes* to the recovery of overhead costs. More specifically, a product or service (a taxi in this case) provides some revenues and incurs some direct costs. The difference between revenue and direct costs (both fixed and variable) is the contribution of that product or service to the organization's overhead costs.

Contribution Income Statement

Returning to the Clearwater Taxi Service example, we can see that the cost data for the analysis can be structured in terms of a *contribution income statement*. An example of such a statement is contained in Table B-3.

As this example indicates, both Taxi 1 and Taxi 2 are contributing to the coverage of overhead costs. Consequently, eliminating either taxi will reduce this contribution and thus will either

Table B-3

Contribution Income Statement for Clearwater Taxi Service

Item	Taxi 1	Taxi 2	Total
Revenue	$30,000	$15,000	$45,000
Less variable costs	12,000	6,000	18,000
Margin (for fixed and overhead costs)	$18,000	$ 9,000	$27,000
Less production-center fixed costs (drivers)	5,000	5,000	10,000
Contribution (to overhead costs)	$13,000	$ 4,000	$17,000
Less overhead costs			15,000
Profit (loss)			$ 2,000

reduce the organization's profit or increase its loss. In fact, it was the $4000 that Taxi 2 was contributing that led to the change from a $2000 profit to a $2000 loss.

SUNK COSTS

One of the most difficult aspects of differential cost analysis is the role of *sunk costs*. As mentioned earlier, an alternative choice decision always looks toward the future rather than the past. This is one reason why full-cost analyses, which typically rely on historical data, are inappropriate for these kinds of decisions. Nevertheless, even when we focus our analytical efforts on the future, we frequently are plagued by history, particularly when it presents itself in the form of sunk costs.

The term *sunk cost* is used to refer to an expenditure that was made in the past and results in an expense on a full-cost report, but that, because it has already been incurred and the decision cannot be changed, is inappropriate when the future is being considered. Consequently, it should be excluded from a differential-cost analysis (which is concerned only with the future). In a very real sense, it is a cost that is sunk.

Sunk Costs and Intuition

For most people, the notion of sunk costs is very difficult to accept intuitively. Since sunk costs are present in many alternative choice decisions, however, you should be comfortable in dealing with them. Let's use a personal example to illustrate their counterintuitive nature.

Problem: Two months ago, you purchased a special vacation package to London, where you plan to spend 1 week. The package includes round-trip airfare, hotel accommodations, meals, and other expenses. This package deal cost you $1000 and is nontransferable and nonrefundable, i.e., if you do not use it, you cannot sell it to someone else or get your money back from the travel agency.

The day before you are scheduled to leave, you learn that, as part of a special promotion, you can purchase an *identical* 1-week vacation package to Paris for $600. You have never been to Paris, but you have always wanted to visit, and you have been to London several times before. You have the $600 in the bank. What are the relevant cost considerations to include in your analysis? Which city would you visit?

If you included the $1000 in your analysis, you, like most people, have difficulty accepting the idea of sunk costs. The $1000 is gone, and there is nothing you can do about it. Your choice now (i.e., 1 day before your departure) is between a free (no additional cost) trip to London and a $600 trip to Paris. The only relevant cost to consider is the $600.

Sunk Costs in Organizational Settings

The classic example of a sunk cost in organizations is depreciation, which is the accounting technique used to spread the cost of an asset over its useful life. Although depreciation will appear on a full-cost report, accountants have traditionally considered it to be inappropriate for differential-cost analysis, since it will not change regardless of the alternative chosen. That is, it is a sunk cost. To examine this idea, let's look first at the accounting view of sunk costs in organizational settings and then examine these costs in a more strategic context.

The Accounting View of Sunk Costs   Accountants typically consider sunk costs from a relatively nonstrategic perspective. In this regard, *nonstrategic* means that we are looking only at the remaining economic life of any assets that are involved in an alternative choice decision and do not consider the longer-term, strategic consequences of the decision. Because of this, the accounting view ordinarily excludes consideration of any decision to replace the assets. Let's look at this from the perspective of a contract-out decision.

Problem: Newton Electric Company (NEC) has a machine with a book value of $40,000 that it is depreciating at a rate of $10,000 per year.

The machine is a highly specialized one, used only to make the coil in the motors used in Newton's vacuum cleaners. Because of technological changes, the machine has a market value of zero—it cannot be sold (a junkyard dealer has offered to remove it at no charge, however).

Assume that NEC's profit before depreciation is $100,000 and that another company has offered to make the same number of coils for NEC for a total price (delivered) of $15,000 a year. Is the book value of the machine a relevant cost to consider in deciding whether to accept the offer?

The answer is no, since the cost is the same regardless of whether or not we subcontract the work. Leave aside, for the moment, the additional cost of the subcontract. If we scrap the machine (i.e., receive nothing for it), we will no longer have any depreciation on it, and our income statements for the next 4 years will look something like Table B-4.

If we continue with the existing situation (i.e., we do not subcontract the work), our income statements for the remaining 4 years of the machine's life would look like Table B-5.

In either case, net profit for the 4-year period is $360,000 and the machine expense is $40,000. The only difference is that in the first alternative, we incur the expense in a single year, whereas in the second alternative, the expense is spread over 4 years.

Table B-4

Year	1	2	3	4	Total
Profit before depreciation	$100,000	$100,000	$100,000	$100,000	$400,000
Less depreciation	0	0	0	0	0
Profit before disposal of assets	$100,000	$100,000	$100,000	$100,000	$400,000
Less loss on sale of machine	40,000	0	0	0	40,000
Net profit	$60,000	$100,000	$100,000	$100,000	$360,000

Table B-5

Year	1	2	3	4	Total
Profit before depreciation	$100,000	$100,000	$100,000	$100,000	$400,000
Less depreciation	10,000	10,000	10,000	10,000	40,000
Profit before disposal of assets	$90,000	$90,000	$90,000	$90,000	$360,000
Less loss on sale of machine	0	0	0	0	0
Net profit	$90,000	$90,000	$90,000	$90,000	$360,000

If we were being completely accurate, we would consider the time value of the cash generated from an earlier reduction in income taxes as a differential item in the first alternative. For purposes of simplicity, this calculation has been excluded from the example.

Because the $40,000 book value of the machine is a sunk cost, we do not include it in our differential-cost analysis. Rather, the analysis looks only at the out-of-pocket expenses that would be eliminated as a result of subcontracting, compared to the cost of the subcontract. These items would affect the "profit before depreciation" figure shown in the income statements. In this case, if NEC can reduce its *out-of-pocket* expenses associated with the coils for the motors by more than $15,000 (the price of the subcontract), then, other things being equal, subcontracting would be financially beneficial.

The Strategic View of Sunk Costs   Although depreciation is a sunk cost and therefore is a nondifferential item in any alternative choice decision, there is a question as to how we should treat depreciation if our perspective is a more strategic one, i.e., one that extends beyond the remaining years of a machine's economic life. The strategic view asks a slightly different question from the accounting view. With the strategic view, the question is what our costs and revenues will be over an *indefinite* time period. When this is the case, depreciation is a relevant item to include.

To state this somewhat differently, when the time horizon is short, the financial perspective generally is a cash-maximizing one. When the time horizon is long (i.e., when it extends beyond the economic life of the asset), the decision becomes more strategic in nature. When this is the case, senior management tends to *include* depreciation (a noncash expense) in the analysis.

The strategic perspective occurs in both contract-out decisions and decisions concerning the elimination of a product or product line. Let's look first at the analysis we might do in a contract-out situation and then look at the decision to keep or drop a product line.

The Contract-Out Situation A contract-out decision typically is not concerned with revenue. Instead, senior management needs to compare costs under two scenarios: (1) manufacture the item or provide the service ourselves, or (2) contract with another company to manufacture the item or provide the service.

Problem: The Arctic Ice Refrigerator Company manufactures a line of refrigerators that contains automatic ice dispensers. The ice dispensers are made in a special department that uses some highly specialized equipment. The department's annual full costs are as follows:

Direct labor	$150,000
Materials	70,000
Department manager	50,000
Depreciation	30,000
Allocated overhead	20,000
Total	$320,000

Arctic Ice has received an offer from a local firm that specializes in ice-dispensing equipment to manufacture the same annual volume of ice dispensers at an annual cost of $280,000. The contract is for 5 years. If Arctic Ice accepts this offer, it will be able to totally eliminate the Ice Dispenser Department. In this regard, management has determined the following:

1. Although the machines used in the department have 5 years of depreciation remaining, they are technologically obsolete and have no market value (they can be removed at no charge, but that is all). However, they can last for another 5 years before they need to be replaced.
2. No inflation is expected.
3. The department manager is willing to accept early retirement (at no additional cost to the company) if the department closes. That is, her salary will be eliminated, and she will draw her retirement income from the company's pension fund, which is a separate entity.
4. None of the allocated overhead is differential; that is, it will be reallocated to other departments if the Ice Dispenser Department is eliminated.
5. The expected number of ice dispensers needed for each of the 5 years of the contract is well known and will be the same as it was during the year in which the figures given were computed.
6. The local firm making the offer has an excellent reputation for quality and delivery.

What are the relevant costs to consider in the analysis of this decision?

If we adopt the traditional approach to this analysis, we will use the following costs to compute the savings from subcontracting:

Direct labor	$150,000
Materials	70,000
Department manager	50,000
Depreciation (sunk)	0
Allocated overhead (nondifferential)	0
Total	$270,000
Less: Cost of contract	280,000
Net financial benefit	($10,000)

If we adopt a more strategic perspective and include depreciation in the analysis (even though it is a sunk cost), we would use the following costs:

Direct labor	$150,000
Materials	70,000
Department manager	50,000
Depreciation	30,000
Allocated overhead (nondifferential)	0
Total	$300,000
Less: Cost of contract	280,000
Net financial benefit	$20,000

Other things being equal, under the first cost analysis we would *not* accept the offer, whereas under the second analysis we would accept it. What should management do?

A short-term, cash-maximizing perspective would lead us to reject the offer. We would save only $270,000 in expenses, and we would spend $280,000 for the contract. The traditional approach, which excludes sunk costs, most certainly would lead us to this conclusion.

From a longer-term, strategic perspective, however, our focus shifts to what might be called "steady-state" operations. This more strategic focus recognizes that at some point we will need to replace the equipment, and thus includes depreciation in the analysis. Under these circumstances, we would accept the offer, since it will improve our financial performance over the long term.

Ideally, of course, we would wait for 5 years to accept the contract. Much could change in the interim, however, that would affect our decision. More important, this option is not available.

Keep or Drop a Product Line   In the decision to keep or drop a product line, senior management must carefully assess the behavior of both revenue and costs, under the scenario that involves dropping the product line, and then compare the results with the option to keep the product line. Again, sunk costs present some analytical difficulties. Consider the following problem:

Problem: Sunshine Pen Company manufactures a line of felt-tipped pens. The annual revenue and full costs of the Felt-Tipped Department are given in Table B-6.

The accountants also have prepared the contribution income statement shown in Table B-7.

The department's manager, arguing that the depreciation expense is a sunk cost and therefore should not be considered in the analysis, has prepared the contribution income statement shown in Table B-8.

The manager's argument is that, at least in the short run, the department is making a contribution to the recovery of overhead costs, and therefore should not be discontinued.

Table B-6

Sales revenue (net)		$600,000
Less:		
Direct labor	$200,000	
Materials	260,000	
Departmental administration	120,000	
Depreciation	80,000	
Allocated overhead	110,000	
Total expenses		770,000
Profit (loss)		($170,000)

Table B-7

Sales revenue (net)	$600,000	
Less variable costs (materials)	260,000	
Margin (for fixed and overhead costs)		$340,000
Less department fixed costs:		
Direct labor	200,000	
Departmental administration	120,000	
Depreciation	80,000	400,000
Contribution to overhead costs		($60,000)
Less allocated overhead costs		110,000
Profit (loss)		($170,000)

Table B-8

Sales revenue (net)	$600,000	
Less variable costs (materials)	260,000	
Margin (for fixed and overhead costs)		$340,000
Less department fixed costs:		
Direct labor	200,000	
Departmental administration	120,000	
Total		320,000
Contribution to overhead costs		20,000
Less allocated overhead costs		110,000
Profit (loss)		($90,000)

Senior management's reaction to these differing perspectives might include the following considerations:

1. In the near future, it makes sense to keep the department, since it is indeed contributing $20,000 in cash to help cover the allocated overhead costs. However, even under these circumstances, we need to ask two questions:
   - Could we, by discontinuing the Felt-Tipped Department, eliminate more than $20,000 of the allocated overhead costs? For example, suppose there were an employee benefits clerk in the administrative service center all of whose time was spent on the employees of the Felt-Tipped Department. This person's salary plus fringe benefits totals $28,000. It might be possible to eliminate this person and save the $28,000. This savings would more than offset the $20,000 contribution, making it financially beneficial to discontinue the department.
   - Assuming that we are capacity-constrained, can we find some other product line to pursue that would generate more than $20,000 in contribution? The difference between the contribution from this new product line and

the $20,000 becomes the *opportunity cost* of keeping the Felt-Tipped Department.
2. In the long run, can we find some other product line to pursue that would cover all of its costs, *including* depreciation and allocated overhead?

Summary of the Strategic Perspective   Traditionally, the strategic perspective is used only when a company is deciding whether to purchase replacement equipment. At that time, management looks at the annual cash flows associated with the proposed investment in new assets and compares them with the amount of the proposed investment. The problem with this approach is that it rarely considers alternatives such as contracting out. Instead, the decision is made in relative isolation.

In an effort to correct for this incremental approach to strategic decision making, senior management must also ask the strategic question when an opportunity to contract out presents itself. To do so, many managers will include depreciation in the cost analysis, since its inclusion provides a good approximation of the company's costs from a steady-state perspective. That is, an analysis that includes depreciation shows what the "typical year" would look like.

Precision of Depreciation   Clearly, depreciation is not a precise measure of steady-state operations, since inflation and technological changes will change the cost of a replacement asset. Because of this, depreciation provides only a rough approximation of steady-state operations. Nevertheless, a rough approximation is better than completely excluding the cost of using up the associated assets.

In short, while depreciation (and any other sunk cost) is *irrelevant* from a cash perspective, it is quite *relevant* from a strategic perspective, since it indicates the annual expense associated with the equipment. Thus, if the purpose of the analysis is to determine whether the program or activity is financially beneficial when all costs are considered, depreciation is a relevant cost to include.

Summary of Sunk Cost Issues in Organizational Settings
The fact that depreciation is a sunk cost does not necessarily mean that it or any other sunk cost should be excluded from all differential-cost analyses. If, for example, the analysis focuses on the continuation of a particular product line or activity over some indefinite time period (which is part of the strategic perspective), senior management would, quite appropriately, include depreciation. Since the continuation of the product line or activity requires eventual replacement of the machines or other assets that are being depreciated, depreciation helps to measure the costs in a steady-state situation.

The Problem of Multiple Assets for One Product Line Treating depreciation as a sunk cost (and thereby excluding it from an analysis of differential costs) suggests that senior management will wait until one of the assets involved in the product line must be replaced before making a strategic analysis. Even when this happens, however, the analysis will not be complete if more than one asset is involved. That is, if a particular product line uses several assets, it is unlikely that the assets will all require replacement simultaneously. Using a strategic perspective for the replacement of a single asset when a product line uses several assets will result in only a partial analysis. Senior management must include either a current or a simulated depreciation amount for all assets associated with the product line if it is to fully analyze the situation under consideration.

Relationship to Changing Strategic Scenarios Increasingly, as companies develop strategic alliances with their suppliers and as their manufacturing operations become more and more automated (i.e., as the number of assets increases), the strategic perspective takes on greater significance in alternative choice decision making. Under these circumstances, it may make sense to move away from the more traditional approach that excludes depreciation (and other sunk costs). In this regard, a key question is whether the decision is a short-term one or one that will have longer-term implications for the company's strategy. If it is short term in nature, excluding sunk costs such as depreciation and the book value of other assets involved in the decision is appropriate. Otherwise, the inclusion of depreciation (and other relevant sunk costs) is quite appropriate.

NONQUANTITATIVE CONSIDERATIONS

The strategic perspective also includes nonquantitative considerations. That is, in any alternative choice decision, there are a variety of factors that cannot be quantified and that can easily tip the balance in one direction or another, frequently overriding the financial analysis. This is especially true if the financial analysis indicates that the two approaches have roughly similar cost and revenue implications.

In the decision to keep or drop a product or product line, nonquantitative considerations usually include product interdependencies, i.e., the extent to which the sales of some of the company's other products are dependent upon sales of the product whose elimination is under consideration. For example, a company that manufacturers both cameras and film would probably find it unwise to eliminate its cameras as a product line, since film sales are highly dependent upon consumers having cameras. Indeed, some companies treat certain products as loss leaders, losing money on them deliberately so as to maximize consumer purchases of their related (and highly profitable) products. The idea is that if the consumer has the loss-leading product in hand, he or she then will purchase some of the company's other products that are used in conjunction with the loss leader.

In an outsourcing decision, nonquantitative considerations typically include factors such as quality, service, delivery, and reputation of the vendor. They may also include market considerations, such as the difficulty and cost of switching from one vendor to another if a particular relationship does not work out. A company that contracts for snowplowing services for its parking lot, for example, typically has an easy time switching from one vendor to another. There are many individuals with pickup trucks and snowplow blades who can provide the service. On the other hand, a company that contracts for the manufacture of specialized packing equipment may have a difficult time switching vendors. The number of such vendors in the market may be quite small.

Another nonquantitative consideration in outsourcing is the cost of switching back to internal manufacture should this become necessary. Once a company contracts out a particular item, it may eliminate the facilities, equipment, and trained personnel required for production of that item. Leasing or purchasing new facilities and equipment and training new personnel may be quite costly. In this regard, the nature of the market for the outsourced item is quite important. In a highly competitive market, a company that is dissatisfied with one vendor can simply hire another. If the market is more oligopolistic, however, it may be difficult to hire a new vendor. Moreover, if the company has eliminated its capacity for internal manufacture, it may find itself at the mercy of its vendor. This is rarely desirable.

THE ROLE OF ALLOCATED OVERHEAD

Additional complexities are introduced into the differential cost analysis when overhead costs are associated with a particular effort for which the differential analysis is to be made. There are two such complexities: allocation bases and the stepdown sequence.

Misleading Allocation Bases

Many companies are attempting to measure the use of service-center resources more accurately. Nevertheless, there are still situations in which a given service center's allocation basis does not necessarily reflect the actual use of its services by receiving cost centers. This becomes an important consideration in alternative choice decisions.

In essence, if a company contracts out some services or if it discontinues the production of a particular product line, it is quite likely that some of the service-center costs *allocated* to the production center in question will decline. In most instances, however, few of those service-center costs will *actually* be eliminated. Only the variable and semivariable costs, and perhaps the step-function costs, in the service center will be eliminated. The remaining costs will be reallocated to other cost centers.

For example, take the case of administration and general (A&G), a service center. A reduction of staff in a given *production* center will lead to a reduction in total salaries in that production center. If A&G costs are allocated on the basis of salary dollars, there will be a reduction in the amount of A&G *allocated* to the production center. It is highly unlikely, however, that there will be any reduction in the staff or other costs associated with the A&G service center. Rather than being reduced, A&G costs will simply be reallocated to other cost centers.

The reverse may happen as well. That is, it is possible that some of a particular service center's costs may be eliminated, even though the costs *allocated* to a given production center from that service center do not fall. For example, assume that cleaning costs are allocated on the basis of square feet. A reduction in the level of the activities in a given production center, or a change in the nature of those activities, may reduce the center's need for cleaning services. This may permit the manager of the cleaning service center to reduce the service center's costs. Yet, unless the space utilized by the production center is reduced, the cost report (which allocates cleaning on a square-footage basis) will not show a corresponding reduction in the cleaning costs allocated to the production center. That is, the costs allocated to the revenue center will fall slightly as a result of the lower amount of cleaning costs *overall,* but the decline will be much less than the actual cost reduction that took place in the cleaning service center. The rest of the savings will be realized by other receiving cost centers, even though they continue to receive the same amount of cleaning as before.

Effects of the Stepdown Sequence

The costs in each service center are allocated to all remaining cost centers (service centers and production centers) as one moves down the steps in the stepdown sequence. Therefore, the total costs of those service centers that are farthest down in the stepdown sequence will include portions of the costs of service centers above them. That is, the total cost allocated from each service center includes its direct and assigned indirect costs *plus* the costs that have been allocated to it from service centers (or "steps") above it in the stepdown sequence.

For example, in a hospital, if social work is a service center that is far down in the stepdown sequence, the total social work service cost allocated to a particular production center will have a significant allocated component (e.g., allocations for administration, house-keeping, laundry and linen, and so on). It may be possible to reduce the use of social workers in a production center by reducing the number of patients treated or by changing the nature of the treatment plans. However, the full impact of that reduction on the costs of the social work service center will be overstated if one uses the fully allo-cated social work totals (which include previously allocated service-center costs). This is because the costs being allocated from the social work service center contain costs from a variety of other cost centers that may not be affected at all by the reduction in the production center's volume of activity or its use of social workers.

The Analytical Effort

Recognizing these complexities and incorporating them into analyt-ical efforts is one of the most challenging aspects of differential-cost analysis. Determining which costs are indeed differential and how they behave is extremely difficult, particularly when a full cost report (such as a stepdown) is the principal source of information. There are no easy answers to this dilemma. Just a lot of hard analytic work.

NOTES

Chapter 1

[1]Michelle Conlin, "Where Layoffs Are a Last Resort," *Business Week,* October 8, 2001.

[2]Ibid.

[3]Darrell Rigby, "Look before You Lay Off," *Harvard Business Review,* April 2002.

[4]Louis Lavelle, "Swing That Ax with Care," *Business Week,* February 11, 2002.

[5]Kathy McCabe, "GE Aircraft Engines to Fire 4,000," *Boston Globe,* October 4, 2001.

[6]Louis Lavelle, "Pressure Is On to Share the Pain," *Business Week,* October 8, 2001.

[7]Conlin, "Where Layoffs Are a Last Resort."

[8]Stanley Holmes, "Is Boeing Cutting Too Close to the Bone?" *Business Week,* November 26, 2001.

[9]Judy Olian, "When Times Are Tough, Smart Companies Invest in People," *Business Week,* December 17, 2001.

[10]Aaron Bernstein, "The Human Factor," *Business Week,* August 27, 2001.

[11]Ibid.

[12]Ken Ryan, "Retaining Talent while Managing HR Costs," *Venture Capital Journal,* June 1, 2001.

[13]Bernstein, "The Human Factor."

[14]"Summer Break: A New Idea in Cost-Cutting," *Business Week,* June 7, 2001.

[15]Lavelle, "Pressure Is On to Share the Pain."

[16]Frank Gibney, Jr., "Survival Strategies," *Time Bonus Section: Your Business,* October 2001.

[17]Eric Wahlgren, "A Longer Wait for That Final Offer," *Business Week,* June 19, 2001.

[18]"Hotel Unfairness," *Boston Globe,* November 2001.

[19]Lavelle, "Pressure Is On to Share the Pain."

[20]Louis Lavelle, "The Gravy Train Just Got Derailed," *Business Week,* November 19, 2000.

[21]Louis Lavelle, Frederick F. Jespersen, and Michael Arndt, "Executive Pay," *Business Week,* April 15, 2002.

[22]Lavelle, "The Gravy Train Just Got Derailed."

[23]Ibid.

[24]Daniel Eisenberg, "Paying to Keep Your Job," *Time,* October 15, 2001.

[25]Ibid.

[26]Justin Martin, "Eli Lilly Is Making Shareholders Rich. How? By Linking Pay to EVA," *Fortune,* September 9, 1996.

[27]Eisenberg, "Paying to Keep Your Job."

[28]Bernstein, "The Human Factor."

[29]Monica Roman, "A Pact Clears United's Runway," *Business Week,* March 4, 2002.

[30]Kimberly Weisul, "Return of the Payroll Scrooge," *Business Week,* November 19, 2001.

[31]Michelle Conlin, "Thinking Beyond the One-Size-Fits-All Pay Cut," *Business Week,* December 3, 2001.

[32]Frederick F. Reicheld, *The Loyalty Effect: The Hidden Force behind Growth, Profits, and Lasting Value* (Boston: Harvard Business School Press, 1996).

[33]Chandrani Ghosh, "When Bean Counters Dispense Medicine," *Forbes,* April 29, 2002.

[34]Randy Myers, "2000 Cost Management Survey: Ship-Shape," *CFO Magazine,* December 1, 2000.

[35]Thomas L. Barton and Frederick M. Cole, "Accounting for Magic," *Management Accounting,* January 1991.

[36]Jack Welch with John A. Byrne, *Jack: Straight from the Gut* (New York: Warner Business Books, 2001).

[37]Faith Keenan, "EMC: Turmoil at the Top," *Business Week,* March 11, 2002.

[38]Wahlgren, "A Longer Wait for That Final Offer."

[39]Joshua Kendall, "Well, Well, Well," *Business Week,* June 18, 2001.

[40]Kevin Tse and Dean Foust, "At Risk from Smoking: Your Job," *Business Week,* April 15, 2002.

[41]Christine Canabou, "A Message about Managing Email," *Fast Company,* August 2001.

[42]Steve Bailey, "Hollywood Tom," *Boston Globe,* November 30, 2001.

Chapter 2

[1]Karen E. Klein, "Make Them Pay," *Business Week Small Biz,* May 21, 2001.

[2]Glenn H. Matteson, "How to Maintain Firm Profits: 94 Ways to Cut Costs in 1994," *Air Conditioning, Heating, & Refrigeration News,* July 11, 1994.

[3]Neil Gross, "Software That Sniffs Out Stolen Property," *Business Week,* December 24, 2001.

[4]Myra Pinkham, "Are Surcharges the Answer to Rising Fuel Costs?" *American Metal Market,* August 6, 2001.

[5]Robyn Meredith, "Car Guy," *Forbes,* January 21, 2002.

[6]Advertisement in the City & Region section, *Boston Globe,* April 19, 2002, p. B3.

[7]Daren Fonda, "Dining in a Din," *Time Bonus Section: Your Business,* April 2001.

[8]Pallavi Gogoi, "Gary Wendt: How's He Doing?" *Business Week,* July 23, 2001.

[9]Joann Muller, "Ford: Why It's Worse than You Think," *Business Week,* June 25, 2001.

[10]Editorial, "How to Control Drug Costs, Simply," *Business Week,* December 10, 2001.

[11]Sanjay Gupta, "Is Your Doctor Too Drowsy?" *Time,* March 11, 2002.

[12]Chester Dawson, "Nissan Bets Big on Small," *Business Week,* March 4, 2002.

[13]Chris Mitchell, "A Herculean Task for an Olympic Leader," *Business Week,* December 17, 2001.

[14]Joann Muller, "Ford: Look to the Lineup, Guys," *Business Week,* September 3, 2001.

[15]David Welch, "Can Lutz Help Steer GM Out of Its Slide?" *Business Week,* August 27, 2001.

[16]Joann Muller and Christine Tierney, "Daimler and Chrysler Have a Baby," *Business Week,* January 14, 2002.

[17]Joann Muller, "Cruising for Quality," *Business Week,* September 3, 2001.

[18]Victoria Murphy, "The Logistics of a Dinner Plate," *Forbes,* January 21, 2002.

[19]President's Private Sector Survey on Cost Control, *War on Waste,* 1984.

[20]Bruce Mohl, "One at a Time, Please: Napkin Dispenser Cuts Restaurants' Costs," *Boston Globe,* March 30, 2002.

[21]Pinkham, "Are Surcharges the Answer to Rising Fuel Costs?"

[22]Sharon Foley and Takia Mahmood, under the supervision of Professors Stephen P. Bradley and Pankaj Ghemawat, *Wal-Mart Stores* (Boston: Harvard Business School Publishing, 1994), Case 9-794-024.

[23]Ken Ryan, "Retaining Talent while Managing HR Costs," *Venture Capital Journal,* June 1, 2001.

[24]Boston University, BSBA Finance Club, interview with Mark Blodgett, CEO, Stocker Yale.

[25]Diane Brady, "A Big Break for Your Postman," *Business Week,* September 10, 2001.

[26]Diane Brady, "Why Service Stinks," *Business Week,* October 23, 2000.

[27]Marty Whitford, "The Heat Is On: Lodging Properties Battle Soaring Natural Gas Prices," *Hotel & Motel Management,* February 19, 2001.

[28]"Enough to Make You Ill," *Business Week Small Biz,* May 21, 2001.

[29]Roberto Ceniceros, "Rising Rates Have Employers Looking for Ways to Cut Costs," *Business Insurance,* October 16, 2000.

[30]Sylviane de Sainte-Seine, "Valeo Cuts Supplier Base to Lower Costs," *Automotive News Europe,* July 30, 2001.

[31]James Muller, "Can This Man Save Chrysler?" *Business Week,* September 17, 2001.

[32]Claudia Hume and Bill Schmitt, "Pharma's Prescription," *Chemical Week,* April 11, 2001.

[33]Lindsay Chappell, "U.S. Suppliers Help Turn On Nissan's Profits," *Automotive News,* September 10, 2001.

[34]Buckley Mintcloud, "Money-Saving Ideas for the Profit-Minded Supervisor," *Supervision,* June 1990.

[35]Muller, "Can This Man Save Chrysler?"

[36]Arlene Weintraub, "Leonard the Giant Killer?" *Business Week,* May 14, 2001.

[37]Robert S. Galvin, "What Do Employers Mean by 'Value'?" *Integrated Healthcare Report,* October 1998.

[38]David W. Young et al., "Value-Based Partnering in Health Care," *Benefits Quarterly* 17 (2), 2001. See also P. E. Greenberg, S. N. Finkelstein, and E. R. Berndt, "Economic Consequences of Illness in the Workplace," *Sloan Management Review* 36 (4), 1995.

[39]Linda Himelstein, "Webvan Left the Basics on the Shelf," *Business Week,* July 23, 2001.

[40]Mark S. Kuhar, "Oil Upgrade: Evaluating the Quality of Oil Being Used May Help Reduce Downtime," *Pit and Quarry,* August 2001.

[41]Milton Roemer et al., "Copayment for Ambulatory Care: Penny-Wise and Pound-Foolish," *Medical Care,* June 1975, pp. 457-466.

Chapter 3

[1]"Oppenheimer Cuts Back on Expenses," *Fund Action,* August 20, 2001.

[2]Robert Galvin, M.D., personal correspondence.

[3]"Lots o' Room at the Inn," *Business Week,* June 25, 2001.

[4]Michael Arndt, "Suddenly, Carriers Can't Get Off the Ground," *Business Week,* September 3, 2001.

[5]Michelle Conlin, "Where Layoffs Are a Last Resort," *Business Week,* October 8, 2001.

[6]Guy Lundberg, personal correspondence.

[7]Conlin, "Where Layoffs Are a Last Resort."

[8]Jerry Limone, "Meetings: Firms Get Creative to Cut Costs," *Travel Weekly,* July 23, 2001.

[9]Tom Lowry and Ronald Grover, "For the Love of the Game and Cheap Seats," *Business Week,* May 28, 2001.

[10]David A. Kunz, "3M Revisited: Evolving for the '90s," *Management Accounting,* October 1992.

[11]James Powers and Michael Connor, "A Quick Hit Approach to Cost Savings," *Harvard Management Update,* September 2001.

[12]Jim Kerestetter, "Silicon Seer," *Business Week,* August 27, 2001.

[13]Pamela L. Moore, "GE Embraces the Paperless Office," *Business Week,* June 25, 2001.

[14]Randy Myers, "2000 Cost Management Survey: Ship-Shape," *CFO Magazine,* December 1, 2000.

[15]Ibid.

[16]Louis Lavelle, "The Case of the Corporate Spy," *Business Week,* November 26, 2001.

[17]Glenn H. Matteson, "How to Maintain Firm Profits: 94 Ways to Cut Costs in 1994," *Air Conditioning, Heating, & Refrigeration News,* July 11, 1994.

[18]Myers, "2000 Cost Management Survey."

[19]Diane Ridge, "Labor Saving Equipment," *Food Management,* August 2001.

[20]Jim Sullivan, "Let's Get Fiscal: Look at the Other Side of Profitability," *Nation's Restaurant News,* July 30, 2001.

[21]David Willis, "Slashing Cost or Value?" *Network Computing,* May 28, 2001.

[22]Andrew Hubbard, "Saving Money by Spending Money," *Mortgage Banking,* March 2001.

[23]Aixa M. Pascual, "Tidying Up at Home Depot," *Business Week,* November 26, 2001.

[24]Buckley Mintcloud, "Money-Saving Ideas for the Profit-Minded Supervisor," *Supervision,* June 1990.

[25]Ibid.

[26]Matthew Boyle, "How to Cut Perks without Killing Morale," *Fortune.com,* February 19, 2001.

[27]Jeffrey Krasner, "Polaroid Pension Plan Underfunded," *Boston Globe,* October 3, 2001.

Chapter 4

[1]Samuel C. Weaver, "Capital Budgeting," *Financial Management,* Spring 1989.

[2]*Financial Times,* May 22, 1998.

[3]For additional discussion of this issue, see Anita M. McGahan, "Sustaining Superior Performance: Customer and Supplier Relationships," Harvard Business School note 797-045.

[4]Sheila M. Cavanaugh and Stephen P. Bradley, *Crown Cork & Seal in 1989* (Boston: Harvard Business School Publishing, 1993).

[5]Monica Roman, "Hyundai Is Alabama-Bound," *Business Week,* April 15, 2002.

[6]Robert N. Anthony and David W. Young, *Management Control in Nonprofit Organizations* (7th ed.; Burr Ridge, Ill.: McGraw-Hill-Irwin, 2003), chap. 9.

[7]Charles J. Christenson, "Disease Control Programs," in Robert N. Anthony and David W. Young, *Management Control in Nonprofit Organizations* (7th ed.; Burr Ridge, Ill.: McGraw-Hill-Irwin 2003), chap 9.

[8]Ann Gibbons, "Overkilling the Insect Enemy," *Science,* August 10, 1990.

[9]Randy Myers, "2000 Cost Management Survey: Ship-Shape," *CFO Magazine,* December 1, 2000.

[10]Joseph Pryweller, "Tough Times Inspire Iowa Thermoformers," *Plastics News,* September 10, 2001.

[11]Dana Dubbs, "Retrofit Chalks Up 501% ROI through Higher Productivity and Lower Costs," *Facilities and Design Management,* April 1991.

[12]Betsy Streisand, "Must-See and See TV," *U.S. News & World Report,* September 10, 2001.

[13]John Y. Lee, "The Service Sector: Investing in New Technology to Stay Competitive," *Management Accounting,* June 1991.

[14]Alice L. London, "Transportation Services for the Disabled," *GAO Review,* Spring 1986.

[15]Health One and Deloitte & Touche, *Managing Care and Costs: Strategic Choices and Issues: An Environmental Assessment of U.S. Health Care, 191-1996* (Minneapolis: Health One Corporation, 1991).

[16]Buckley Mintcloud, "Money-Saving Ideas for the Profit-Minded Supervisor," *Supervision,* June 1990.

[17]Kathleen Kerwin and Joann Muller, "Bill Takes the Wheel," *Business Week,* November 12, 2001.

[18]William S. Symonds, "Razor Burn at Gillette," *Business Week,* June 18, 2001.

[19]Spencer E. Ante and David Henry, "Can IBM Keep Earnings Hot?" *Business Week,* April 15, 2002.

[20]Kerwin and Muller, "Bill Takes the Wheel."

[21]Michael J. Mandel et al., "Productivity: The Real Story," *Business Week,* November 5, 2001.

[22]Frank Gibney, Jr., "Survival Strategies," *Time Bonus Section: Your Business,* October 2001.

[23]Chuck Salter, "This Is One Fast Factory," *Fast Company,* August 2001.

[24]Linda Himelstein, "How Cheap Is My Valley," *Business Week,* November 19, 2001.

[25]Dean Foust and Christopher Palmer, "Against the Flow at Duke Energy," *Business Week,* November 5, 2001.

[26]Richard S. Dunham (ed.), "Anchors Away?" *Business Week,* July 9, 2001.

[27]C. Douglas Poe, Gadis J. Dillon, and Kenneth Day, "Replacing Assets in the Construction Industry," *Management Accounting,* August 1988.

[28]"Burying Trash in Big Holes—on the Balance Sheet," *Business Week,* May 11, 1992.

[29]Loc. cit.

Chapter 5

[1]William S. Symonds, "Razor Burn at Gillette," *Business Week,* June 18, 2001.

[2]"Haggar Makes the Modular Move in Slacks Production," *Bobbin,* 33 (10), June 1992.

[3]Sharon Foley and Takia Mahmood, under the supervision of Professors Stephen P. Bradley and Pankaj Ghemawat, *Wal-Mart Stores* (Boston, Mass.: Harvard Business School Publishing, 1994), Case 9-794-024.

[4]Robert J. Pisapia, "The Cash Manager's Expanding Role: Working Capital," *Journal of Cash Management,* 10 (7), 1990.

[5]Jan W. Rivkin and Michael E. Porter, *Matching Dell* (Boston: Harvard Business School Publishing, 1999), Case 9-799-158.

[6]"GM Slices and GM Slashes, but the Flab Survives," *Business Week,* December 23, 1991.

[7]"Anything under Zale's Tree?" *Business Week,* December 23, 1991.

[8]"A Stampede for Cheaper Money," *Business Week,* January 20, 1992.

[9]Emily Thornton, "Innovative Financing," *Business Week,* August 27, 2001.

[10]"Hefty Sell-Offs May Help to Fix Goodyear's Flat," *Business Week,* April 15, 1991.

[11]Gene Koretz, "Warning Sign: Low Dividends," *Business Week,* April 22, 2002.

[12]John T. Mulqueen, "Money Matters—When It Doesn't Pay to Buy-Lease," *Communications Week,* July 20, 1992.

[13]Ibid.

[14]Barbara Rudolph, "Why Didn't the Creditors Notice?" *Forbes,* October 11, 1982.

[15]Laura Saunders, "Too Little Is Not Enough," *Forbes,* November 7, 1983.

[16]Heather Timmons, "Do Household's Numbers Add Up?" *Business Week,* December 10, 2001.

[17]"The Shake-Up in the Barclays Boardroom," *Economist,* April 25, 1992.

[18]Brian Bremner, "Cleaning Up the Banks—Finally," *Business Week,* December 17, 2001.

[19]Emily Thornton, "Who Can Afford to Go Broke?," *Business Week,* September 10, 2001.

[20]David Henry, "The Numbers Game," *Business Week,* May 14, 2001.

Chapter 6

[1]Michael J. Mandel et al., "Productivity: The Real Story," *Business Week,* November 5, 2001.

[2]Ibid.

[3]"25 Leaders for a Dangerous Time," *Business Week e.biz,* May 14, 2001.

[4]Desa Philadelphia, "Global Briefing," *Time Global Business,* October 2001.

[5]Amy Barrett and Diane Brady, "At Honeywell, It's Larry the Knife," *Business Week,* November 26, 2001.

[6]Roger O. Crockett, "Wireless Work," *Business Week,* August 27, 2001.

[7]Diane Ridge, "Labor Saving Equipment," *Food Management,* August 2001.

[8]Bridget McCrea, "Shrinking Is Not an Option," *Industrial Distribution,* April 2001.

[9]Timothy J. Mullaney and Darnell Little, "Online Finance Hits Its Stride," *Business Week,* April 22, 2002.

[10]Ibid.

[11]Jonathan Fahey, "Dealers 1 Internet 0," *Forbes,* April 29, 2002.

[12]Edward Teach, "The Great Inventory Correction," *CFO Magazine,* September 1, 2001.

[13]For details of these and other examples, see Larry Downes and Chunka Mui, *Unleashing the Killer App: Digital Strategies for Market Dominance* (Boston, Mass.: Harvard Business School Press, 1998).

[14]See Robert G. Cross, *Revenue Management: Hard-Core Tactics for Market Domination* (New York: Broadway Books, 1997).

[15]Amy Borrus, "How Marriott Never Forgets a Guest," *Business Week,* February 21, 2000, p. 74.

[16]Laird Harrison, "A New Crystal Ball," *Time Global Business,* April 2002.

[17]Sylviane de Sainte-Seine, "Valeo Cuts Supplier Base to Lower Costs," *Automotive News Europe,* July 30, 2001.

[18]"25 Leaders for a Dangerous Time."

[19]Jim Kerstetter, "Silicon Seer," *Business Week,* August 27, 2001.

[20]Peter Burrows, "The Era of Efficiency," *Business Week,* June 18, 2001.

[21]Harrison, "A New Crystal Ball."

[22]Darnell Little, "Bringing Bad Beef to Light before It Hits the Shelves," *Business Week,* December 3, 2001.

[23]Faith Keenan, "Opening the Spigot," *Business Week e.biz,* June 4, 2001.

[24]Janet Ginsburg, "Plastic as High as an Elephant's Eye," *Business Week,* July 9, 2001.

[25]Burrows, "The Era of Efficiency."

[26]George Taninecz, "Value-Chain Fulfillment," *Industry Week,* May 15, 2000.

[27]Randy Myers, "2000 Cost Management Survey: Ship-Shape," *CFO Magazine,* December 1, 2000.

[28]Diane Brady, "Why Service Stinks," *Business Week,* October 23, 2000.

[29]Ibid.

[30]Ibid.

[31]Ibid.

[32]Charles Haddad, "Bucking the Odds by Slashing Costs," *Business Week,* November 26, 2001.

[33]Chandrani Ghosh, "When Bean Counters Dispense Medicine," *Forbes,* April 29, 2002.

[34]Fahey, "Dealers 1 Internet 0."

[35]Anthony P. Hourihan, personal correspondence.

Chapter 7

[1]Jack Welch with John A. Byrne, *Jack: Straight from the Gut* (New York: Warner Business Books, 2001).

[2]James Powers and Michael Connor, "A Quick Hit Approach to Cost Savings," *Harvard Management Update,* September 2001.

[3]See Frederick F. Reichheld, *The Loyalty Effect: The Hidden Force behind Growth, Profits, and Lasting Value* (Boston, Mass.: Harvard Business School Press, 1996).

[4]Editorial Comment, "Keeping Clients Happy Is the Best Way to Cut Costs," *National Underwriter/Property & Casualty Risk & Benefits,* September 21, 1998.

[5]Robert Berner, Gerry Khermouch, and Aixa Pascual, "Retail Reckoning," *Business Week,* December 10, 2001.

[6]"The Global Economy: Who Gets Hurt?" *Business Week,* August 10, 1992.

[7]Monte Burke, "Back to Life," *Forbes,* January 21, 2002.

[8]For a discussion of ABC, see Robin Cooper and Robert S. Kaplan, "Profit Priorities from Activity-Based Costing," *Harvard Business Review,* May 1991.

[9]"Determining the Savings of Reduced Cycle Time," *IIE Solutions,* March 2001.

[10]Michael Crane and John Meyer, "Focusing on True Costs in a Service Organization," *Management Accounting,* February 1993.

[11]Joseph A. Ness and Thomas G. Cucuzz, "Tapping the Full Potential of ABC," *Harvard Business Review,* July 1995.

[12]"How to Escape a Price War," *Fortune,* June 13, 1994.

[13]Charles H. House and Raymond L. Price, "The Return Map: Tracking Product Teams," *Harvard Business Review,* January-February 1991.

[14]President's Private Sector Survey on Cost Control, *War on Waste* (Washington, D.C.: U.S. Government Printing Office, 1984). For current efforts to improve performance in the federal government, see *Management of the United States Government,* a report prepared annually by the Office of Management and Budget.

[15]Al Gore, *The Best Kept Secrets in Government* (Washington, D.C.: U.S. Government Printing Office, 1996). For a critical appraisal of the National Performance Review, see Barbara A. Coe, "How Structural Conflicts Stymie Reinvention," *Public Administration Review,* March-April 1997.

[16]Michael Hammer and James Champy, *Reengineering the Corporation* (New York: HarperCollins, 1993).

[17]Michael Hammer and Steven A Stanton, *The Reengineering Revolution* (New York: HarperCollins, 1995).

[18]For additional discussion of operational auditing in nonprofit organizations, see Robert N. Anthony and David W. Young, *Management Control in Nonprofit Organizations* (7th ed.; Burr Ridge, Ill.: McGraw-Hill/ Irwin, 2003), chap. 11.

[19]Hammer and Stanton, *The Reengineering Revolution.*

[20]Eliot Marchal, "Tiger Teams Draw Researchers' Snarls," *Science,* April 19, 1991.

[21]Jack Welch with John A. Byrne, *Jack: Straight from the Gut.*

[22]Ibid.

[23]Amy Barrett and Diane Brady, "At Honeywell, It's Larry the Knife," *Business Week,* November 26, 2001.

[24]James Don Edwards, Cynthia D. Heagy, and Harold W. Rakes, "How Milliken Stays on Top," *Journal of Accountancy,* 167 (4), 1989.

[25]These factors are explained in greater detail in David W. Young and Leslie Pearlman, "Managing the Stages of Hospital Cost Accounting," *Healthcare Financial Management,* April 1993.

[26]Douglas Stanglind, "What Are You Trying to Do," *U.S. News & World Report,* March 3, 1997.

[27]Jim Carlton, *Apple: The Inside Story of Intrigue, Egomania, and Business Blunders* (New York: Times Business/Random House, 1997).

[28]Bruce Einhorn, "Quanta's Quantum Leap," *Business Week,* November 5, 2001.

[29]Spencer E. Ante and David Henry, "Can IBM Keep Earnings Hot?" *Business Week,* April 15, 2002.

[30]Ellen Neuborne, "Should You Outsource?" *Business Week Small Biz,* October 8, 2001.

[31]Joe Cyr, "Managing Activities at General Motors' Suppliers," *CMA Magazine,* 1993.

[32]James P. Womack and Daniel T. Jones, *Lean Thinking: Banish Waste and Create Wealth in Your Corporation* (New York, Simon and Schuster, 1996).

[33]See Alfred D. Chandler, Jr., and Stephen Salsbury, *Pierre S. duPont and the Making of the Modern Corporation* (New York: Harper & Row, 1971).

[34]Peter Burrows, "The Era of Efficiency," *Business Week,* June 18, 2001.

[35]S. Chatterjee, "Delivering Desired Outcomes Efficiently: The Creative Key to Competitive Strategy" *California Management Review,* 40 (2), 1998, p. 78.

[36]Ibid.

Chapter 8

[1]This chapter contains a brief discussion of some important management control system principles, problems, and potential solutions. A more complete discussion can be found in Robert N. Anthony and V. J. Govindarajan, *Management Control Systems,* 10th ed. (Burr Ridge, Ill.: Irwin-McGraw-Hill, 1999). For a discussion of management control in a nonprofit context, see Robert N. Anthony and David W. Young, *Management Control*

in Nonprofit Organizations (7th ed.; Burr Ridge, Ill.: McGraw-Hill/Irwin, 2003).

[2]See Richard F. Vancil, "What Kind of Management Control Do You Need?" *Harvard Business Review*, March-April 1973.

[3]Sheila M. Cavanaugh and Stephen P. Bradley, *Crown Cork and Seal in 1989* (Boston, Mass.: Harvard Business School Publishing, 1993).

[4]Margaret Reber and David W. Young, *Franklin Health Associates* (a disguised name) (Cambridge, Mass.: Crimson Press Curriculum Center, 1996).

[5]Jack Welch with John A. Byrne, *Jack: Straight from the Gut* (New York: Warner Business Books, 2001).

[6]Janet Anderson, David Young, and Fred Foulkes, *Kelmscott Rare Breeds Foundation* (Cambridge, Mass.: Crimson Press Curriculum Center), Case 102-07, 2002.

[7]For details, see the "New York City Sanitation Department" case in Anthony and Young, *Management Control in Nonprofit Organizations.*

[8]The classic book on transfer pricing is David Solomons, *Divisional Performance: Measurement and Control* (Homewood, Ill.: Dow Jones-Irwin, 1965).

[9]See Fred Thompson, "Management Control and the Pentagon: The Organizational Strategy-Structure Mismatch," *Public Administration Review,* 51 (1), 1991.

[10]Anthony and Govindarajan, *Management Control Systems.*

[11]Samuel C. Weaver, "Capital Budgeting," *Financial Management,* 18 (1), Spring 1989.

[12]"Feature: A Conversation with Gary Hamel, Author of *Leading the Revolution* (Harvard Business School Press, 2000)," *Innovation Alert from Harvard Business School Publishing,* July 11, 2000.

[13]John F. Rockart, "Chief Executives Define Their Own Data Needs," *Sloan Management Review,* March-April 1979.

[14]Robert S. Kaplan and David Norton, *The Balanced Scorecard* (Boston, Mass.: Harvard Business School Press, 1996).

[15]James Don Edwards, Cynthia D. Heagy, and Harold W. Rakes, "How Milliken Stays on Top," *Journal of Accountancy,* 167 (4), 1989.

[16]Kaplan and Norton, *The Balanced Scorecard.*

[17]Steven Spear and H. Kent Bowen, "Decoding the DNA of the Toyota Production System," *Harvard Business Review,* September-October 1999.

Chapter 9

[1]See the discussion of Dell's cash conversion cycle in Chapter 5.

[2]Reported in Constantinos C. Markides, *All the Right Moves* (Boston, Mass.: Harvard Business School Press, 2000).

[3]Michael E. Porter, "What Is Strategy?," *Harvard Business Review,* November-December 1996.

[4]For details on Wal-Mart, see Sharon Foley and Takia Mahmood, under the supervision of Professors Stephen P. Bradley and Pankaj Ghemawat, *Wal-Mart Stores, Inc.* (Boston: Harvard Business School Publishing, 1994).

[5]Stephen P. Bradley, *Wal-Mart Stores, Inc., Teaching Note* (Boston, Mass.: Harvard Business School Publishing, 1995).

[6]Ibid.

[7]Wendy Zellner, "How Well Does Wal-Mart Travel?" *Business Week,* September 3, 2001.

[8]Michelle Conlin and Wendy Zellner, "Is Wal-Mart Hostile to Women?" *Business Week,* July 16, 2001.

[9]Geoffrey Colvin, "Smile! It's Recession Time!" *Fortune,* October 29, 2001.

[10]This paragraph and the next two are based on Jan W. Rivkin and Michael E. Porter, *Matching Dell* (Boston, Mass.: Harvard Business School Publishing, 1999).

[11]For additional details on Dell, see Rivkin and Porter, *Matching Dell.* See also Andrew Park and Peter Burrows, "Dell, the Conqueror," *Business Week,* September 24, 2001.

[12]Gary McWilliams, "Price War Squeezes PC Makers," *Wall Street Journal,* March 26, 2001.

[13]Park and Burrows, "Dell, the Conqueror."

[14]Jack Welch with John A. Byrne, *Jack: Straight from the Gut* (New York: Warner Business Books, 2001).

[15]Cate Reavis, Carin-Isabel Knoop, and Jeffrey F. Rayport, *Disney's "The Lion King" (A): The $2 Billion Movie* and *Disney's "The*

Lion King" (B): The Synergy Group (Boston, Harvard Business School Publishing, 1998), Cases 9-899-041 and 9-899-042.

[16]Toby Stuart and David Collis, *Cooper Industries' Corporate Strategy* (Boston: Harvard Business School Publishing, 1992), Case 9-391-095.

[17]Welch, *Jack: Straight from the Gut.*

[18]David Thielen, *The 12 Simple Secrets of Microsoft Management: How to Think and Act Like a Microsoft Manager and Take Your Company to the Top* (New York, McGraw-Hill, 1999).

[19]For additional thinking on this point, see David W. Young, "The Six Levers for Managing Organizational Culture," *Business Horizons,* September-October 2000.

[20]Clayton M. Christensen, *The Innovator's Dilemma: When New Technologies Cause Great Firms to Fail* (Boston, Mass.: Harvard Business School Press, 1997).

[21]Welch, *Jack: Straight from the Gut.*

[22]Ben Elgin, "Inside Yahoo!," *Business Week,* May 21, 2001.

[23]Steven L. Goldman, Roger N. Nagel, and Kenneth Preiss, *Agile Competitors and Virtual Organizations: Strategies for Enriching the Customer* (Cincinnati, Van Nostrand Reinhold, 1995).

[24]Herbert A. Simon, *Administrative Behavior* (New York: The Free Press, 1945).

[25]See Bradford D. Smart, *Topgrading* (Englewood Cliffs, N.J.: Prentice-Hall, 1999).

[26]For details, see Bill Capodagli and Lynn Jackson, *The Disney Way* (Chicago: McGraw-Hill, 1999).

[27]Howard Schultz and Dori Jones Yang, *Pour Your Heart into It: How Starbucks Built a Company One Cup at a Time* (New York: Hyperion, 1997).

[28]Pamela L. Moore, "This Scandal Changes Everything," *Business Week,* February 28, 2000, pp. 140-143.

[29]Welch, *Jack: Straight from the Gut.*

[30]Robert Slater, *Jack Welch and the GE Way* (New York, McGraw-Hill, 1999).

[31]Thielen, *The 12 Simple Secrets of Microsoft Management.*

[32]Suzy Wetlaufer, "Common Sense and Conflict: An Interview with Disney's Michael Eisner," *Harvard Business Review,* January-February 2000.

[33]Warren Bennis and Patricia Ward Biederman, *Organizing Genius* (Reading, Mass.: Addison-Wesley, 1997).

[34]Wayne Burkan, *Wide Angle Vision: Beat Your Competition by Focusing on Fringe Competitors, Lost Customers, and Rogue Employees* (New York: John Wiley & Sons, 1996).

[35]Jeffrey Pfeffer, *The Human Equation: Building Profits by Putting People First* (Boston, Mass.: Harvard Business School Press, 1998).

[36]Dorothy Leonard and Walter Swap, *When Sparks Fly: Igniting Creativity in Groups* (Boston, Mass.: Harvard Business School Press, 1999).

[37]Bob Nelson, *1001 Ways to Energize Employees* (New York: Workman Publishing, 1997).

[38]Pfeffer, *The Human Equation.*

[39]Philip H. Mirvis and Edward J. Hackett, "Work and Work Force Characteristics in the Nonprofit Sector," *Monthly Labor Review,* April 1983.

[40]Nelson, *1001 Ways to Energize Employees.*

[41]Judith M. Bardwick, *In Praise of Good Business* (New York: John Wiley & Sons, 1998).

[42]Don Peppers and Martha Rogers, *Enterprise One to One: Tools for Competing in the Interactive Age* (New York: Doubleday, 1997).

[43]Pfeffer, *The Human Equation.*

[44]Slater, *Jack Welch and the GE Way.*

[45]Schultz and Yang, *Pour Your Heart into It.*

[46]Ken Melrose, *Making the Grass Greener on Your Side* (San Francisco, Calif.: Berrett-Koehler Publishers, 1995).

[47]Robert S. Kaplan and David P. Norton, *The Balanced Scorecard* (Boston, Mass.: Harvard Business School Press, 1996).

BIBLIOGRAPHY

Amelio, Gil, and William Simon. *Profit from Experience: The National Semiconductor Story of Transformation Management.* New York: John Wiley & Sons, 1997.

Anthony, Robert N., and V. J. Govindarajan. *Management Control Systems,* 10th ed. Burr Ridge, Ill.: Irwin-McGraw Hill, 1999.

Anthony, Robert N., and David W. Young. *Management Control in Nonprofit Organizations,* 7th ed. Burr Ridge, Ill.: McGraw Hill/Irwin, 2003.

Burkan, Wayne. *Wide Angle Vision: Beat Your Competition by Focusing on Fringe Competitors, Lost Customers, and Rogue Employees.* New York: John Wiley & Sons, 1996.

Capodagli, Bill, and Lynn Jackson. *The Disney Way.* Chicago: McGraw-Hill, 1999.

Christensen, Clayton M. *The Innovator's Dilemma: When New Technologies Cause Great Firms to Fail.* Boston, Mass.: Harvard Business School Press, 1997.

Cooper, Robin, and Robert S. Kaplan. *The Design of Cost Management Systems.* Englewood Cliffs, N.J.: Prentice-Hall, 1991.

Davis, Stan, and Christopher Meyer. *Blur: The Speed of Change in the Connected Economy.* Reading, Mass.: Addison-Wesley, 1998.

Deming, W. Edwards. *Out of Crisis.* Cambridge, Mass.: The MIT Press, 1986.

Downes, Larry, and Chunka Mui. *Unleashing the Killer App: Digital Strategies for Market Dominance.* Boston, Mass.: Harvard Business School Press, 1998.

Doyle, James S. *The Business Coach: A Game Plan for the New Work Environment.* New York: John Wiley & Sons, 1999.

Drucker, Peter. *Management Challenges for the 21st Century.* New York: HarperCollins, 1999.

Goldman, Steven L., Roger N. Nagel, and Kenneth Preiss. *Agile Competitors and Virtual Organizations: Strategies for Enriching the Customer.* Cincinnati, Ohio: Van Nostrand Reinhold, 1995.

Hamel, Gary, and C. K. Prahalad. *Competing for the Future.* Boston, Mass.: Harvard Business School Publishing, 1994.

Hammer, Michael, and James Champy. *Reengineering the Corporation.* New York: HarperCollins, 1993.

Hart, C. W. L., J. L. Heskett, and W. E. Sasser, Jr. "The Profitable Art of Service Recovery." *Harvard Business Review,* November-December 1990.

Ishikawa, K., ed. *Guide to Quality Control.* White Plains, N.Y.: Kraus International Publications, 1986.

Juran, J. M. *Juran on Planning for Quality.* New York: The Free Press, 1989.

Kaplan, Robert S., and David P. Norton. *The Balanced Scorecard.* Boston, Mass.: Harvard Business School Press, 1996.

Kotter, John P. *What Leaders Really Do.* Boston, Mass.: Harvard Business School Press, 1999.

Labovitz, George, and Victor Rosansky. *The Power of Alignment: How Great Companies Stay Centered and Accomplish Great Things.* New York: John Wiley & Sons, 1997.

Leonard, Dorothy, and Walter Swap. *When Sparks Fly: Igniting Creativity in Groups.* Boston, Mass.: Harvard Business School Press, 1999.

Markides, Constantinos C. *All the Right Moves.* Boston, Mass.: Harvard Business School Press, 2000.

McKenna, Regis. *Real Time: Preparing for the Age of the Never Satisfied Customer.* Boston, Mass.: Harvard Business School Press, 1997.

Melrose, Ken. *Making the Grass Greener on Your Side.* San Francisco, Calif.: Berrett-Koehler Publishers, Inc., 1995.

Mendelson, Haim, and Johannes Ziegler. *Survival of the Smartest: Managing Information for Rapid Action and World-Class Performance.* New York: John Wiley & Sons, 1999.

Nelson, Bob. *1001 Ways to Energize Employees.* New York: Workman Publishing, 1997.

Peppers, Don, and Martha Rogers. *Enterprise One to One: Tools for Competing in the Interactive Age.* New York: Currency/Doubleday, 1997.

Pfeffer, Jeffrey. *The Human Equation: Building Profits by Putting People First.* Boston, Mass.: Harvard Business School Press, 1998.

Reichheld, Frederick F. *The Loyalty Effect: The Hidden Force behind Growth, Profits, and Lasting Value.* Boston, Mass.: Harvard Business School Press, 1996.

Schultz, Howard, and Dori Jones Yang. *Pour Your Heart into It: How Starbucks Built a Company One Cup at a Time.* New York: Hyperion, 1997.

Slater, Robert. *Jack Welch and the GE Way.* New York: McGraw-Hill, 1999.

Sloan, Alfred E. *My Years with General Motors.* New York: Macfadden Books, 1965.

Spear, Steven, and H. Kent Bowen. "Decoding the DNA of the Toyota Production System." *Harvard Business Review,* September-October 1999.

Thielen, David. *The 12 Simple Secrets of Microsoft Management: How to Think and Act like a Microsoft Manager and Take Your Company to the Top.* New York: McGraw-Hill, 1999.

Unseem, Michael. *The Leadership Moment: Nine True Stories of Triumph and Disaster and Their Lessons for Us All.* New York: Random House, 1998.

Welch, Jack, with John A. Byrne. *Jack: Straight from the Gut.* New York: Warner Business Books, 2001.

Womack, James P., and Daniel T. Jones. *Lean Thinking: Banish Waste and Create Wealth in Your Corporation.* New York: Simon and Schuster, 1996.

Index

ABOUT THE AUTHOR

David W. Young is a professor of accounting and control at Boston University's School of Management and a principal in The Crimson Group, Inc., which provides its clients with customized in-house management education programs.